DANCING WITH DISCOMFORT

Dr. Carey Borkoski

First published 2021

by John Catt Educational Ltd,
15 Riduna Park, Station Road,
Melton, Woodbridge IP12 1QT

Tel: +44 (0) 1394 389850
Fax: +44 (0) 1394 386893
Email: enquiries@johncatt.com
Website: www.johncatt.com

ISBN: 978 1 913622 71 8

Set and designed by John Catt Educational Limited

To my wife, Susan, and my kids, Colby, Henry, and Sara.
I am forever grateful for your love, laughter, and family dance parties.
Thank you for giving me the time and space to do this work.

CONTENTS

ACKNOWLEDGMENTS

If you have ever undertaken a sizable project, you know first-hand that nothing gets accomplished without the love and support of so many others. Writing a book is no different and so I want to take a moment to thank the many people who made this book possible. This support took the shape of physical and virtual togetherness, exchanges of ideas and edits, and memories and stories of those no longer with us.

First, to my wife, Susan, for giving me the space, encouragement, and feedback to help me write and finish my first book. This book does not get completed without her love and support so thank you for pushing me and believing I could do this work. I also want to say thank you to my kids who managed to provide just the right mix of laughter and play to keep me energized to write the next chapter.

Thanks also to my amazing contributing authors, Drs. Barbour, Clark, and Roos. Our conversations, podcast chats, and collaborations set the foundation for this book. I would also be remiss if I did not offer a special thanks to Dr. Brianne Roos who is one of my closest friends, fellow podcaster, and research partner. Brianne, thank you for listening to me dream, plan, and finally write this book. Thank you for staying interested in and reading early drafts of chapters. Please know that you are appreciated. I would also like to thank Dr. Laura Shaw and Dr. Christine Eith, two dear colleagues and friends, who may not know it, but their online and text conversations were invaluable to my writing process. I am grateful for their support and especially all our virtual laughs together. I would also like to thank my mom, Cathy, who, in many ways, has grown along with me during many of the transitions shared throughout this book. Much gratitude to her for teaching me the value of determination, commitment, focus, and love of family.

The beautiful visuals within the book are all thanks to Tonio Nguyen, one of my doctoral students and friends. Thank you for the collaborative work, great conversations, and our shared love of The Cure! I look forward to our next project.

I would also like to thank my editor Mark Combes for his knowledge, experience, patience, and keen eye. Your suggestions, conversations, and skills helped to make this book what it is.

Even in memory, heart, and spirit, Coach Shelton and Sara Downey, my grandmother, remain a constant influence on me. Although these incredible ladies are no longer with us, their love, life lessons, and lasting stories remain with me and countless others. I am grateful to have known and loved both amazing women.

Thank you to readers who took a chance and bought this book. I hope you enjoy reading this as much as I have enjoyed writing it.

Again, thank you to my community of family and friends. I am eternally grateful to each one of you and for your curiosity, kindness, and support throughout this whole process.

CONTRIBUTING AUTHORS
Chapter 6, Dr. Kristin Barbour and Dr. Paula Clark
Chapter 7, Dr. Brianne Roos
Illustrations, maps, and visual aids, Tonio Nguyen

INTRODUCTION

"It is okay to lose to an opponent. It is never okay to lose to fear." – Mr. Miyagi

Dear reader,

Before you read this book, I have a confession to make. I am a huge fan of the sports movie genres. When I say sports movie, I am referring to *Rocky* (one, two, and three), *The Karate Kid*, *Rudy*, *Remember the Titans,* and so many others. If you are too young to remember those movies then check them out now. In each one, the main character often comes to a new town and struggles mightily to fit in, to make a team, join a group, or just be enough in their eyes. I love a great underdog story and I used to think that my attraction to these movies was about an escape from my reality. I could bury myself deeply into the lives of these characters, imagine how nicely and neatly, with a steady, predictable rhythm their stories unfolded and eventually the main character, our underdog, emerged victorious and joyful. Then I realized, it was not that at all. Well, maybe a little, but that was not the main reason I loved these movies. I am drawn to these stories because I just love to root for an underdog. I crave those stories of defeat, grit, messiness, self-doubt, confusion, and conflict all in service of the joy and celebration at the end of the movie. Admit it, you love these stories too! I think we also love these stories because we can relate. At some time in our lives, we have been in these stories, probably a lot of times. Sure, most of the time our stories are way bumpier, less predictable, and we do not get the Hollywood ending, but these struggles, this mess and uncertainty, is familiar to each of us.

The characters in these movies, Rocky Balboa, "Rudy" Ruettiger, and Daniel LaRusso in Karate Kid, all experienced a similar trajectory or should I say roller coaster ride. Take Daniel LaRusso, he and his mom moved from New Jersey to California where they knew no one. He starts in a new school, meets a girl, and, of course, they become friends only to realize that her ex-boyfriend is not so nice and starts picking on Daniel. Daniel is struggling to find his place; he is stuck in between wishing he was back in New Jersey with the familiar places and faces and the reality of living in California tangled in uncertainty and the unknown. In walks Mr. Miyagi and we know the rest of the story. Mr. Miyagi helps Daniel to pick his head up, pay attention to the moment, focus on the now, adjust, grow, and thrive. Now, I am not suggesting that we should all go out and take up karate. What I am suggesting is that we love a good underdog story because it tells the story of an individual who struggles, eventually reveals their vulnerability, and gradually, with support and practice, becomes aware of and present in these moments. Each character, usually with help from someone or some team, recognizes the moment – the transition, and this is where the movie, their story, and our story start to turn. This is the key piece. In every sports movie I have watched the athlete or team has a shifting or hinge moment, a realization that there is no "should" only what "is." It might still be hard but there is a path, some direction, some intentionality and purpose. With a focus on the here and now, the character commits to exploring what is possible. They train for the big fight, practice on the football field, or finally see the value of focusing when painting a fence. When Daniel starts his training with painting a fence, "up...and down...," and polishing cars, "wax on...wax off...," he is not happy but then he and Mr. Miyagi begin to build a trusting relationship. Mr. Miyagi offers feedback without judgment, makes connections between Daniel's personal experiences, thoughts, and feelings, and this practice and eventually, Daniel is better able to embrace and leverage these moments of dissonance and uncertainty.

We all have stories of struggle, uncertainty, self-doubt, and imposter syndrome. What do you replay from your own stories? What do you notice when you are in one of those stories? Do you even take notice or just try to ignore or avoid those moments? Too often, we take a deficit approach and focus on the negative, the mistakes, our failures. What if Daniel had kept his head down, stayed unaware of these opportunities, and walked away when Mr. Miyagi invited him to train? I used to spend a lot of time focused on my mistakes and struggles. I could get right back in those situations, feeling the embarrassment and shame of transitions until one day, my therapist said, "thank goodness you were able to do that because look at what you have been able to accomplish! Carey, you need to show your younger self some kindness, some gratitude." In that moment, my therapist shined a light on these experiences and did what cognitive behavior therapists refer to as guided discovery. She journeyed with me to understand my views and then challenged me to extend or shift my thinking. We need to stop beating ourselves up, stop with the regret, let go of the deficit thinking and embrace these moments for what they are: beautiful uncertainty full of possibilities to grow, learn, and develop.

Too often in our schools, communities, businesses, and other organizations, individuals focus on and only celebrate winning outcomes. We want higher profits, better grades, and more of some identified outcome. Getting the right answer or a correct outcome is too often valued over the process. And, while this is NOT a book on the US educational systems or how we arrived at an outcome-centered focus, I would suggest and have experienced as a student and teacher, the paralysis, fear, anxiety, and missed opportunities that derive, in part, from this celebration of a "thing" rather than our journeys or progress. Even as I write this book, I suffer from imposter syndrome. For those who are unfamiliar with this term, it is the idea that individuals experience and believe that they are not as competent as others perceive them to be. In Richard Bach's (2011) book *Illusions: The Adventures of a Reluctant Messiah*, he says "we teach best what we need to learn." I did not hear that quote until recently but have always thought that it was the universe's sense of humor that continues to put me in a community with students and colleagues where I am working to cultivate belonging, build awareness of how they are feeling in these learning moments, and what we might do to create a space for embracing these opportunities. I hear myself telling students not to worry so much about grades and focus on the process and think that a building might fall on me or lightning might strike.

I once was that student and still feel much of the anxiety and worry over "achieving." The difference between me as a student and now is that I see the moment unfold. It is like I am watching a movie of myself. When I start a new project, try a new hobby, engage in a new community of friends, whatever the transitions moment—I see it start. I would love to tell you that I do not worry, get nervous, or even experience an emotional spiral, but I cannot. This book is *not* a key to avoiding the moments. On the contrary, this book and the transitions practice is about buying a ticket to your own movie, crying when needed, laughing at the funny parts, and embracing the mess. Good things can happen if and when we pay attention.

Most individuals do not have a Mr. Miyagi to help focus on the here and now and watch their own movie, ask about and point out emotions and reactions, and celebrate progress instead of counting the missteps. It is no coincidence that I favor a good sports movie. My own experiences as a player and later as a coach helped me to recognize that great coaches, much like great teachers, value growth and development over wins. Nathan Drucker (2014) in an Edutopia article shared his research with coaches for a book he wrote. In his interviews, he discovered that all of these amazing coaches described the key to their success as a focus on process. Most coaches he spoke with noted that with this keen focus on progress, development, and growth outcomes eventually emerged.

Aiming for the right answer, the highest score, or any outcome loses sight of the discovery, the journey, and conjures a tremendous sense of fear and anxiety in many individuals. Being "right" also is not always a measure of growth or positive change. Very rarely are real-world questions answered with a black and white response. I can remember teaching an undergraduate microeconomics course and, almost like clockwork, after a lecture and discussion of an economic theory, my students would ask, "but what if...." There are infinite scenarios that alter the result, change the analysis, and soon we realize that the only universal response to those what if scenarios is, "it depends." We need to sit up and pay more attention to our process, focus on the here and now. Drs. Nagoski and Nagoski (2019) in their book about burnout, remind us that we spend too much time, energy, and stress in the space between what we think *should* be and what actually *is*. This book is my attempt to situate and center our attention and energy on that space in between, the here and now, our present thoughts, images, and emotions no matter the discomfort. We need to learn to embrace these moments and stay in the process instead of avoiding, closing our eyes, and hoping for a good result.

Recently, I was catching up on a Netflix series—not a sports movie! I was in the middle of my morning row, with the episode playing through my earbuds and one of the characters, a senior surgical resident, was asking a first-year resident how she felt about treating her first patient. Without giving away the whole episode, this senior resident was concerned about the new resident's potential for success. According to her record, she had scored high marks on the requisite exams, earned excellent grades, and received strong recommendations, and yet she was not performing well. He wanted to better understand her situation to provide some guidance and support, so he asked her about it. With some trepidation, she shared that "she hated first days." She explained further with a story of when she was in fifth grade. She painfully recalls answering a question incorrectly and the class laughing because she gave an incorrect response. Now, she finds herself in another first—her first day as a resident but this time is acutely aware that, as a doctor, getting something wrong could mean someone might die. She did not like first days because, according to this first-year resident, it conjured up those feelings of self-doubt, uncertainty, and embarrassment from old experiences with other firsts. How would her story change if, in these moments, she could embrace the moment, run towards the transition, and focus on what *is* not what *should* or, in this case, what *was*?

Why do I bring up this story? This story and her story is also my story, your story, and everyone's story. We have all had "firsts" and they continue throughout our lifetime, regardless of who we are or where we are professionally, emotionally, spiritually, or geographically. This resident's story illustrates how our change in roles, in this case, from medical student to doctor, happens quickly. We graduate, pass a test, or are appointed to a new role or position. Interestingly, however, the resident's process of *becoming* a doctor, owning and integrating this identity, takes much longer. Like this new resident and *The Karate Kid*, firsts are full of possibility and excitement but also taking that first step, entering that classroom, a boardroom, a different role or context, engaging in that first step, or any event, represents change and the transition process brings self-doubt, fear, uncertainty, and a great risk of looking foolish or getting it wrong. I spent much of my early life trying to avoid, sidestep, or just ignore these worries and fears. In the best case, individuals learn to manage the fear and doubt, build resilience, and, even with the stress and anxiety, move through it. However, in the worst case, individuals choose *not* to engage, miss out on opportunities, and spend too much time reflecting on what might have been, regretting.

These firsts are transitions, change, and an evolution in an individual's state. These in-between moments come in all shapes and sizes, but they are ubiquitous. Students tell me about their nervousness and trepidation. They describe the self-doubt and wondering if they will ever belong. Friends, colleagues, students, and family members recount asking how do I act like an academic, doctoral student, manager, or a leader?

Businesses, universities, K-12 schools, communities, and other organizations are good at what they do; bringing products and services to market, creating, disseminating, and translating knowledge, and preparing individuals to be good citizens and productive individuals. For example, graduate programs are great at building students' knowledge, skills, and disposition including academic writing, critical thinking, data analysis, and relevant subject matter. Primary and secondary schools offer frameworks and strategies to prepare young people to meet state standards and pass required tests and businesses select and train individuals for specific tasks and roles needed. What these entities often forget or devote insufficient time to is caring for the actual person *doing the work*. Individuals are not the role, there is a learner in the learning, a leader in the leading, and a worker in the working. Parker Palmer (1997) reminds us that, "If we want to grow as teachers—we must do something alien to academic culture: we must talk to each other about our inner lives—risky stuff in a profession that fears the personal and seeks safety in the technical, the distant, the abstract."

We often fail to design, implement, and attend to our human development—the uncertainty and anxiety, where an individual stands somewhere between their current (now, old) identity and a potential new addition to their identity. Through my own journey and experiences, I recall moments of doubt, have listened to and observed student trepidation, anxiety, and uncertainty, and interviewed countless others who shared similar experiences. What all of this has taught me is that we often focus on the wrong problem. As design thinking suggests, we often fall in love with a solution before we fully understand the problem or challenge. With time and patience, I realized that individuals often struggle and experience stress, worry, and self-doubt, not because an academic program is too hard, or students cannot manage the workload or the learning environment. Nor is it a matter of individuals being underprepared for a new role, position, or responsibility. The "problem" is not a problem at all. It is an opportunity, an awareness that transitions happen, and individuals experience dissonance, discomfort, and a push-pull between where they were and where they are going (literally and metaphorically). We need to realize that these moments and our human identity development happens throughout our entire lives. Remember, we cannot avoid or prevent these reactions entirely. We can, however, build our awareness, learn to stay in the moment, examine the processes, embrace the struggle, and train to navigate these moments head on. We can pay attention to our own stories. This also means that leaders, teachers, and colleagues also need to buy admission to their students' and employees' movies. We need to listen to our community of learners to see and provide support for each individual's unique transition. Attending to our own and others' development in these ways means we have an opportunity to grow, develop, and thrive and emerge victorious like the underdogs who get the Hollywood endings!

With this book, I hope to talk with readers about these all too familiar transitions, share personal stories and experiences of success and failure, and offer a practice that I have used myself, with my classes, and in my work. This training includes learning strategies and supports to navigate the transition stages, practice with a training routine, and ultimately aims to normalize the practice of noticing, naming, and effectively navigating transitions.

As we will discuss, transitions are a paradox; they involve mess, discomfort, uncertainty, and stress, and also offer opportunities for discovery, creativity, growth and learning. We cannot leverage these rich moments unless we learn to take notice, stay in them, and embrace the journey and process. This book is about those moments, transitions we all experience throughout our lives whether it is a first— new school, grade, job, or a more predictable milestone like adulthood, marriage, college, coming out, parenting, or something else entirely. These transitions could also be familiar and different. For example, entering graduate school or taking another job may not be the *first* time you experienced this kind of a moment, but it is unique and different for other reasons. It is possible that you have transitioned into other roles during your career but even that familiarity comes with new and different experiences. This book is about noticing, naming, and learning to navigate the transitions in ways that honor the struggle, celebrate the mess, and contribute to our development.

In order to lean in and embrace these transitional moments, individuals and organizations need to adopt practices to change our perceptions of and habits during these transitions. This book includes reflection prompts, visual artifacts, and other strategies as opportunities to start this process of change. These pauses will, hopefully, help readers make the topics relevant by connecting them to personal experiences and focusing us on noticing and changing our automatic negative responses to the discomfort and uncertainty of these transitional moments. As you read this book,

I would encourage you to make space in your daily routine for a notebook (virtual or physical) and time to actively engage with these activities. To practice one of these pauses, open up your notebook and consider the following:

CHECKPOINT:
Powerful questions often help us bring attention to our thoughts, actions, and experiences.
Consider a recent transition.
- What do you notice about the moment?
- What does it look like?
- How do you feel?
- What are you telling yourself in this moment?
- What are you learning?

We all have a story to tell, we each have our underdog moments. Instead of leading with stress, worry, and doubt in those moments, how can we cheer for ourselves and bring the same vigor and energy we call on to cheer for the underdogs, the Rocky Balboa's, Rudys, and Daniels in our sports movies?! How can we turn our moments of transition and discomfort into delight and anticipation? Okay, maybe delight is pushing it, but this book is all about learning to detect those transitions, examine the moment, embrace the worry and self-doubt, normalize the discomfort, and leverage the opportunity. If we do not pay attention, we just might miss it. The stress and worry of a moment is the same energy required to get excited and anticipate the moment. What if we could turn the channel or flip a switch and embrace our own underdog moments? If you have ever cheered for or celebrated the triumph of an underdog or felt like one yourself—this book is for you, your team, and your organization.

HOW TO USE THIS BOOK

"I am a work in progress." This is not an idea that I thought about or articulated until a few years ago. Like most people, I grew up with signposts, mile markers, and checkpoints signaling what was next on my journey, the expected milestones or transitions many of us experience. These transitions look different for different individuals and groups but each of us has used some sort of mental checklist to navigate and move through these moments in our lives. This might include going to kindergarten, entering high school, or winning a competition, contest, or spot on a team. These transitions or markers may also involve passing a driver's test, graduating from college, or getting a first job. I recall finishing college and thinking to myself, "now what?" Whatever these markers or signposts, these goals or outcomes guided my path and measured my progress. After this series of milestones, grades, and metaphorical finish lines, had I arrived? Was I grown up? Did I have an answer to the question of what I wanted to be when I grow up?

Looking back, the idea of asking or answering a question like, "what do you want to be when you grow up" is well intended and, sometimes, a good conversation starter. This question, however, is much more complex than this all-too-common inquiry. The idea that we can measure our change and growth in discrete terms like a checkbox, signpost, or finish line seems funny now. The more I learn and the older I get, the more I realize that I am and will continue to be a work-in-progress.

For so long I thought growing up meant achieving a certain something. I would arrive and accomplish some set of tasks that would somehow make me complete. I also thought "arriving" required some form of perfection – having the right answers, no cracks, no bumps or bruises, and being happy without self-doubt or insecurity. It is all of these things and none of these things.

Transitions and our signposts or markers represent those in-between moments with fuzzy boundaries and myriad thoughts and feelings. They embody problems and possibility and discomfort and discovery. Over time, I realized any one accomplishment or signpost does not make you "enough." Moving into and successfully through these milestones and transitions are not what define us or lead to our success. If we do not feel or believe we are enough before the signpost, event, accomplishment, or transitional moment, we are not going to change that view of ourselves after it.

Life is never one thing. Our transitions come in all shapes, sizes, duration, and intensity. They are gray, messy, and often uncomfortable. They include moments of paradox, seemingly conflicting ideas that upon examination are often true, and our willingness and ability to notice, name, embrace, and sit in these paradoxes is what makes us whole. Paradox might include discovery in discomfort, the beginner mindset of an expert, kindness within the rigorous expectations of a teacher or leader, or an expression of courageous vulnerability. It is staying still and present to grow, moving slow to go fast, and enjoying the process as much as any outcome.

Our fears, anger, and hurt often stem from our unwillingness and difficulties with experiencing these paradoxical moments embedded in our expected and unexpected transitions. This book offers an approach for learning and practicing staying in and being present for these transitional moments. To embrace and lean into the self-doubt and discomfort to experience and leverage the opportunities to learn and grow. Through stories, research, my own professional and personal experiences, and some intuition, I offer a framework to try and see, feel, notice, and effectively navigate our beautiful mess of possibilities.

This book includes a few warm-up/background chapters, suggestions for "equipment" you may find useful on your own journey, and a map or training plan to do the work. It also includes visuals and checkpoints that provide a way to reflect on and intentionally engage in what comes up as you read this book. Treat the checkpoints as your own personal coach. I have found that in my own experiences and doing my work, the most useful developmental tools have come from individuals who show up coach-like. For me, this means bringing a willingness to listen, being present, staying engaged in conversation, and asking powerful questions. They don't offer advice, share their own experiences, or provide mentoring. They stay curious and act in the service of the other person engaged in the connection.

The checkpoints may also help you lean into the words on the page, consider your transitional moments, and notice your own thoughts, feelings, and actions as you reflect on and experience transitions. These reflection prompts serve to help each reader name, notice, and be in whatever thoughts and feelings come up while reading this book. The prompts might also represent an invitation to explore your own discomfort, doubt, needs, and goals related to your transitions work. We are all on our own unique and beautiful journey. There are highs and lows and twists and turns. There are moments in life that will bring us to our knees and moments that will send us soaring.

This book and the strategies contained are not meant to be prescriptive. Everyone is different and each journey and transition offers its own possibilities and challenges. What is universal, however, are these moments of self-doubt and anxiety. No matter your credentials, accomplishments, or status, if we pay close enough attention and look carefully at our own transitions, we will see moments of hesitation and worry. Using research, personal stories, sample plans, and strategies, I hope that everyone will find a useful nugget to apply to their own transitional moments. These moments happen to all of us all the time and rather than side-stepping, avoiding, or running through, we must stay, be present, and lean into the discomfort. It is only through this willingness to own these uncomfortable moments that we will learn and grow.

To me, the answer to the question of what I will be when I grow up is to move in and through each moment. To notice and celebrate the signposts and slow down, stay in, and experience the in-between moments. This book and the strategies contained within aim to help us resist the urge to sidestep, bury, or run from our discomfort and self-doubt. Being a work in progress is not growing *up*, it is growing *through* our moments and staying present for whatever comes up. Our lives are full of transitions big and small, hard and easy, expected and unexpected. This book, I hope offers an opportunity to practice ways to leverage the possibilities of these in-between moments.

As a coach and someone who values being coached, I have learned setting intentions and naming small steps towards those intentions is paramount to doing this work. It is not about accomplishing a goal or reaching an accomplishment as much as it is about cultivating habits of presence, awareness, and intention in everything we do. As you consider your reasons for reading this book, consider setting an intention or two. Then, I would encourage you to notice, name, and navigate each of these intentions. Notice how you are feeling and what you are thinking. Name the intention. It might be curious, presence, or any other intention you set. Finally, consider a few strategies to navigate or honor those named intentions. The maps at the end of this chapter offer a guide for this work. If you find them helpful, I encourage you to try using these artifacts in other aspects of your life.

What do I wish for you as you read this book? I love this question because I do not wish anything for you—that is the point. If I honor my own core values of authenticity, inclusivity, and curiosity and the words on the pages of this book, I must remain unattached to your journey. I will stay curious, present, and ready with powerful questions that I do hope will help you to see and know yourself. This work does not make life easier; it will not make the hurt go away. What it can do, however, is open each of us to the possibility of experiencing all of the beautiful mess that life has to offer us.

INTENTIONS MAP

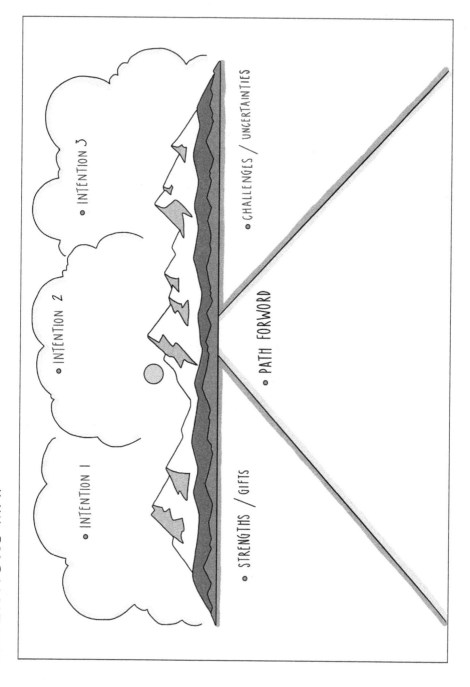

PLANNING MAP

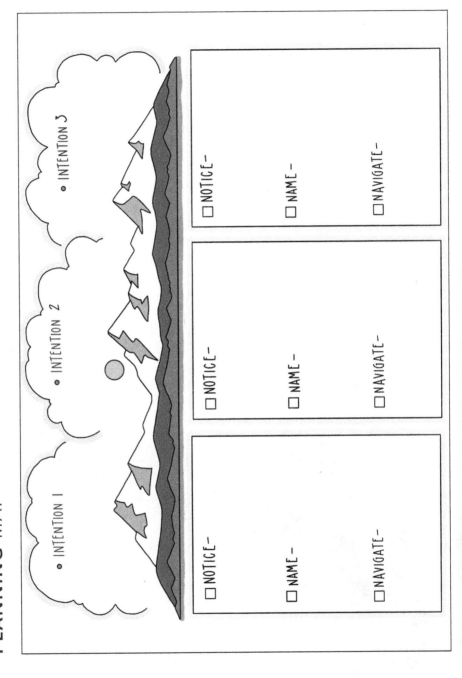

- INTENTION 1
- INTENTION 2
- INTENTION 3

□ NOTICE –

□ NAME –

□ NAVIGATE –

□ NOTICE –

□ NAME –

□ NAVIGATE –

□ NOTICE –

□ NAME –

□ NAVIGATE –

CHAPTER 1: THE ROADMAP

"If you feel lost, disappointed, hesitant, or weak, return to yourself, to who you are, here and now and when you get there, you will discover yourself, like a lotus flower in full bloom, even in a muddy pond, beautiful and strong." – Masaru Emoto

As we begin, I will introduce and explore concepts, definitions, and ideas related to transitions, firsts, and these moments of discomfort and discovery. This first chapter provides a roadmap for our journey and scratches the surface of relevant topics that include questions to consider as we start, required training accessories, a proposed practice to effectively notice and name these transitions, and strategies to navigate back to your whole self. Chapter 1 represents a chance to ease into the work and consider where and how you will begin your own journey to embrace these transitions.

QUESTIONS TO CONSIDER: WHO, WHAT, WHERE, WHY, AND HOW?

On March 12, 2020, during the very early days of the 2020 pandemic, my family received an email that our kids (aged five, five, and nine) would transition to remote learning for two weeks. Then, we received another notice that remote learning would extend for another two weeks, and another, and suddenly, well, you know the rest of the story. It felt like the whole country—really the world—had to immediately pivot in a variety of ways that included our routines for school, business, social gathering, grocery shopping, and traveling. These pandemic-related changes happened quickly but our transitions into these new experiences took much longer and many of us are still navigating these moments, thoughts, and feelings as I write and you read these words.

According to William Bridges (2009), change represents a situational or external experience while transitions involve an often longer and mostly internal process. Victor Turner described the process of adaptation to change as being "neither here nor there; [we] are betwixt and between" (1969). While I can only speak for myself and my family, I think that we still often feel like we are hovering somewhere between what used to be (pre-pandemic) and what is. It is an exhausting and challenging place to be, in the thick of the discomfort, and while I recognize that the pandemic represents an extreme on the transitions spectrum, it is in these outlier moments when the signs, features, and characteristics of a concept emerge with clarity. These moments can be nebulous and uncertain, full of hesitancy, disappointment, and self-doubt. My own students, colleagues, friends, and neighbors report a sense of this doubt, uncertainty, and fatigue, and often describe feeling like they are never doing enough, doing too much, and getting nowhere.

Long before the pandemic was a thing, I was thinking about the idea of transitions. I have been teaching, advising, and mentoring students for a while and, repeatedly, students describe those all too familiar feelings and thoughts. They report anxiety, worry, and doubt as they enter new academic programs, start internships, and accept jobs. Students express similar sentiments even when they share exciting news of marriage, parenthood, relocation, and other milestones. I remember one student, let's call him Lenny. He was a great student, smart, and was thriving in our program. He was preparing to take a great job after graduation when one afternoon he stopped by my office to share the good news that he and his wife were expecting their first child. Lenny possessed a strong sense of self and clear goals and plans. Yet, in this very exciting moment, he felt nervous and unsure about this new adventure. Would he be up for the task? How would he juggle a new job with a new baby? Regardless of our accomplishments, degrees, and stance in our lives, transitions unnerve us all.

Transitions take all kinds of forms. They can be short-lived or long-lasting, structured and supported or unstructured with minimal support. They sometimes have certain outcomes like adolescence to adulthood or leaving single life for marriage while at other times the outcomes are unpredictable or incomplete (Merriam, 2005). Interestingly, transitions in my mind also represent "firsts." Some might be familiar like starting a new job or new grade or even moving for the third time in four years. While individuals may have experienced a similar transition, the circumstances and conditions are often new, at least, in some ways.

I, too, have experienced transitions, questioning, trying mostly to push down and ignore the tremendous anxiety and stress that sometimes accompany these moments. I vividly recall starting a doctoral program. Now, I should be honest, this was my second doctorate—a story for another day. Even though I had been down this seemingly familiar path, I had so many worries, doubts, and questions: Would I connect to my new peers? What was I thinking by going back to school? Do I belong here? Who do I think I am? Did the admissions committee make a mistake when they accepted me into this program? The all too familiar uncertainty and wariness crept into my mind. Much like our love of the underdog story, these experiences and transitional moments are universal. Regardless of age, location, identity, context, or other factors, everyone knows the sense of dread, worry, and doubt in these moments. The stories we tell ourselves—

getting stuck on a channel that repeats these defeating images and comments of how we do not belong and cannot do this—make it almost impossible to leverage the possibility and tremendous potential for learning, growing, and developing. Therein lies the rub. At the end of the day, transitions—no matter the type, kind, or duration—are a paradox. Nature's attempt at humor, I guess. Within the muddiness, the mess of the confusion and dissonance, rests beautiful possibilities. If only we could notice, name, and navigate these transitions to harness their true power and anticipate and prepare for these moments. We all need a Mr. Miyagi. Someone to help us mark the moment, act as a bridge, noticing and naming these moments helps us better explore, make connections, and seize these wonderfully messy transitions. Imagine what could happen.

CHECKPOINT:
- Who or what is your Mr. Myiagi?
- What wisdom does your Mr. Myiagi bring to a current transitional moment?
- What does he/she notice?

WHAT AND WHERE?

The stories we tell ourselves about our personal failings and the perceived successes of others in these very same moments—these are the songs, the movies, the stories on replay. We get stuck on a channel that repeats these defeating images, comments, thoughts, and feelings. We believe we do not belong and cannot do whatever the moment requires. It is almost impossible to pause to recognize the possibility and potential for learning, growing, and developing. Bridges (2009) refers to this transition, this in-between moment, as the neutral zone. While I appreciated his description of this space, I grew up watching a lot of football with my dad and brother so I could not help but think about the familiar football penalty known as a neutral zone infraction. When a player or players commit a neutral zone infraction it means that he or they entered a space that is reserved for the player with the ball. Everyone else is prohibited from entering. Knowing this, Bridges's definition of a neutral zone to describe transitions did not work with my own understanding. Even Bigger and Stephen's (2009) characterization of Turner's (1974) transition phases as having clear attributes and boundaries did not quite resonate. For me, transitions represent an in-between space that is more dynamic, not an "off limits" or indifferent, neutral space. On the contrary, this is an active space swirling with confusion, excitement, doubt, anticipation, energy, and possibility. When we focus, live in the now, and when navigated effectively, these spaces are occupied by multiple people, engaging in connections, communication, and collaboration to check in, listen, learn, kindly question, and manage and leverage the possibilities in those moments. To me, it is an integration of offense and defense, practice and performance, teaching and learning, and reflection and presence.

One afternoon, while watching my son quickly learn to ride his new hoverboard, it occurred to me that hovering might better characterize transition for me. Webster-Merriam's defines hovering as "position[ing] over something without select[ing] it;" "remain[ing] suspended over a place or object;" and "mov[ing] to and fro near a place." In my experience, transitions are active spaces alive with potential. We hover in these moments. How we move to and fro depends on what we do with and in these moments.

I should be clear about this idea of firsts. For me and, in this book, firsts are really any kind of transition. They involve a period of change over time in a variety of circumstances. It doesn't necessarily have to be the *first* time you are doing something but there is something about the moment that is different, that involves a change to your current state, often a shifting or evolution of your perspectives, profession, location, whatever the relevant status. The change taking place looks and feels different, *new in some way.* Transitions include development, change, movement, addition, passage, transformation, adjustment, alterations, metamorphosis, and shifts. These transitions can be small or large and anticipated or not. We move in and out of transitions throughout our entire lives whether we are aware of them or not.

CHECKPOINT:
- What picture would you design, draw, paint, or imagine to best describe a transition to you?

WHERE?

The "where" of transitions is complex and will be discussed in much more detail in Chapter 3. As I considered the where and location of transitions, I was reminded that transitions include a physical, mental, and spiritual state or place. Some transitional moments may include all three while others are limited to one of these features. For example, when an individual decides to take a job in another location, this transition most likely includes at least a mental and physical shift or change. The individual, their belongings, and maybe their family will literally need to shift into a new home, geographic location, and routine. Additionally, there are mental transitions that happen. Bridges (2009) reminds us that we need to attend to our physiological adjustments as well as our physical changes. It is often easier to notice the external changes in our environment and routines. We must remember that as we hover in those in-between spaces of transitions, the location or setting of these moments may extend far beyond the physical environment we can see and feel.

THE WHY AND HOW OF THIS WORK

Transitions represent a paradox—so much discomfort and so much discovery. What are those possibilities if I/we do the work? When I first started signing up for running races, I needed a goal and a reward. Admit it—exercise is NOT always a result of internal motivation. We all love the "swag," the shirts, jackets, medals, mugs, hats, and all sorts of other rewards. So, it is fitting to think about what we might "get" from this transitions work.

Transition training offers many kinds of swag. Engaging in this work provides opportunities to decrease our anxiety and worry over new and unfamiliar situations. It represents a way to get to know ourselves in ways that may help us to pay attention to our reactions, emotions, thoughts, and feelings so that we can interrupt the self-doubt and leverage what is possible. Lowering our own stress and paying more attention to our own thoughts and reactions also means that we can "put on" or "wear" a mindset that embraces the learning and unknown of a transitional moment. This transitions training also includes practical strategies that can be adopted and used during these transitions and, like a new water bottle or running hat, might support you on your transitions journey. Ultimately, the rewards of this transitions training offer a means to better align the reality of our internal selves with the external world. We no longer need to battle so hard with the "shoulds" and can stay present and navigate these moments with a true sense of ourselves. Parker Palmer (2004), in his book *A Hidden Wholeness,* encourages us to show up with our unique gifts and true value and to live our authentic selves. He suggests that we are born integrated, our internal aligned with the external. This transitions training offers an approach and strategies to work towards what he calls living an "undivided life." This work helps us to show up in these transitional moments as our true selves willing and able to share our truth and vulnerabilities.

We have established that transitions have common features and yet, they are uniquely our own in numerous ways. Variations in our transitional experiences are as real as the diversity of the flowers, trees, frogs, and human beings we see. Paying attention and learning to recognize these moments means we can help ourselves and others effectively navigate these events. Identifying individual-specific strategies, designing and implementing relevant techniques, and offering appropriate support may lead to more equitable experiences and opportunities. Moreover, this work, a recognition of our thoughts and feelings in these new, unfamiliar moments may also create and cultivate inclusive work, school, and community places. Noticing, naming, and navigating the transitions means we may see each other, be seen as ourselves and see the uniqueness and contributions of every individual. It also means that we can recognize and name our collective and different struggles and care for the humans in our spaces. Together, these actions cultivate and contribute to our sense of belonging.

No one should hate, tolerate, or waste valuable energy avoiding or ignoring their first day, moment, or any other kind of transition. It is critical that we do the work outlined in this book so that we are better equipped to normalize the discomfort and embrace the possibility in the uncertainty. We have all been in those moments and regardless of age, expertise, profession, or other individual characteristics, firsts represent a paradox of possibility and self-doubt. Let's face it, the disequilibrium, disorientation, dissonance, and just plain messiness of transitions are filled with self-doubt, uncertainty, and stress and yet, we know that from a great mess can come beautiful results (Merriam, 2005). Admittedly, I can appreciate the paradox of possibility and uncertainty—hovering on that line of falling apart and claiming victory. What I struggle with is being in those moments of mess and being able to know, in my bones, that good will emerge from this mess! This is about normalizing discomfort so that you embrace and appreciate the moment so the transition no longer feels like adversity that you must battle or struggle with, rather this is an opportunity to thrive in the moment and shape and create the outcomes.

Take a simple, seemingly trivial example. Our kids love projects— any kind of project where they can imagine, design, create, and build amazing objects. Here is the thing, to do that work, and you know what is coming, requires a great deal of mess—there is just no way around it. Truth be told, I usually leave the management of these projects to my spouse because it elicits too much stress for me. The point being, our kids, have this great tolerance and appreciation for the potential of the moment—what that mess might mean if they just hang in there and stick to it. More accurately, our kids do not even see a mess—they only see the enjoyment, fun, creativity, and the potential in their efforts—imagine if we could all see our transitions with that view, even just a little. Now, doing an art project may not actually constitute a *transition*, but the messiness, unexpectedness, and uncertainty within those moments may be similar to how we feel and what is possible during a transition.

Transitions are universal. Individuals, regardless of status, context, location, and other characteristics, experience these moments of discomfort. Even the most accomplished individuals suffer from imposter syndrome. Transitions represent these hovering moments described as in-between status. These periods are dynamic, full of uncertainty and self-doubt, should include supportive relationships, trust, and collaboration, and represent tremendous possibilities. The key to unlocking this potential is not to rush through, ignore, or avoid this dissonance, individuals who focus on the moment in front of them and what IS, embrace the uncertainty, and lean on their own learning and the support of others to successfully navigate and thrive in these moments.

Transitions bubble over with possibilities but if we do not expect them or are unprepared, we often react in less-than-optimal ways.

Activity bias refers to the human tendency to favor some action over doing nothing (Patt and Zeckhauser, 2000). Moreover, experts including Aiko Bethea (2019) and Patt and Zeckhauser (2000) suggest that this need to act often results in worse outcomes. When faced with change and subsequent transition, our tendencies are to:

- Rush through the moment which may lead to confusion, poorer outcomes, and ultimately frustration at not being successful.
- Abort or escape the moment—complete avoidance —either never starting or quickly quitting.
- Ignore and discount the importance of the moment.

While our responses to these transitions will vary, the point is that we miss tremendous opportunities. Remember, the hovering area is filled with a chance to create, renew, grow, and develop. When we put ourselves out in the world, it is a gift to the world.

CHECKPOINT:
- What strategies do you use to manage and navigate your transitional moments?

As a kid, I struggled mightily with any kind of first. I am a recovering perfectionist. I can recall many moments where I engaged all three reactions: rushed through, escaped, and sometimes ignored these transitions. For me, these firsts were not moments of opportunity but the possibility to make a mistake. I was enveloped with a fear of making mistakes, stress about making a mess, worry about not belonging to a community, and an inability to see the potential. There were things I wanted to try, join, be a part of that I just missed out on. I did take advantage of many opportunities and am grateful for each one of those. But my point is that I often took the safe route and I believe, in my bones, that choosing safety over courage, confidence, and audacity meant that it took me a lot longer to achieve goals I had set for myself.

Deciding to engage in this work requires a commitment to investing in some new (or used) training equipment. Even if you do not love trying new things, I hope we can all admit that buying new shoes, clothes, or equipment is fun. I must admit that I love buying new running shoes, a new jacket, and even a great hat or a comfy pair of running socks. The point is transitions training has its own set of equipment. This training toolkit includes several items but this book will focus on a Gr-attitude, dance with discomfort, learning identity, and reflection "gear." In subsequent chapters, I will describe the features and functions of this equipment. In an attempt to provide a quick review, I offer the following.

CHECKPOINT:

Who? What? Where? Why? How?

- If you were to sketch an image, write a scene, or paint a picture of a recent transition, what would be included?
- Who are the individuals in the visual?
- What does it look and feel like?
- Where is the setting for this transition?
- Where were you mentally and physically?
- Why were you experiencing this in-between moment and how did you feel and react in these moments?

Go through this exercise a couple of times for different transitional moments. What do you notice and learn about your own transitions?

ATTITUDE

My high school field hockey coach, Lilian Shelton, the coach of teams who won 31 county titles, 29 regional titles and 20 state championships, stands as the winningest coach in all sports in Maryland. She led our team with a quiet, kind, and strong determination. There are so many gestures, quotes, practices, and routines that she instilled in her players. She listened fiercely, enthusiastically cheered for us, and whole-heartedly celebrated our joys, all while disciplining, guiding, and teaching us with great care and concern.

Yes, we practiced hard, running, executing passing drills, shooting on goal, and strategizing but attitude mattered—in Coach Shelton's philosophy—more than natural ability or any skills. It was evident in her demeanor and her message. Transitions training is about our mental awareness, curiosity, and fortitude, the stories we tell ourselves, the care we show (or don't) ourselves and each other.

We have already established that transitional moments are hard and uncomfortable. Preparation and practice are also hard and require a shift in attitude. This is not a Pollyanna kind of approach to adjusting our attitudes. This is an intentional and serious commitment to changing our mindset. I like to call on the three "Gr's" (think growling sound) which include grace, gratitude, and greatness. An attitude of grace means that we grant ourselves and others kindness in and through these periods of transition. It is important to care for ourselves as we move in the in-between. Give yourself a break and show patience.

With grace, we must also find gratitude. This work is hard, and the question is can you shift your attitude to find appreciation for something in the moment? Not after the transition is over and the outcomes are known. That would be too easy. In the mud, through the self-doubt, and during the discomfort.

Finally, expect greatness. By traditional standards this might seem boastful. I, however, want to submit that aiming for greatness means seeing the ball into the net and visualizing crossing some finish line. Greatness means that it is possible to be kind (show grace) and rigorous all at the same time. We can have high expectations, expect big things, raise the standards, and be kind. Success in and during transitions starts with adjustments to our attitude. Changing our perspective about what hard work requires and what translates to ours and others' successes. Starting with a focus on grace, gratitude, and greatness will make a huge difference in the way the work is done, the process flows, and the outcomes eventually emerge.

CHECKPOINT:
Imagine your favorite music.
- What do grace, gratitude, and greatness sound like in this tune or song?
- What instrument is playing?
- What energy does it bring to you?

DANCING WITH DISCOMFORT

Dancing with discomfort requires connecting with and cultivating, integrating, and executing awareness, learning, practice, training, in and through transitions rather than trying to avoid or eliminate them. Transitions practice focuses on our ability, individually and collectively, to embrace the discomfort. We will no longer worry about "if" we will fail. We will know and accept with certainty that we will fail; we will step into the arena and own, embrace, and celebrate it.

Over the years, after many of my own trials and tribulations, I began to realize that perfection is overrated. Moreover, as Brene Brown, in the *Gifts of Imperfection* (2010) reminds us, perfection is unattainable and actually creates shame, blame, and more judgment which just leads us into a terrible continuous cycle.

I slowly began to change the channel. I shifted from a voice of self-doubt to one that offered support, interrogated the doubt, showed up with curiosity, and embraced the uncertainty of a moment. These shifts take time sometimes only lasting for a second, but then with time, the change remains for an hour, and then a day or even for longer. The new channel included questions like:

- What am I feeling?
- Does the feeling match what is occurring?
- What is the worst that can happen if I...?

I soon realized a couple of things, (1) sometimes I succeeded in making new connections, joining a community, feeling a sense of belonging, and achieving the desired results, and (2) sometimes I failed and survived.

The second realization was the most important. Failure happens.

We survive and usually do better than survive. We name the moment, examine the experience, and use the new knowledge to better manage the next transition. We get up, wipe ourselves off, and begin again with more and richer information.

Out of those moments of failure, I also realized that it empowered others around me to do the same. Opening yourself up to vulnerability sends a message to those around you (who are also equally nervous and worried about these new moments) to explore and embrace the possibilities of these firsts. When this happens—a collective embracing of these moments—that is beauty. That is the magic.

In the midst of any first, the messiness of metaphorical art supplies spilling and tossing around the space; there is energy, hope, and excitement of what will come when we effectively navigate that moment. Learning to notice, name, and navigate those moments is like coming up for air after swimming deep in the ocean. It is releasing the stress valve so we can take a collective exhale and get on with the work at hand. Learning to gradually or momentarily lean into these transitions and dance in the mess helped me permanently shift my mindset to one of calling out those times of uncertainty. I no longer embrace the practice of perfectionism and I now, proudly, have come out as a work-in-progress, embracing the practice of change, the oscillation of transitions, and the development that emerges from this work.

CHECKPOINT:
- How does gratitude show up in your transitions?
- When was the last time you showed gratitude to yourself?
- What do you hear in the moments of discomfort?
- What are you telling yourself in these moments?

LEARNING IDENTITY

Much of what I know and share in this book comes out of some combination of my academic training and experience but more importantly, my own trials, errors, and critical reflections on my own transitions. While I do bring lots of professional experience and many academic credentials to this discussion, I do not like the word "expert." Webster defines an expert "as a person who has comprehensive and authoritative knowledge in any particular area." I understand this definition but believe this idea of expert, at least in practice, ignores an important element of being an expert. True expertise includes a learning identity. This identity incorporates an individual's innate understanding, learned knowledge, and experiences with a desire and valuing of the role of continual learning. With this concept in mind, I prefer the notion of someone who earns and gains wisdom from integrating knowledge and experience and a person who possesses a tolerance for uncertainties in life and an optimism that problems can be overcome. The notion of wisdom as compared to expertise also aligns better with the conception of transitions. I think it is possible and necessary to consider ourselves as in progress and on a journey. Expertise, in my view, implies a static and finished way of being whereas transitions training acknowledges and embraces the idea that growing, developing, and learning is part of our continuing journey. To that end, each transition and the relevant practice in our transitions accumulates a few nuggets of wisdom to share along the way. To me, expertise connotes a finish line or completion, but this is not my view of knowledge, development, or learning. Like transitions, learning and development are part of our journey.

In my view, learning and the accumulation of knowledge is ongoing, oscillating, and ever-changing. According to psychological research, wisdom derives from cognition, reflection, and compassion (Baltes and Smith, 1995; Bierly et al, 2000). Cognition includes knowledge and experience, reflection involves an ability to examine situations, and compassion is about the ability to take other perspectives and maintain an open mind and intellectual humility. And there it is—humility, intellectual humility (Resnick, 2019; Ryan, 2020). When individuals approach and begin to navigate new experiences or transitions, most of us feel nervous, anxious, uncomfortable, and a level of stress about this unknown. In these moments, try to remember that we have choices. We can push away this dissonance and pretend that we are "fine", or we can "push it down" and just "deal with it", or we can admit feeling uncertain and that we do not have an answer. Successfully navigating transitions and leveraging these moments of uncertainty and discomfort requires a level of vulnerability and humility. Coming to the experience with a beginner's mindset (Vanderbilt, 2021), a willingness to hold a novice frame of mind, and the ability to acknowledge that "I don't know" stimulates curiosity that helps us to lean into the discovery in our transitions.

"I don't know." Admitting those three words is not easy and, for many of us, they are almost impossible to say. Our egos and confidence will not allow us to admit otherwise. Being right, identifying as an expert, knowing the answer, winning the game, and earning the money is what is valued and rewarded by traditional systems and structures. The combination of these internal and external cues means that we spend a lot of time and energy pretending that we are "in the know." Why is this a problem? Why not "fake it until you make it?" What if we changed the channel or the voice in our heads? What would happen?

REFLECTION IN AND AFTER ACTION

Reflection is a critical part of transitions work and while it is identified as the final step in this framework, it really occurs throughout as a way to check-in, reestablish our presence in a moment, and process just-in-time information to adjust to the moment as needed. For example, leaders, whether in a classroom, in a team, or with a project workgroup must engage in critical reflection. Individuals and groups must build in time during and after activities to review, assess, and adjust as needed. Reflection, as an intentional practice, can offer ways to slow down when our instinct is to rush through an uncomfortable moment, learn important lessons from decisions or interactions, and adjust our approach or strategy to improve a situation or relationship. Reflection practices come in all shapes and sizes and are used for a variety of purposes. As we will consider in Chapter 7, reflection is a tool for focusing our attention and intentions to stay with these uncomfortable and uncertain transitional periods. Critical reflection also represents one strategy that contributes to our readiness for change discussed in the next section.

CHECKPOINT:
- What do you notice when you show up as a learner?
- What is true in those moments?
- What does your learning mindset look like?
- What wisdom does a learning perspective provide?
- How do you want to stay connected with this learning identity?

TRAINING PLAN: READINESS FOR CHANGE

Kroger (1993) suggests that a time of readiness contributes to changes and growth in our identities. In order for these disparate moments to be integrated into new insights (Baumeister, 1986), individuals need to notice, name, and effectively navigate these thoughts, feelings, and events. Mentors, guidance, and institutional structures are critical supports but an individual's own reflections and perspectives on the moments of transition also contribute to the resultant outcomes. As I have worked with students and reflected on my own experiences with a variety of transitions, I recognize that this "readiness for change" is this idea of noticing, naming, and engaging in whatever moment we find ourselves. It is not enough to know the stages of the transition or the expected path, we need to help ourselves and others prepare for change, be present in the transition, and leverage our connections and community, practice, and reflection to succeed. This readiness for change could help to mediate the relationship between our development, growth, and these often stressful and uncertain events (Baumeister, 1986).

In this practicum, together we will learn to recognize our own and others' transitions, describe the thoughts and feelings associated with this period, practice and adopt strategies to prepare for, and navigate these transitions. This practice includes structures and training strategies and remains flexible to be inclusive and accessible to a variety of individual needs and situations. Transitions are naturally disruptive and unsettling, and this transition practice will help to mitigate those feelings. Fenge (2001) suggests that individuals need to consolidate, clarify, and settle into their evolved identity and attending to our thoughts and feelings in these moments may help individuals, groups, and organizations to develop, cultivate, and embody outcomes of any transitions. We need time to reflect, experience, and adjust. Moorehead (2019) also reminds us that individuals "did not enter new lives as complete, rather [individuals] were working to consolidate, clarify, and settle into an identity."

Given that these transitions are often unstructured, unanticipated, and unfamiliar, individuals and groups require support. This may include intention, self-monitoring, structured programs, and/or some form of coaching. Whatever form this support takes, individuals need to notice and name these transitions so that they can be intentional and learn to stay in these moments with strategies that lead to growth and opportunities.

Noticing, naming, and being present in these transitions depends, in part on structures and supports in place to contemplate and explore in these moments of in-between (Ibarra and Obodaru, 2016). This possibility makes it paramount that individuals do the work to prepare for these moments. Ottaie (1996) suggested that examining and identifying stages of change are critical. He offered evidence that individuals who gain awareness and engage proactively reported more distress and he posited that this distress motivated them to actively prepare for purposeful change. It stands to reason—and here is that transition as paradox again—if you notice the transition and start to work through the mud, the discomfort will follow. The readiness for change, preparation, and practice will help individuals wade through the mud and emerge in a new and beautiful space full of opportunities.

This book offers a process or training program for what Baumeister (1986) refers to as readiness for change. There is so much literature about development—identity, mental, emotional, that includes stages, descriptions, activities involved, but what is missing and needed to leverage these moments is intentionality, purposeful work to recognize, name, practice for, and be in our moments of transition. Without a readiness for these transitions, we may not know when, why, or how a transition will emerge, but we know there is probably one just around the corner. Individuals, groups, and organizations cannot harness the possibilities locked within the messiness of these transitions without intentional preparation and practice. This book offers one way to prepare and effectively leverage these moments; a framework to design preparation suitable for your needs, context, and goals.

WHAT THIS BOOK IS AND IS NOT

This book includes discussions of the interconnectedness of emotions and cognition, identity development, resistance training, intervals, and active recovery, and other topics related to transitions. I am not, however, a neuroscientist, psychologist, or exercise physiologist or trainer. My own experience as a learner and my professional endeavors as a teacher-researcher have provided valuable insights, ideas, and strategies for making the most of these transition moments to grow, learn, and develop as individuals.

This book is a first step of learning, knowing, and growing. We need to hold an intellectual humility about our transitions. I spent most of my life avoiding, hiding, covering up, and badly managing the discomfort of transitions. Perfectionism, fear of being wrong, worry about failure and looking bad or stupid meant that I missed out on a lot of opportunities and possibilities. I also thought that by grinning and bearing it and making it through a transition I would be "better" and somehow more fulfilled but that was not the case. If you are not enough before the transition, you will not be enough as you move through the transition.

Transitions offer us an opportunity to focus on and value the journey, to gain insights and benefits from the process rather than making the effort and work all about the final outcome. Individuals often find themselves setting and focusing on one or a set of goals. These outcomes or milestones represent an external motivation to keep moving forward, to do the work, and commit to something. What happens if and when this same individual misses this goal even by a little bit? A personal trainer once told me that data is valuable, measuring progress and our successes are important to the process. She also said, however, that data should *empower* us not have *power over* us. Goals, achievements, and other outcomes are only one piece of the journey, they do not define our success or growth. Thinking that we will be good enough, smart enough, or fast enough only after we complete some identified goal misses the value, benefits, and importance of the journey *to* that goal.

It was not until I recognized that my most energized, productive, and powerful moments of learning happened when I embraced discomfort. When I realized that embracing the discomfort of an ultramarathon—owning the moment of fatigue, fear, and soreness—meant that that moment eventually shifted to one of strength and learning. Or, when I gained excitement and energy from becoming a doctoral student—not worrying that I would fail but embracing the suck and the possibilities simultaneously. Transitions are all of this and more, discomfort, uncertainty, fear, worry, challenge *and* excitement, novel, full of opportunities, potential for growth, and learning. What will you do with your next transition? Could you change the channel, normalize the discomfort, and embrace the transition and—during the challenge—leverage the opportunities?

This book offers insight into how we could change that channel and develop a learning identity, provides strategies to normalize the discomfort of these important moments, and explores a framework or training process to fully engage with and leverage the opportunities in our transitions. We need to study, practice, rehearse, get ready—train. This book, in many ways, is a training program, a routine, framework, and a process that includes several steps when practiced individually and collectively. A commitment to this process will contribute to our individual, group, and organizational ability to successfully notice, name, be present in, and effectively navigate transitions we encounter. It represents one way to help us learn how to notice, name, and form habits for effectively managing our transitions and create learning, growth, and development. Learning theorists Piaget (1958) and Mezirow (1997) described these notions as disequilibrium and disorienting dilemmas and suggested that attending to these moments, *being intentional* and *doing* something with the discomfort and moments that emerge during transition contribute to learning new knowledge. It is my hope and aim that reading this book, learning the signs of our own transitions, and simulating moments of transition may contribute to our ability to turn and face our self-doubt and make the most out of these opportunities.

CHECKPOINT:
Setting intentions contributes to our ability to be present and act with intention. Articulating our intentions includes goals but the point of this exercise is to help us notice and name the moments during the journey rather than those that result *after or because of* the journey.

TRANSITIONS MAP

Date:

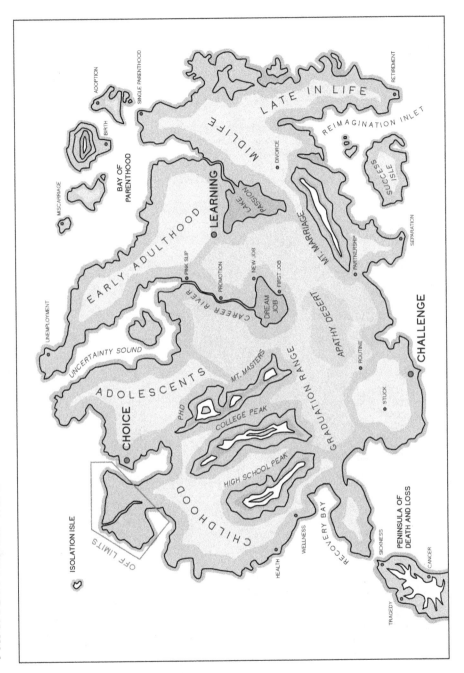

CHAPTER 2: WHO AND WHAT?

"The only constant in life is change." – Heraclitus

In this chapter, I will introduce the "who" engaged in these transitions. I will give you a hint, we are *all* characters in this story. I will also explore the "what" of transitions with a brief look at the researchers and evidence that informs how I think about and approach these pivotal moments.

THE WHO

During the pandemic of 2020, it was never more certain that individuals, groups, organizations, and countries expressed a sense of nowhere and somewhere. As Victor Turner suggested, we were "betwixt and between" conventional professional roles, career paths, and family and school contexts. Parents, students, professionals, families, and others entered new roles with old rules and structures, hovering, almost suspended, exiting an old role but not fully clear on the new role(s).

Merriam-Webster defines transition as "one state, stage, subject, or place to another; change; a movement, development, or evolution from one form, stage, or style to another." Everyone has experienced many transitions and they come in all shapes and sizes and do not discriminate by gender, race, sexual identity, age, experience, profession, location, or any other characteristic. Transitions encompass myriad emotions ranging from excitement and anticipation to doubt and worry. They also stir up lots of questions such as, "Am I ready?" "Can I do this?" "Will people think I am good enough?" "What if I fail?" While full of possibility, transitions conjure up a sense of uncertainty and the unknown and we might often feel as if we are wading into the deep end of a pool or a murky, muddy swamp. Whatever the metaphor, we have all been there, asked ourselves these questions, *and* successfully navigated these moments.

CHECKPOINT:
- What emotions do you notice during your own transitions?
- What metaphor would you use to describe a transition?
- What colors emerge?
- What do you hear?

Prior to landing on this idea of transitions, I attempted to better understand an individual's identity development. Early on, from personal and professional experiences, I was keenly aware that teaching and training organizations including K-12, higher education institutions, and businesses or governmental organizations were willing to invest in an individual's knowledge, skills, and dispositions, and most have figured out how to implement the skills training piece efficiently and effectively. What is often missing, however, is attention to the simultaneous development of self, the identity of the students, workers, colleagues, and members and the relevant or contextual knowledge, skills, and dispositions.

The neglect of human development and inattention to identity development is not done to cut corners nor is it to harm anyone, it's probably not deliberate. Leaders, managers, and other decision makers rely on their assumptions. I hear it all the time, program leaders suggest that these students received admission to this program so they should already be prepared, or project managers assume that their employee is an expert in her profession and transition to a directorial position should be a smooth one. Others assume that individuals find mentors who "teach" and "develop" them, or they learn through observation and practice. Accomplished, smart, and innovative companies, organizations, and individuals underestimate the sometimes-paralyzing nature of transitions. This imposter syndrome, discomfort, and self-doubt are real and represent the difference between just doing the job or assignment and thriving in the job or project. I have spent much of my teaching career forging connections, listening, cultivating community, and belonging to all with the goal of providing support to individual personal and professional development.

Erikson (1959) reminds us that a well-developed identity means individuals internalize goals, values, and beliefs. There is consistency in self over time and identity is formed, molded, and augmented through exploration and commitment to some form of identity. While we often think about identity development in adolescence, the reality is that development happens throughout our life and adapts and changes, in part, as a result of an individual's experiences with change and this process of transition. As Erikson suggested, failure to establish an identity during our adolescence can create confusion. Similarly, it is the case that confusion about identity can occur when a transition involves a clashing or incongruence of well-established identities with a potential new identity emerging out of this transitional moment.

Take Janet. She was admitted to a doctoral program as a result of her stellar academic records, the strong articulation of her research goals, and her professional expertise and experience. She came with a well-established professional identity as an educator and school leader and walked into a new and unfamiliar academic space. In this new state of being, Janet identified as a novice and, in her own words, "I asked myself what am I doing here? I was thinking that XX University must have made a mistake when they accepted me into the program." In that moment, even with her expertise, she felt like a beginner. These conflicting feelings of expert-novice in this example contributed to challenges to Janet's transition. Incongruence and even consolidation of our current and new identities during these transitions put individuals in-between then and later. Individuals, depending on their attention and focus to the now, hover in discomfort and uncertainty during these periods of transition.

It is critical to remember that this change—the choice to go back to school—happened quickly and yet Janet's transition to a scholar-practitioner occurred gradually over the course of her three-year doctoral journey. Transitions may not always encompass such stark contrasts in identities, nonetheless it is critical to remember that the potential of this in-between space is not just about learning, productivity, and growth. It also contributes to the development of us as human beings.

Janet's description of her transition back to school is common. Over the years, I have worked with hundreds of students who report similar feelings of trepidation and uncertainty. I have also observed new faculty, leaders, managers, and school-aged kids describe doubt and worry over being "up for a task." They question their preparation, how they will fit in, adjust, be accepted, and succeed. Whether we are working with students, colleagues, employees, leaders, or on ourselves, it is critical to attend to identity development and realize its role in human development. Affirming individual anxiety, doubt, and confusion, introducing a diversity of role models and talking about and supporting values, goals, and identities contribute to more effectively navigating these transitions. Transitions training, attending to identity and human development in these moments needs to happen throughout our entire lives (Bridges, 2009). We cannot lose sight of this and we cannot avoid these moments. Adults re-explore and redefine their identity commitments over their lifetime (Stephen, Fraser, and Marcia, 1992).

I can recall so many transitions or those dreaded firsts the doctor in the Netflix series described. Moving into a new house when I was in third grade and meeting my neighbor for the first time. Starting high school and walking through what felt like these giant, long hallways while worried about how I was ever going to find my classes or where I would sit in the cafeteria.

I also recall transitions that included *not* achieving a goal or moving into a new position. I had taken a semester off from college and moved back home where I was working until I figured out my next move. I decided that what made the most sense for me was to transfer to a university closer to home. I completed the paperwork, sent in the application to the local university, and continued to work all the while planning for the summer and fall semesters closer to home. Later in the spring, I received a letter from this university letting me know that I had been waitlisted. What?! This was not expected—what was I going to do now? How would I navigate this unexpected moment? After some time to reflect and consider my options, I decided to go back to the same, out-of-state university. I finished up that next year and moved into my professional endeavors. The point is transitions are as diverse as the trees and animals all around us. They can be tall or short, anticipated or not, smooth or bumpy, and, even with support, they are still confusing, complicated, and challenging. Yet, if we turn the channel or change the station on our approach to these transitions, they can also be fruitful, full of potential and possibility, and present an opportunity for growth and success.

Everyone experiences and some individuals, groups, and organizations even prepare and train for these transitions. Pilots, soccer coaches and athletes are just a few examples of individuals who notice, name, prepare, and navigate these transitions. Pilots transitioning to unfamiliar aircraft require specific training. In what is referred to as Pilot Transition Training, individuals receive instruction, train with a qualified trainer who has previously experienced these normal, abnormal, and emergency procedures, and the pilots practice, practice, and practice some more. In soccer, coaches and players also practice transition scenarios. They design and implement different sequences of events and try out strategies to help individual players and the team adopt and execute relevant steps to navigate transitions. For example, these strategies might include communicating (i.e. naming) the team's shift to a transitional moment, connecting and engaging through a particular series of passes, coordinating through positioning and their use of space which all culminates to coordination required to support each other in these moments. Successfully navigating these transitions requires both coaches and players to notice the moment of transition on the field, name the specific transition, and stay with and navigate the moments according to their plan and practice. This support and assistance come from coaches on the sidelines and players on and off the field. After engaging in those transitions, coaches and players engage in self and collective coaching to reflect on what worked and how to improve on those moments that did not go as well.

To prepare and navigate for these transitions require awareness, an ability to see the moment, identify the signs, and lean into the discomfort (Merriam, 2005). The following section discusses some of the research about what we can expect and what to look for in these transitional moments.

CHECKPOINT:
- What do you notice before and during your transition?
- What do you see in your surroundings?

THE "WHAT" OF TRANSITIONS

"A sense of identity is never gained nor maintained once and for all. Like a good conscience, it is constantly lost and regained." – Erik Erikson (1956)

Psychologists, anthropologists, and many other individual "ists" use a variety of terms and concepts to describe the ideas of transitions. Erik Erikson (1963) studied adolescent identity development and cultural anthropologists Van Gennep (2019) and Turner (1965) researched tribes in Rhodesia and studied distinct phases of transition they called Rites of Passage and liminality. Dr. Nancy Schlossberg, a counselor and psychologist, also examined transitions through social work and counseling and later as it relates to retirement. As I discussed in the previous section, regardless of context, perspective, or age, everyone experiences transitions in some way, shape, or form.

As I first tried to clarify my thinking on the idea of transition, I further explored Erikson's (1963) research on adolescent development. He defines identity development as finding out who one is and describes an identity crisis as a critical moment or turning point in an individual's life. Initially, the concept of identity crisis seemed to align closely with my understanding of and experiences with transitions. As I read further, I also learned that Marcia (1966) expanded his work to include four distinct identity statuses characterized by various levels of exploration of and commitment to an identity. These include identity diffusion with no commitment or exploration, foreclosure where individuals commit quickly with no exploration, moratorium with no commitment and lots of exploration, and completion where individuals explore and ultimately commit.

While these stages and the theories of identity development are intertwined with transitions and represent one consequence or application of transitions, it was not exactly describing the moments I had experienced or had heard described by students and others. I continued my journey to understand my sense of transition.

Although chronologically, Schlossberg's work came almost two decades after Turner's ethnographic study and research on transitions, I discovered her articles and books first and they immediately aligned with my thinking and experiences with transitions. Dr. Scholossberg conducted research and has written numerous books on her theory on transitions "as a vehicle for analyzing human adaptation to transition" (Evans et al, 1998). Schlossberg (1984), in her comprehensive studies on transitions across the lifespan, suggested that individuals experience, on average, seven major career shifts over a lifetime and everyone goes through countless firsts.

In her Transition Theory (Schlossberg, 1981), she describes the catalyst for transition as one where some triggering episode initiates a change. Moreover, she suggested that the availability of resources like supports, strategies, and ourselves contribute to how well or poorly individuals and groups "move in, through, and out" of these transitions (Schlossberg, 1984). Schlossberg's ideas about transition apply to events like attending college, beginning a new career, and entering retirement. These transitional moments can be expected or unexpected, positive or negative, or a change that creates the presence (i.e., new job, child, location, bonus) or the absence (i.e., applied for a job but did not get it, failed an entry exam, did not have a child) of a desired outcome. Regardless of the outcomes, these moments alter our individual or collective place, space, and views in and of our context or environment.

Greta Bradley's (2008) applied these ideas of transition to the induction process for new social workers. She describes a rite of passage where "newly qualified social workers have to learn and adjust to their new roles." The notion of a rite of passage emerged from Van Gennep (1960) and Turner (1974) and their conception of rites of passage as "transition period marked by distinct phases...." In the context of his research, Turner examined these rites of passage or transitions as exclusively anticipated moments like adolescence to adulthood, single life to married life, having kids, and other milestones. Turner described individuals experiencing transitions to be no longer or not yet where individuals, teams, and organizations are exiting one moment and facing another new moment. These new moments and this process are, just that, in process—incomplete. Turner also characterized this process as ambiguous, neither here nor there, "betwixt and between" (Wels, van der Waal, Spiegel, and Kamsteeg, 2011). This image of betwixt and between resonated with me but exclusively focused on structured, supported, and known moments with outcomes which were almost certain.

Ibarra and Obodaru (2016) adapted Turner's idea of liminality and the process by which individuals experience these moments. Unlike Turner, they embraced the idea that these transitions and in-between moments could be more fluid, and they incorporated the idea of and/both rather than an either/or. These transitional moments did not have to represent a shift from one state to another or a change in social status but could blur the lines of status and coalesce into a hybrid form of an old or new state of being. Their conception of transitions included a range of self-guided and structured supports, a sometimes-incomplete narrative and voluntary in nature, and the outcomes may be uncertain with multiple outcomes, regressive change or even an unresolved status. Together, Turner, Schlossberg, and Ibarra and Obodaru offered a clear and representative characterization of transitional moments I have experienced, observed, and heard described by friends, students, colleagues, parents, and others.

CHECKPOINT:
- What do transitions represent for you?

For me, and throughout this book, transitions represent the whole "mess" of what individuals face. These moments represent a change in status or state of an individual, team, or organization. These moments vary in duration, level of structure and support, predictability, and certainty of results. Some transitions will be voluntary and familiar while others are forced and unfamiliar. As Turner (1969) noted, transitions or rites of passage also include stages, but these steps are far more blurred than he suggests. Individuals shift to and fro within the process and the features of the steps vary according to individual, context, role, and other factors. Many of these transitions, for reasons I will discuss later, go unsupported and sometimes are felt and experienced but go unnamed. As a result, the entire experience may represent an incomplete or unfamiliar trajectory that may or may not be voluntary and whose outcomes are more likely to be unpredictable. To sum it up, transitions and the thoughts and feelings related to these moments are messy. They are exactly what our activity area looks like during and after our kids do a project. They provoke self-doubt and questions and yet, they are beautiful, exciting, and full of possibility. These moments and projects are often unpredictable and uncertain but what they do have in common is that they:

- happen to everyone.
- contribute to individual identity development.
- elicit discomfort, uncertainty, and confusion.
- represent rich opportunities for learning and growing.

- require awareness, openness, preparation, practice, support.
- include ongoing reflection and recalibrating.

So, the question is, if we know with great certainty that transitions happen, how do we shift our mindset, change the channel in our heads, and stay curious and remember that transitions are part of the creative process. It is messy and it is a little nerve-wracking and there is tremendous chance for learning and development. How do we prepare and effectively engage in our own creative process?!

Over the next several chapters, I will dive more deeply into the requisite training accessories, my proposed training plan, and some suggested strategies and activities. Journeying through transitions is hard and uncomfortable but evidence suggests that:

- individuals should achieve success staying in and attending to these transitions.
- intentional responses to these moments matter more than the actual adaptation.
- early action contributes more.
- success requires coaches, teachers, and leaders to identify the needs and strengths of individuals and design and implement appropriate programming.

In education, transitions happen all the time whether it is starting a new teaching position, a student entering a new grade again and again each year, or graduating from high school and heading to college and then leaving college for the workforce. Transitions and firsts are ubiquitous and no matter the age or experience, they still bring feelings of worry, uncertainty, and self-doubt. The only thing certain in transitions is that individuals will experience another one.

CHAPTER 3: WHERE? WHY? AND HOW?

"When it comes right down to it, wherever you go, there you are. Whatever you wind up doing, that's what you've wound up doing. Whatever you are thinking about right now, that's what's on your mind." – Jon Kabat-Zinn

It is important to also consider the "where," "why" and "how" of this transition practice. This chapter explores where transitions occur and a rationale for adopting a practice of transitions training for yourself, students, and colleagues! Then, we will briefly explore how individuals, teams, and organizations can use this book, and their knowledge of transitions themselves and with their colleagues and employees to design and engage in the transitions training presented in later chapters.

Transitions involve embracing exploration and eventual commitment to a new and evolved status, stance, or identity (Bussolari and Goodell, 2019). In the first chapter, we reviewed how transitions are universal and involve a change catalyst followed by some period of transition. The ebb and flow, intensity, and duration of these transitions vary but what is true of all of these moments is the self-doubt, uncertainty, worry, stress, and opportunity.

WHERE?

The "where" of transitions is complicated. We often think of the where of transitions as a physical relocation. While that can be true, the where of transitions can also result from changes in context, role, profession, standing, or a variety of other factors. Transitions yield a great deal of discomfort because they alter our relationships, roles, assumptions, perspectives, and routines (Schlossberg, 2011). The reality of transitions and what is often the most difficult and overlooked element of this moment is that change significantly alters individuals. The catalyst initiates a transition that in some ways alters our internal "where" which creates a shift into an in-between state of being. We hover between who we were, what we did, and what we thought into a place where we face who we might become, what we might do, and how we might think.

I recall a time when I relocated from Winston-Salem, NC to the nearby town of Greensboro. It was only 25 minutes from where I completed my undergraduate studies and then worked for a few years and yet, Greensboro felt like a brand-new place. I moved to a new town and was starting a new graduate program and was trying very hard to find a community. I also tried to get to know my new neighborhood, establish a home, and settle into a familiar routine. Here is the thing, this was definitely a transition marked by a new geographical location and an exit from the workforce back to poor graduate student, but there was also a mental shifting, a relocation of sorts.

What I did not realize at the time was that I moved to a new physical location but was hovering in a less certain and ambiguous mental place, "betwixt and between." As I started this economics master's program, I was actually mentally sitting in my first undergraduate economics course remembering the struggle, self-doubt, and worry. I vividly remember coming home after my first day of graduate school and crying at the kitchen table as I attempted to complete my homework. I was stuck in the memory of being unsuccessful in a similar academic space, worrying and anxious that I would once again fail. I was not an undergraduate student anymore and I was too scared to commit to my graduate student role.

On the surface, change happened—I appeared to be a graduate student. In reality, the change occurred but the transition was just beginning. I was paralyzed by my own fear making the period much more difficult and drawn out. Eventually, with some time and practice, I managed my stress and anxiety but it never quite subsided. These are the moments where individuals, students, colleagues, friends, and neighbors need support and would benefit from a practice of transitions training. During transitions, even with a physical change, we remain in the same place or space, hovering. With practice and preparation, these transitions should represent a beginning and opportunity to be in the here and now, as a graduate student, new learner, teacher, parent, whatever the role and effectively navigate the physical and mental "where" of these beautiful transitional moments.

This process of development, identity consolidation, or evolution takes time, attention, and work. We may remain in the same place or space, hovering, but transition represents the beginning of what can be a slow, progressive shift of our mental "where." Bridges (2009) reminds us that organizational change requires leaders to attend to the psychological transitions of participants. Individuals who join primary and secondary schools, higher education institutions, and professional organizations all struggle with the where of their new locations, context, roles, and the internal struggle. It is critical that teachers, advisors, mentors, and others take Bridges's heed and design and implement programming and strategies to support individuals in their unique journey into and through these transitions.

WHY?

I like to believe I have learned a lot during my life, and I am happy to share that much of what I know has come from my amazing students. For example, after a few years of teaching, I realized that this question of why matters a lot. Sharing the why of teaching and learning or a decision to change or adopt a new process or strategy is important. While I have usually been able to build trusting relationships with my students, transparency and having an answer to the why always went a long way. I no longer take for granted or expect anyone to follow my lead or my directions without some explanation from me.

When, for example, I introduce assignments to my students, I explain my thought process, the connections between tasks, and how the work will be relevant and prepare them for the next step. In the spirit of that practice, I want to offer a brief discussion about the why of this training, this transitions practice.

My rationale for inviting you to commit to this work includes multiple reasons. While much of this "why" discussion will center on the return on investment from this work, I will also briefly revisit the ways in which organizations, educational institutions, and other entities currently operate. This will also include a consideration of how the assumptions or myths held by leaders and other decision-makers also warrant consideration and commitment to transitions training and programming. The why discussion will conclude with a brief discussion of the relationship between emotions and cognition, including a note about the effects of fear of failure on our transitional moments and, lastly, a detailed discussion of the potential to experience a variety of economic and psychic benefits.

ASSUMPTIONS WE MAKE

According to an article by Larry Kim (2015), people make decisions about individuals in just seconds. He notes that psychologists call these split-second judgments, "thin slicing." Each of us faces numerous decisions throughout the day and so we use past experiences, existing information, and other easily and quickly accessible data in lieu of an authentic, exhaustive, and time-consuming search. As a result, these "thin slices" mean it is possible that decision-makers overgeneralize or draw incorrect conclusions about people. For example, when I first started working as a faculty member, I noticed that many of our graduate students would benefit from some additional academic writing support. When I crafted and presented a proposal to the leadership, their response suggested that any individual who earned admission here could already write. While my experience told me otherwise, leadership denied my proposal and students did not gain access to these much-needed resources. Like this erroneous assumption, each of us has made assumptions about our own students, colleagues, and employees.

While individuals are actually struggling to navigate a transition or expending a great deal of energy to avoid, push down, or rush through these moments, these transitional moments appear to someone on the outside as underperforming or failing to show up in their current roles. Those around them may assume the individual was not prepared, the task was too hard, the program faculty, leadership, or supervisor did not do a good job, or any of a variety of reasons as a way to explain what they actually refuse or are unable to see—a transition. Individuals, groups, and organizations need this book and this training so that they can notice, name, and mark these transitions. Individuals need to focus on this present moment, learn language to describe their thoughts and feelings, and practice navigating or supporting individuals during their transitional periods.

Assumptions we make represent one barrier to effectively supporting individual development during transitional moments. Like assumptions, our tendency to act rather than pause and consider can also create problems in these moments. Knowing that we are certain to experience lots of firsts, what can (or should) we do? The answer is not always clear or easy.

Aiko Betheo (Brown, 2019) suggests that in these moments we tend to favor action over inaction, or what is known as *action bias*. This describes the idea that individuals, groups, and organizations feel the need to act even when there is little to no evidence that this decision to act will lead to better outcomes. In fact, there are researchers like Bar-Eli et al (2007) who suggest that this quick action often leads to improper responses, poor outcomes, and interventions that try to address a problem that has yet to be accurately defined. Moreover, societal norms and expectations view inaction as wrong.

How is this related to transitions? Well, as we move into these firsts and face choices, we need to be fully aware of our natural human need to act and then we need to fight that act, pause, intentionally avoid acting until we have had some time to familiarize ourselves with the moment, to recognize, name, and engage in this important moment. Whether because of assumptions made or our tendency to act hastily, these inclinations keep us and our teachers and leaders from noticing and marking transitions. Ultimately, individuals missing out or suffering through these important moments could have been supported with a commitment to and practice with transitions training.

EMOTIONS AND COGNITION

Like assumptions, research and experts' evolving understanding of cognition and emotion helps to explain our neglect of these critical transitions. Early research on human development and information processing considered cognition and emotion as separate systems (Ye, Quifang, and Xiaolan, 2000). According to Ye et al (2000), Thomas Aquinas, in the 13th century, saw behavior as two categories, cognition and affect. Emerging research now suggests that emotions and cognition work as integrated and interconnected systems (LeDoux and Brown, 2017; Plass and Kaplan, 2016). Negative emotions contribute to more time needed for learning and lower performance (Brand et al, 2007) while enjoyment can actually facilitate learning. Emotions can also serve to motivate learning and broaden resources for decreasing our intrinsic load or they can narrow cognitive resources and increase extraneous processing requirements. This notion of affect and cognition being integrated is critical to the why of transitions practice because it supports the idea that educators, employers, and others must attend to the emotional needs of their students and workers in these pivotal moments. Transitions are already confusing and uncertain and when we layer on the requisite tasks, projects, and assignments in our daily lives, these experiences, together, culminate into less-than-ideal performance and circumstances.

Human learning is complex. Sweller (2011) developed the Cognitive Load Theory (CLT) which refers to the working memory required from an individual to perform a task. One of the many reasons it is critical to consider CLT and working memory is because this working memory comes with limited capacity and duration. If we assume that emotions and cognition are intertwined, it stands to reason that negative emotions like confusion, struggle, worry, stress, self-doubt, and anxiety—the telltale signs of a transition—could crowd out the productive load required to learn and/or perform a task. For this reason, it is paramount that individuals, teachers, coaches, mentors, leaders, and others learn to notice transitions and devise a plan to help others navigate these often challenging and important moments.

Growing up I attended church regularly. I joined a youth group, played handbells, and sang in the choir. One Christmas season, I decided to audition for a duet with one of my good friends. We got the parts and our rehearsals began. Now, this is not exactly a textbook kind of transition although, in my view, it represented a change in roles from member of the choir to soloist. I tell this story to illustrate the power of our emotions. We started choir rehearsal and it was time for our duet. I was nervous, scared, worried I would miss a note, forget a line, just fail. The intensity of my emotions was so strong I could not get through the song. I knew the words, had practiced, but could not do it.

These transitions, no matter how small or short-lived, can have a paralyzing effect. The associated fear, confusion, and worry can emerge as a shy kindergartener, an absent middle schooler, a co-worker who refuses to share their project idea, or a leader who cannot make a decision or makes it without the team's input. These transitional periods, if ignored, can do harm to the individual or team and represent a missed opportunity.

Emotions researcher, Mark Brackett (2019), tells us that everything we do and learn is filtered by our emotions. These transitions represent an amazing chance to learn and grow and when we fail to attend to these moments, we can actually hinder our own progress.

CHECKPOINT:
Think about a moment of transition in your own life.
- How did you feel?
- How did you react?
- What emotions were you feeling?

I have plenty of examples of transitions—some good and some bad. What makes one bad? I can remember entering college. I was a strong high school student, ready for the rigors of college studies, or so I thought. I signed up for my first classes and for many reasons struggled at the start. I kept quiet, did not reach out for help, and the worry, embarrassment, questioning, and uncertainty built up. I just assumed that I should be doing better and must be doing something wrong. Remember I had been a good student in high school and this was new and uncharted territory for me. Consequently, I suffered unnecessarily for the entire semester. I was afraid to make another mistake and I was fearful of admitting that I was in unfamiliar territory and was not "in the know."

Emotional experiences, like transitions, are ubiquitous and critical in any learning setting (Tyng, Amin, Saad, and Malik, 2017). Teachers, leaders, and others must consider these transitions and related emotions carefully. Individuals' attention, memory, problem-solving, and other cognitive processes are affected by these emotions and thus significantly contribute to an individual's ability to flourish and perform. Understanding the intricate relationship between emotions and cognition means we might be able to use this transition training to design and implement strategies that match the transition journeys of different individuals.

The previous discussion provided a rationale that suggested this work is needed to challenge assumptions we make and to better reflect the role that transitions and the associated emotions play in the day-to-day management of our school, work, and other responsibilities. The subsequent section explores a variety of potential benefits individuals, groups, and organizations stand to gain by investing time, effort, and commitment into this important work.

IMPROVED PERFORMANCE AND WELL-BEING

According to Gray (1987), fear is a subjective emotion that contributes to physiological changes including increased heart rate and muscle tension. Individuals experience fear as a response to a perceived threat that they want to avoid or escape. Researchers examined the fear of failure in a group of elite junior athletes and found that this fear can lead to higher levels of anxiety, lower performance in their sport and school, and lower levels of well-being (Sagar, Lavallee, and Spray, 2009). The study demonstrated the need for coaches and practitioners to teach athletes effective coping strategies to teach individuals how to confront their fears and how to rehearse and reframe. Like athletes, educators, leaders, and other individuals would benefit from strategies that include intentional practice to challenge perspectives and practice managing the discomfort as it emerges. Leaning into transitions practice may mitigate fear of failure and contribute to our ability to notice, name, and effectively be in these uncomfortable moments.

RETURN ON INVESTMENT

I have a dear friend and colleague whom I respect, trust, and often rely on to serve as a sounding board for some of my crazy and not-so-crazy ideas. As I write this section, I can hear her saying, in her most supportive way, this is a really interesting idea and I am intrigued but I have to ask, "What is the return on investment? What would someone gain by reading this book or doing this work?" This discussion is for her, but also for you. In considering this important question, I recall my own economics training and the undergraduate courses I taught. A quick answer to this "return on investment" question would be an accumulation of human capital.

Economists categorize economic resources as land, labor, and physical capital, and later, as there was increased attention on the quality of labor, economists introduced the idea of *human capital (*Becker, 1964*)*. Human capital is a quick but complicated answer because this concept encompasses the accumulation of knowledge, skills, and other personal attributes which vary greatly from person to person. Heckman and Rubenstein (2001) delineated cognitive (skills and knowledge) from non-cognitive human capital accumulation (i.e., motivation, problem-solving, adaptation) and while I understand these differences, I have never loved the term "non-cognitive" or "soft" skills. In my view, it undervalues the importance of this aspect of human capital, yet another example of why this work matters so much.

As discussed earlier, transitions represent a paradox of discomfort and discovery, and an opportunity for growth and development if we notice, name, and attend to these critical periods. Attending to these transitions could be equated with making important investments in human capital. For the purposes of this discussion, the return on investment or human capital benefits include what I will refer to as economic and psychological well-being, and while these categories do not perfectly align with the positive outcomes of transitions practice, they do provide a good starting point for this discussion.

Transitions training as a method of human capital investment may yield benefits related to economic well-being. These include increased satisfaction and productivity, which may contribute to lower attrition or higher retention of students, teachers, and other workers. I hope "the why" of adopting transitions practice is apparent. Investing in this work, making time, and committing to this practice may, in the short run, leverage the benefits of the moment and also build a foundation for improvement and reflection, emotion regulation, openness, and flexibility. All of which will contribute in positive ways to transitions and really all stages of our development.

In addition to economic well-being, a practice in transitions training that includes focusing on the work, being here and now, and committing to a shift in attitudes, it reflects the importance of psychological well-being, and, perhaps, a more humanistic approach to the care and attention required for our individual development. This kind of well-being includes personal growth, self-acceptance, and the belief in supporting that growth and potential. Economic well-being, on the other hand, includes knowledge, skills, and an accumulation of factors that promote consumption and wealth. While the following discussion is not an exhaustive articulation of the benefits, the return on investment from this work, I do think that the included list provides strong evidence of why this work matters, and individuals and organizations need to commit to a practice of focusing on and engaging more effectively with personal and collective transitions.

As suggested in previous chapters and supported by research evidence, transitions are ubiquitous and uncertain which can leave us doubtful and stressed. Moreover, individuals are certain to experience these transitions numerous times across their lives. This stress, confusion, dissonance, and ambiguity contribute to lower psychic well-being and may also result in reduced satisfaction in an individual's program of study, classroom, professional role, and other contexts. Moreover, this lower satisfaction contributes leads to burnout, higher turnover, and attrition (Maslach, Schaufeli, and Leiter, 2001; Nagoski and Nagoski, 2019).

With respect to psychic well-being, transitions training offers opportunities to promote metacognitive skills (Hayes, 2011), reduce psychological stress in the short run, and cultivate long-term changes to general stress which includes decreasing individual tendency to ruminate or cycle in the worry and discomfort for prolonged periods of time (Hayes, 2011). Focusing on the moment, being present, and attending to what *is* rather than what *should* be also promotes emotion regulation (Hayes, 2011), cultivates creativity and cognitive flexibility, and improves individual and team social skills.

Transitions training, in teaching individuals to notice their own experiences, describe and share their own story, and remain alert to their thoughts and feelings in these moments. This training could improve self-observation and improve management of or immediate reaction to situations and experiences. It can raise awareness of stressors and warning signs work to align emotions to the realities of the event and learn to accept individual limitations (Malpass, Binnie, and Robinson, 2019). By way of example, I have worked hard to notice my own reactions, emotional experiences, and thoughts in various situations. Please understand, this does not mean that I do not react or that another person does not see my expression. What it means is that I am able to better navigate short and long periods of transitions because I just know myself better.

For instance, while I identify as a teacher-faculty, part of my role eventually needed to include a researcher identity. As my professional identity continued to evolve, I started to take on small research and writing projects. I remember receiving those first rounds of feedback from the editor of one of my first journal submissions. The feedback sent me into a spiral, defeated, questioning, and doubting my own abilities and my novice research identity. I was truly stuck. With reflection and coaching from colleagues, I paid more attention and focused on recognizing the moments, my reactions, my thoughts, and feelings in relation to the feedback received. I still feel defeated when I receive tough and critical feedback, but it is short-lived. I do a better job of putting it into perspective and talking it through and applying the comments to effectively use and leverage the feedback.

Even starting new projects and research papers represents a form of transition and even after preparing and practicing with these transitions, we experience them, feel nervous, uncertain, and doubtful. These moments do not and will not disappear. Individuals will always experience these periods of gradual change. The difference is that, with practice, individuals acquire knowledge, some awareness, new habits, and a set of skills to effectively navigate and leverage these important moments.

In addition to those benefits already mentioned, research also suggests that attention to these moments of development contributes to greater energy, openness, and adaptability (Block and Richmond, 1998). By working in the present, wrestling with the emotions and thoughts, individuals learn to question with curiosity, remain open to perspectives and possibilities, and navigate these critical transitions with self-compassion and care. This training invites individuals into moments of disorientation that, with training, lead to reorientation or what Hudson (1999) refers to as a cycle of renewal.

HOW?

> *"Like it or not, this moment is all we really have to work with." – Jon Kabat-Zinn*

In order to experience the aforementioned benefits, we need to talk about the "how" of this training. The details of the transitions practice, features of the training, and sample strategies are discussed later in the book. For now, let's take a quick look at how we might approach this work.

Transitions training incorporates ideas of mindfulness that include paying attention, focusing on the here and now, and cultivating an ability to sit with difficult and often conflicting thoughts and feelings, to hover in-between. In research about mindfulness as a way to navigate identity development, Dong, Campbell, and Vance (2017) remind us that it is critical to foster acceptance of individual thoughts and emotions rather than trying to push them down or control them. John Kabat Zinn (1994) also said that being present and mindfulness represent "paying attention in a particular way: on purpose in the present moment, and nonjudgmentally." Masicampo and Baumeister (2007) also noted that welcoming challenging images and emotions may contribute to a greater ability to tolerate our thoughts and feelings. In a structured but adaptable way, transitions aim to offer a deliberate practice to learn to effectively navigate moments of transition.

Transitions training, in some ways, incorporates opportunities and strategies to practice being present, to learn to pay attention, attach language to our experiences, and kindly and with curiosity explore these moments. Similar to mindfulness training, the transitions training activities and techniques help individuals raise their awareness of individual stressors and teach us to detect early signs of a transition. It trains us to cultivate new connections and responses to our thoughts by asking questions, checking and comparing our perception and our reality, and eventually changing the channel away from the discouraging images and thoughts. By adopting this kind of practice, individuals can teach themselves and others to notice these moments and approach them with awareness and engage in these reflections with non-judgmental and non-reactive attention (Kabat-Zinn, 1990).

While later chapters offer a much more detailed account of the transitions training the following offers a sampling of how to engage in this training.

WARM-UP
- check-in
- engage in familiar conversations with new people
- ask for individuals to share their views and ideas
- cultivate trusting relationships
- create an inclusive space for exploration

INTERVALS
Noticing, naming, and marking the transition
- Communicate openly – describe the experience with words and images

- Describe emotions
- Express grace and gratitude

Hovering

- Acknowledge the dissonance and the muddiness of the moments
- Engage in dialogue, provide feedback, practice self-compassion
- Identify quick wins
- Aim for greatness (kindness and rigor)

REST AND REFLECTION

- Own the transition
- Practice reflection
- Establish goals
- Engage in new learning

OTHER STRATEGIES

- Focused attention – specific object
- Open monitoring – take in the surrounding environment, not any specific object

Learning to identify these transitions and preparing and practicing for these moments contributes to successful shifts through and out of these moments, increases satisfaction of individuals moving through the transitions, contributes to a person's sense of belonging, self-efficacy, and self-concept. Pilots receive instruction and train with a qualified instructor and, of course, practice, practice, and practice some more. Soccer coaches and players run drills, focus on key principles, and teach players to connect, coordinate, and collaborate on and off the field in order to build support, relationships, and communication. Coaches of all sorts listen to their clients, students, and colleagues, devise a plan to train for and through a transition, prepare and practice, and debrief and reflect on the previous transition. Continuing to name the experiences, train for these experiences, and reflect contributes to improved success and while this practice may not prevent future transitions, training can support individuals to leverage the possibilities rather than bowing to the uncertainty.

This chapter offered insight into the where, why, and how of transitions and the training program. While some transitions feature a physical or geographical location, almost every transition also includes a mental relocation of sorts. Individuals, teams, and organizations may find themselves moving to and from an old reality and a new one. Naming and attending to this back and forth may yield benefits that include economic and psychic well-being. While learning to manage transitions may increase productivity and employee and student retention, equally important, this work will contribute to improved emotion regulation, lower levels of stress, and improve observation and reflection skills. Doing this work requires time, effort, and commitment to the practice.

This chapter offered a glimpse at the strategies and later in the book I will review, in great detail, the program framework and each step of the program. In the end, teachers, leaders, facilitators, and supervisors who engage in this training program may better support diverse learners in schools, businesses, and other organizations, design and implement equitable strategies and techniques from the program, create inclusive spaces and places for individuals to explore their transitional moments and, hopefully, this work leads to increasing belonging in our organizations and institutions and for individuals who engage in this work.

CHAPTER 4: TRAINING WITH ATTITUDE

"Talk to yourself like you would to someone you love."
– Brene Brown

"Although many of us think of ourselves as thinking creatures that feel, biologically we are feeling creatures that think." – Jill Bolte Taylor

When I was a senior in high school, our field hockey team made it to the state finals. I remember it like it was yesterday, a crisp, cool November morning, warming up on beautifully manicured fields surrounded by friends, family, and other hockey fans and media. We were playing one of our archrivals, I was in goal, my best friend led the defense in front of me, and the whole team was ready for this game. We were coming off of another great season and entered today's game with one of the best records in the state. Throughout both halves, the game was tight, we were playing well but just could not seem to get the ball in the net. By late in the second half, we were tied and towards the end of the game, one of the other team's forwards got loose with the ball. She was headed to goal, she penetrated our midfield line, dribbled through our defense, and I was the last player between her and the goal. Unfortunately, for me and the team, she scored and that ended up being the goal that gave the other team the State Championship.

It was my last game of my last season of my last year as a high school field hockey player. To say I was devastated is an understatement. The team was upset, I was upset, and it was an all-around awful situation. When it came time for the short ceremony to award trophies, well, let's just say I was not my best self. Looking back, it is hard to believe I reacted the way I did. Our players each received a runner-up plaque, and, in a private moment, I dropped the plaque on the grass and slid my cleated shoe across the face leaving several scratches on the award. My mother, of course, was furious with me. She pulled me aside to remind me that my family and friends had come to support and cheer me on, but I wanted nothing to do with them after the game. I just wanted to be alone or, more accurately, disappear. Later, my mom said I needed to work on my bad attitude.

Throughout much of my young life and into my college years, this was a recurring theme. The poor sportsmanship, fortunately, did subside but my attitude about letting a goal in the net, underperforming in a road race, earning less than an 'A' on an exam, and just doing less than I thought I should in *any* situation lead to an attitude that included tears, anger, upset, surrender, and even quitting things I loved. Now, in my defense, I had a lot going on. I was struggling with my sexual orientation, grappling with perfectionism (remember – I am a recovering perfectionist), and desperately trying to grow into my own identity. Like all of us, I still had a lot of work to do and still do to this day.

Looking back, I recognize now that my "bad" attitude may not have been that after all. Sure, my reaction and lack of interaction with my family and friends were not appropriate because it may have hurt them, but it is not evident to me that my attitude, my evaluation of the moment, was bad. In fact, in preparing for this chapter and reading more about moods, emotions, attitudes, and mindset, I have come to believe that attitude may not be good or bad, positive or negative. Buddhism, for example, teaches that an important path to enlightenment is accepting things as they are in this moment. Buddhism promotes equanimity—"it is what it is."

Individuals need to avoid pushing reality away, rejecting reality, and wanting something different. Negative and positive, this binary thinking quickly values one state over the other, when in fact, there may be tremendous opportunities to learn in those uncomfortable (i.e., negative) moments. This binary thinking limits our view and focuses attention on outcomes rather than a journey. In my view, that moment on the field hockey field might be better described as my reaction to or attitude towards myself and my failing to achieve an outcome that I hoped for and, quite frankly, had expected. We were a great team with strong players and it seemed reasonable to believe we would win. This transition to a different and unexpected outcome was difficult. My response and attitude in that moment were related more to my own inability to see my own and my teammates' successes, our journey, and our growth. In these moments, individuals, including myself, often have a low tolerance for discomfort and negativity and, as a result, tend to act hastily in less-than-ideal ways. In those moments, it is important to acknowledge the struggle, recognize that we cannot run from the moment, embrace it, and allow space for myriad feelings and experiences, staying open to what is happening.

I know I mentioned a Netflix series earlier in the book and, as I was falling asleep last night, I was listening to another show. I have a love of medical dramas and in this scene a nurse was caring for a Buddhist monk receiving hospice care. A few moments later the nurse, pushing this monk in a wheelchair through the ER, saw a woman and man noticeably upset, holding hands, and it was clear from the scene that the woman needed medical attention. The nurse commented on how sad it was to see them so distraught and the monk asked the nurse to look again, to notice the love that had to exist between these two people for them to experience this intense sadness and worry. I understand that a Buddhist monk is a special and unique individual who, over time, trains to practice equanimity. But I also believe anyone can find peace in what is, and practice to remain present focusing on the here and now, and catch glimpses of the love, kindness, and goodness often hiding in, under, or behind a mess.

CHECKPOINT:
Find a nearby window and look out of it.
- What do you see?
- What do you notice?
Now, move your body slightly to the right.
- What do you see?
- What is different?
- What has changed?

Looking back at that field hockey game and, in that transition, I did not have the knowledge, skills, experience, or training to focus on the moment. I could not effectively grapple with the discomfort of losing so I pushed the feelings down, pushed people who supported me away, and tried to quickly move through the experience. I may never achieve a commitment or practice to focus on the present like a Buddhist monk, but this work and this book can contribute to shifting and teaching us to embrace these moments, the transitions. It can provide us with the awareness and fortitude to name and notice what we hoped for in that moment and the reality of what actually occurred. Successfully navigating transitions requires us to be present, in the *actual* moment, not in our minds wondering about and dwelling in what *could* or *should* have been.

One fundamental difference between younger me and older me is my mindset and attitude. Reflecting on my reaction to the hockey game and other, similar moments, I realize that I think my reaction, my "bad" attitude was a reflection of my mindset. For many reasons, that is a story for another book. I believed that I would be liked, loved, and accepted if I achieved some designated outcome, won the game, or earned the top score or grade and anything short of that bar was failure. As Brene Brown suggests, talk to yourself in the way you would to someone you love.

How would I have talked or responded to my best friend who played defense in front of me? Would I have scolded her for our failure? Would I have expressed my frustration or shown anger with metaphorical scratching of the award? No! Of course not, for some reason our humanness allows us to find that equanimity, to focus on what is, and notice the good when our friends, family, and loved ones are involved. I know with certainty, that I would have responded with kindness and love. I could sit quietly in that terrible moment and easily see and name her successes, strengths, and contributions to our season and our four years as a successful hockey team. I would and did see her disappointment and tried to react with kindness, a listening ear, and empathy. The attitude I expressed in that moment was more about my inability to be in that actual moment, to quiet my own judgmental voices, show myself some kindness, navigate the gap between *should* and *is*, and give myself some grace.

CHECKPOINT:
- How do you speak with your friends?
- With yourself?
- In a moment of your friends' struggle, how do you respond?
- How is it the same or different than your response to yourself and your own struggle?

As you engage in transitions practice and training, you will find that this work not only encourages and motivates you to focus on the here and now, the current journey, it will contribute to your ability to adopt attitudes that reflect caring for ourselves, acknowledging the journey, and valuing the process over the outcomes. This does not happen with one change or even several, it is gradual and oscillating. Eventually, continuing this transitions practice will shift your mindset away from outcomes and "things" towards an appreciation and valuing of the journey, the process, the transition, and all of its mud and chaos.

Part of shifting mindset is beginning to accept the realities of these transitions, not to roll over and do nothing, but to act and react in ways that honor being present and, in the moment, noticing and experiencing whatever arises. In my experience, acceptance starts with working to adopt different attitudes or ways to evaluate situations and scenarios. The following chapter offers three such attitudes on which to focus to begin your journey towards noticing, naming, and embracing your transitions.

Attitude represents a way of thinking, an individual's views of a person, place, or thing, and is often revealed in our behavior or actions. As I considered how attitude matters in transitions work, I had to examine my own understanding of attitude. To my untrained eye, attitude and mindset were synonymous. As I read a little more about these terms, it became apparent that these related terms were, in subtle ways, different.

I came across a definition of mindset that made sense to me. Mindset is like a mental operating system or, as Mezirow (2000) suggests, habits of mind that include skills, attitudes, cues, and experiences. Mezirow also noted that a mindset can contribute to being "more inclusive, discriminating, open, emotionally capable of change, and reflective" (2000). Mindset contributes to our walk towards clarity, vision, thought, actions, and results.

Throughout our lives, mindset adapts and evolves to change and promotes growth (or not). Mindset encapsulates our attitudes, thoughts, feelings, and beliefs related to our worldview and approach to engaging with the world. In some way, mindset feels like a personal strategic vision and our attitudes, perhaps, represent tactics or actions steps as one way to operationalize, implement, or apply our mindset to a situation.

With mindset as the operating system or a collection of viewpoints, attitudes represent our interactions with the world, groups, students, colleagues, friends, and ourselves (du Plessis, 2015). Arguably, transitions training, the practice of noticing, naming, practicing, and reflecting has the potential to contribute to transformative learning and developing a mindset that reflects the ability to stay present, open, and curious about and during these transitions. In my own experience, mindset and attitudes share a sort of reciprocity, a possible chicken and egg situation. Changing attitudes can contribute to shifting mindset while changing or influencing mindset may also force us to amend, augment, or drop attitudes that align with this adjustment to mindset. Later, in the book, I will discuss the importance of adopting a learning identity which, as you will read, also embodies a particular mindset and is consistent with the attitudes discussed in this chapter. For now, I want to make the case that the three "Gr's", Grace, Gratitude, and Greatness represent accessories needed to engage in this transition training.

Sure, I could have started this part of the book with a discussion of mindset but, for me, mindset feels big and expansive, a state of being that emerges and evolves gradually over time. I wanted to start Part II of the book, not with lofty and longer-term goals, but something achievable, realistic, and appropriately matched to most readers of this book. High expectations and greatness will be covered later in this chapter so suffice it to say, I wanted to set kind and rigorous expectations for our work around attitudes (see what I did there!).

For the purposes of this discussion, I conceptualize attitude as a short-term response, change, or action that both contribute to the moment at hand—our awareness and evaluation of a transition, and long-term progress towards a shift in mindset about these transitions. Desmond Tutu reminds us that the way to eat an elephant is one piece at a time. While changing and adopting a learning mindset to effectively face and navigate transitions is the goal, we have to start with one piece, one step at a time, one attitude at a time.

In my own experiences and observations, I have come to firmly believe that focusing on grace, gratitude, and greatness represents a good first step in shifting our mindsets away from avoiding, ignoring, and rushing through our transitions to one of embracing and learning and benefiting from these moments. Looking back at that moment on the hockey field, I understand that my reaction was less about having a positive or negative attitude and more about adopting a set of attitudes that could extend grace, gratitude, and greatness to myself and others. As a Buddhist monk reminds us, these transitional moments require us to find equanimity, be in the moment and lean into our reality rather than push it away. This set of attitudes offers an important tool to help navigate transitional moments and contribute to cultivating this learning mindset and identity.

GRACE

CHECKPOINT:
- What does grace mean to you?
- What does it look like to give yourself grace?
- What happens if you give yourself permission to embrace the uncertainty of a transitional moment?
- What would happen if you shared this moment with someone else?

When was the last time you made a misstep? A mistake? Competed at work, in some sort of race, or even just a friendly conversational debate and, you immediately began to critically evaluate your own performance, your choice of words, actions, or responses to questions. How did you speak to yourself? How did you feel? What did you say? Knowing the conversation, you had with yourself, now ask yourself, would you speak to a friend in that same way?

I recall a conversation—or should I say argument—I had with my nine-year-old son. It was in the midst of the 2020 pandemic, he was tired of us and, well, we could all use a break from family time. We love spending time together and we have so much fun, but it has been almost a year of isolation, remote schooling, infrequent playdates, and social distancing for everything and everyone. He and I have been battling over him taking more responsibility for his actions—engaging in an appropriate way when we call his grandparents, cleaning up his room, putting away toys, books, and other activities when finished, so on and so forth. One night, in my fatigue and exasperation, I got upset and sent him to his room where he ate his dinner by himself and had some time alone. He eventually came down and apologized but, overall, it was a rough night.

As is typical for me and my parenting, I spend a lot of time trying to figure out how to help him with some of the tasks and responsibilities I think are appropriate for his age. I also spend time thinking about how I could help myself and how I could have handled the situation better. There is always room for me to improve and learn to be a better parent. On that night, I was feeling bad, questioning my approach, doubting my insistence on my latest parenting demands. I grew impatient with myself, frustrated that I just never seem to get these moments right. As I mentioned earlier in this book, the pandemic has really made me and many others feel like we are doing as much as we can and never doing enough, never getting it right.

These are the moments when we need grace the most. Grace is an act of kindness and, in this case, I am referring to the idea of giving ourselves some grace. Beating ourselves up contributes to an inaccurate evaluation of what we did or did not achieve. It also misaligns our perceived reality with the actual reality and possibilities. Even as we fail, make mistakes, or stumble, it is critical that we avoid judgment and forgive ourselves. It is paramount that we recognize and accept that human beings are imperfect, and failure is a shared human experience. We must also allow ourselves to feel bad, find some perspective in our errors, and learn from and move on after these moments. It is possible, with grace, to feel bad, express hurt, and also admit we are doing the best we can and that we will keep trying.

Showing yourself some grace during these transitions and feelings of uncertainty and dissonance opens us up to the possibility of giving ourselves permission to forgive mistakes, to welcome failure, and engage in trying without worrying about perfection (Tungend, 2015). Expressing kindness may mitigate fear, decrease feelings of being overwhelmed by uncertainty and self-doubt and prompt a sense of forgiveness. Importantly, practicing an attitude of grace may also close the gap between the "should" and "is" statements which could, ultimately, also reduce the uncertain feelings of those transitions and increase our willingness to tolerate and embrace the possibilities. Practicing grace means we are more likely to navigate these in-between moments, stay in the present, and engage in ways that contribute to our own development.

As discussed earlier, being in these moments prompts a need to control the situation, push past the dissonance, ignore the uncertainty, and schedule and plan for the discomfort. Movement, action, decision making, and being productive are our attempts to manage the dissonance of the transition rather than providing ourselves with some grace to admit we do not know, we are unsure, and that we are just feeling our way through. Perhaps, taking a pause and being open to vulnerability might just make these transitions more manageable. In these in-between moments when you are neither here nor there, could you just listen to how you talk and respond to yourself in these moments? Could you try to address and walk with yourself without judgment or defense? Extending ourselves some grace may eventually elicit a sense of emotional courage (Bussolari and Goodell, 2009) where we can admit that we are not in control and we just do not know.

Imagine the power you might feel if you could just let go and see what happens. Change the channel and ask yourself: How can I *allow* myself to change rather than how *should* I change? What might happen if, with some grace, you stayed present, named the discomfort, and stood in the feelings? Sure, you might fail, the expected outcome may not be achieved, but so what? We name that moment in the transition and stand in the mud again recognizing that it is possible to navigate this moment and learn from this. Grace is a powerful attitude that when unlocked may help us lean into these transitional moments of possibility.

GRATITUDE

"I don't have to chase extraordinary moments to find happiness—it's right in front of me if I'm paying attention and practicing gratitude." – Brene Brown

Now, you might be thinking, okay, grace I understand. I *might* be able to show myself some grace, some kindness in those difficult transitional moments. We have already established that periods of transition are hard and they can be difficult to effectively navigate. I deserve kindness and to give myself some perspective on the moment. But gratitude? It is reasonable, even a little possible, knowing the challenges of transitions, that I and/or we might be deserving of some kindness, and even just a little moment of perspective. But now you want me to be thankful for these moments of dissonance, real or potential failure, discomfort, and uncertainty? You cannot be serious!

I am serious and I know this work is hard. At first, it may feel like you are being disingenuous, trying to find happiness in difficult moments of transition and doubt. Yet, these are the moments when we have to dig deep and work hard to find something for which we authentically might express gratitude. I am not asking you just to say that you are thankful for the dissonance or even the transition. This is critical.

This expression of gratitude cannot be a surface, fleeting, or even pretend kind of gratitude. This attitude is not adopted by pretending that you are psyched about uncertainty or self-doubt. That would be disingenuous and untrue. This kind of gratitude means that we are present, focused on the here and now of this discomfort, and monitoring the moment in a way that we can authentically find gratitude. The point is not to casually and inauthentically say thank you for the uncertainty. The goal is to find something that you actually are thankful for in that moment, during this transition. Could you find gratitude in being with colleagues while you wrestle with the challenge, or express thanks for having the determination to just show up for the competition, the new job, the new school, or any other kind of transition?

CHECKPOINT:
Think about your most recent challenge, a transition.
- How might you express gratitude for the moment?
- What about the moment could you be thankful for?

This description of gratitude reminds me of my new Peloton bike and some of the training sessions I voluntarily joined very early in the morning. Recently, I did a 60-minute ride, intervals of varying duration, frequency, and intensity. As we were about 25 minutes into the ride, I was winded, tired, and my legs were on fire—no exaggeration. Then, the trainer looked into the camera and said, figure out why you are here, how are you grateful for this moment? I was stumped. I was barely keeping pace, wanting to just stop (I didn't) and now she wants us to be thankful for the moment? This is not a shake my hand or pat you on the back kind of thankful. This kind of gratitude has to come from your gut, your core. You have to really believe it in your bones or it is not real gratitude and it will not help in these moments of transition. At the almost halfway point of the ride, I thought to myself, I am grateful that I got up and on my bike this morning. I am grateful that I made it this far in the ride. Who knows what is coming but so far, so good. You see, being grateful and showing gratitude to yourself does not have to be lofty nor should it be untrue. The important feature of this transitions practice of gratitude is that it is truthful and authentic in the moment about something in the moment. You need to be able to look yourself in the mirror or the reflection of your Peloton screen and make that gratitude statement and then believe it.

No matter how small it is, finding true gratitude in the moment contributes to self-compassion, self-acceptance, and might just reshape our relationship with ourselves. This is critical to transitions practice because our ability to genuinely appreciate the moments of dissonance, to express thanks for the uncertainty, means that we are no longer focused on the *should* of the moment and actually focused on the here and now and being thankful for even small parts of the present. Grace and gratitude, together, may also change the ways in which we evaluate any moment. It is possible that adopting these attitudes may also help diminish the importance of our typical sources of self-worth like perfectionism, body image, or external approval which might allow us to notice and embrace these important moments of transition. A statement, observation, or awareness of true gratitude certainly will contribute to shifting our mindset. It is also true, however, that an attitude of gratitude helps us to stay focused and present in these periods of transition.

GREATNESS

> *"Never underestimate the power of dreams and the influence of the human spirit. We are all the same in this notion: The potential for greatness lives within each of us." – Wilma Rudolph*

I know I have already talked about field hockey and, I realize now, that the story I am about to share might give the impression that field hockey was always tough, difficult, and sometimes heartbreaking. Well, that is true *and* it was amazing, fun, silly, and inspiring. Experiences can be all of that—tough and terrific.

My field hockey coach was a leader, parental figure, mentor, and cheerleader. She also valued schedules, routines, and traditions. Every Monday afternoon, at the start of practice, like clockwork, our team engaged in what was fondly known as "dribble-jog-sprints." This conditioning drill was known far and wide among players, around school, between parents of players, and alumni of the program. This training activity, at the time, represented one of the most challenging routines we did, and we did it *every* week.

Players paired off, got a ball and stick, and lined up on the sideline of the field. When coach blew the whistle to start the drill, players, already on the sideline, dribbled the ball across the field, dead stopped the ball on the opposite sideline, jogged back to the side of the field where this drill began, and then sprinted back to the ball. Our legs were burning, lungs were on fire, and the team would look around at each other all thinking the same thing. It was only our first practice and completing those three, little activities meant we had only finished ONE of the fifteen dribble-jog-sprints of the workout!

Each Monday afternoon, Coach Shelton would put a number on her office door. This told us how many dribble-jog-sprints we each needed to complete during the drill. We would usually approach the door with trepidation, often designating some brave soul to go and check her door. Early on in the season, the numbers started at fifteen, and, believe me, this felt nearly impossible but by the end of the season, we would complete thirty. Now, consider for a moment, what if on the first Monday of the fall season, Coach Shelton tacked the number twenty-five on her office door? Some would say that she is pushing us towards greatness, to championship level. Others would say, of course, the team needs to be tough and must be able to do this kind of work to win games. Here is the thing—and this is one of the many reasons Coach Shelton stands as one of the best and most loved, respected, and accomplished coaches in high school sports—Lil Shelton understood greatness and she would never start a team's transition to greatness at twenty-five.

The award-winning actress, Helen Hayes, said "the expert in anything was once a beginner." Coach Shelton always began the season with fifteen dribble-jog-sprints because for her, cultivating greatness in her players and achieving greatness as a team meant standing in the present with her beginners and seeing fantastic achievement now, on that first day of practice. She knew what greatness looked like and how to cultivate it in others. She understood that setting high expectations and designing a series of related, daily goals coupled with kindness, patience, and discipline contribute to greatness in individuals and her teams.

This chapter, I hope, has already made a good case for the value of integrating and practicing attitudes that include grace and gratitude. I am also confident that this last "Gr" attitude needed for a successful way forward through these transitions includes adopting an attitude of greatness as we practice, learn, and are present in the discomfort and uncertainty of our numerous transitions.

HIGH EXPECTATIONS

Robert John Meechan said "set your classroom expectations high, the higher the better. Expect the most fantastic things to happen, not in the future, but right now!" Like Coach Shelton, Meechan understands the value of the "right now." Lil understood where our team was both mentally and physically and used this awareness to design a path for the team to develop and grow. She led and supported the team with small, daily steps, right-now victories that pointed to a larger goal like winning a state championship. She knew that to find greatness, to cultivate our individual and collective greatness meant focusing on the here and now. It is not possible to successfully complete thirty dribble-jog-sprints or develop as a researcher, graduate, leader, novelist, adult, parent, or any evolving identity until you engage in and live those first few steps.

Grace and gratitude are fundamental to our transitions practice but without high expectations, being nice to ourselves and others will not be enough. Sonia Nieto (2005) reminds us that harm may be done when teachers do not apply the same level of rigor with their students of color as compared to similar white students. Being nice, or easy, and lowering expectations only leads to lower levels of confidence and increased self-doubt in ourselves and those we teach, lead, and work alongside. In fact, the evidence is clear that NOT setting our sights on greatness contributes to an individual's belief that he or she cannot achieve a set goal (Muenks, Wigfield, and Eccles, 2018). Expecting less from ourselves and others may contribute to us and them struggling to believe in our and their capability and competence.

Importantly, we can expect and achieve greatness when we combine attitudes of grace and gratitude with high expectations. Decoupling these ideas may lead to more self-doubt, uncertainty, and feeling like we are not enough. Like dribble-jog-sprints, greatness involves setting high expectations while also working to notice and calibrate the uncertainty, doubt, and stress associated with these transitional moments.

CHECKPOINT:
- What high expectations are you setting for yourself?
- How do these expectations honor your core values?
- How do you celebrate meeting these high expectations?

Rudland, Golding, and Wilkinson (2019) characterize stress as paradoxical. Stressors, like conditioning drills, performances, exams, assignments, firsts, and other projects may inhibit and contribute to an individual's learning and successes. The framework of high expectations includes setting and seeing those high expectations and having awareness of our own and others' experiences, abilities, needs, and context in order to translate these expectations into actionable daily steps. High expectations only contribute to navigating transitions effectively when individuals, groups, and teams remain focused on this moment, this step, and this work—realizing what matters.

There is no formula for exacting this process. It is iterative and requires individuals to be present and self-aware. As we consider our own and others' experiences with transitions, the associated uncertainty, and the self-doubt, it means avoiding standards and goals that are inflexible, unrealistic, or inadequately supported and learning to notice, name, and monitor the related stress. Unproductive stress contributes to anxiety and low self-esteem and inhibits our ability to effectively see and navigate these important transitions.

An article by Melbourne Child Psychology offered five ways to set high expectations while also exerting patience rather than pressure. The author suggested teaching individuals to value the process, to set clear and realistic expectations, mark personal bests, welcome mistakes, and provide encouragement throughout the process.

KINDNESS, PATIENCE, AND DISCIPLINE

Lil Shelton knew how to set high expectations but the real secret to her success was her kind and patient leadership. Some coaches, leaders, and even parents believe that great leadership includes motivation by fear, loud voices, and meanness. This was not Coach Shelton and she had over 300 wins as evidence of the effectiveness of her kind and caring approach.

Our field hockey team made the state semi-finals my sophomore year in high school. It was a close one. The game was tied at the end of regulation so we played sudden death overtime, and found ourselves in a shootout to decide the game. In this scenario, each team chooses five players who each go head-to-head with the goalie. The team whose players score the most wins the game. As you might imagine, I was nervous, worried, and wondering if I could do this. I was trying to prepare myself mentally for the fact that these next few minutes of me in the goal with each of the opposing players would decide if we made it to the state finals. I looked up from my preparation and saw Coach Shelton approaching. She grabbed the cage of my helmet and smiled at me. Yes, she smiled, we had a moment that I will never forget. In the midst of all of the stress, anxiety, and nervousness of this big moment, we had a moment. Coach smiled and quietly said, "you've got this." She did not give me a speech about my preparation and how hard we had all worked. She also did not focus any of my attention on the fact that this moment determined our *future* plan. She was here, in this moment, walking with me through this time. Coach Shelton, with just her smile, said she believed in me, had confidence in our team, and could see the greatness.

Greatness includes expressing a sense of kindness to ourselves and others in order to set high expectations and recognize our own experiences and knowledge to set reasonable goals. It is about mixing high expectations and kindness in those most crucial of moments. Greatness is not just about reaching a goal, achieving an outcome, or being the best. High expectations and kindness are not mutually exclusive. It is possible for teachers, leaders, colleagues, and peers to be kind to each other and themselves and still maintain high expectations.

The thing about Coach Shelton's approach and transitions training, in general, is that a mix of greatness and kindness only works if you work, if we work. Coach Shelton set a goal and offered a plan to achieve that goal and each player had to buy in, commit, and train. Only we can be present, focused, and disciplined enough to do the work, take the steps in the mud, and wrestle with discomfort. This includes days where the work feels easy and you want to do more, but the plan calls for recovery and rest. For example, during the week, I usually include a 20 or 45-minute low-impact ride in my exercise schedule. The trainer and the sequence of the ride represent a way for me and others to work hard and also give the body a respite from the stressors of high impact and hill intervals sessions earlier in the week. During these moments of transition, it is often tempting to push ahead, go a little faster, add more resistance. We need to find and practice the discipline to stay the course, work the plan, and remember the reason we are here.

First-year doctoral students also often struggle with this kind of discipline. They often want to get ahead, do more reading, work on their papers, and do something that might provide an edge. This always happens as we enter the conclusion of the fall semester and move into the winter break. I always urge them to rest, take a break, and do something else. At first, they are skeptical, but they usually trust this developmental process and end up thanking us for encouraging the break! An attitude of greatness means having the discipline and patience to stay the course, do the 20-minutes of work, take time off from your studies, and NOT push harder, past the plan in the moment. Staying present, aware, and focused on that moment allows individuals to achieve their own greatness. It is not about a "should" or "could", it is the "now" and the "is" where the development and growth happens.

This need for discipline and patience extends to varied transitions at a variety of ages in different contexts. These are the days, regardless of context and transition type or duration, when we must focus on fundamentals and the task at hand. These routines are sometimes less-than-exciting but are paramount to our success. For example, my twin son and daughter are in kindergarten and slowly making the transition from listening to stories to reading letters, words, and eventually books. Right now, however, they need to focus on letter recognition and letter sounds. My daughter often sighs or momentarily quits because she is frustrated that she is not reading yet. These are those moments during a transition where she must stay the course, focus on the moment, the here and now, and feel the frustration and do the work.

Just like the dribble-jog-sprints, our kids cannot complete twenty-five intervals and read until they recognize the letters in the words in the sentences of their favorite books. Rushing through, ignoring, or even avoiding transitions often happen when individuals set their sights on a final outcome, a state championship, reading, or another identity. It takes patience with ourselves and discipline to stay the course and trust the process.

CHECKPOINT:
- What process do you need to trust?
- What is keeping you from trusting the process?
- What kindness could you extend to yourself?

GREATNESS ALL YOUR OWN

Greatness is a mix of high expectations, kindness, patience, and discipline. Also, critical to cultivating an attitude of greatness is to remember that greatness is in us and others and should not be defined by an external measuring stick or standard. We define and create our own path to greatness. My grandmother, Sara Downey— one of my most favorite people in the world—had a knack for seeing the greatness in others. I spent a lot of time with her and my grandfather, they appear in almost all of my significant memories. I loved her to pieces, and she had a way of always being amazed at and excited by hearing or experiencing other people's victories and successes.

I once thought she was just an optimist, just trying to see the bright side and, honestly, I would sometimes think it just cannot be as good as she thinks. Whenever she would attend a sports event, school performance, or any celebration, she expressed so much cheer and excitement. What I came to realize is that she really saw me, saw my family members, her friends, and neighbors. She could see the unique greatness and contributions in everyone. The writer and historian, John Buchan, said that "the task of leadership is not to put greatness into humanity, but to elicit it, for the greatness already there."

Coach Shelton and my grandmother saw the greatness present in individuals in their lives. Coach Shelton could smile and laugh with her players in the tensest of moments and could capture a quiet second with her players during a moment of celebration. My grandmother did not focus on the future or what should, she marveled at, revered, and expressed excitement at being in these moments with her grandkids, friends, and family. Both of these women, in their own and unique ways, expressed grace and gratitude and saw and cultivated greatness in others. While neither may have identified as or called themselves leaders in the traditional sense, they certainly tried to and did see greatness in their friends, family, players, and teams. In our moments and periods of transition, those in-between feelings, can we stay present and aware enough to see our own greatness?

CHECKPOINT:
- What does your own greatness look like?
- What is the name of your greatness?
- List two or three of those now.

Grace, gratitude, and greatness represent three key attitudes that individuals need to work to adopt as they engage in transitions training. Self-kindness, expressions of gratitude, and thankfulness while simultaneously setting high expectations will lay the foundation for individuals to embrace the dissonance of transitional moments. These attitudes contribute to improved self-confidence, self-acceptance, reduction of fear, openness to uncertainty, and valuing process over outcomes (Busolari and Goodell, 2009; Schlossberg, 2011). Attitude adjustment often connotes a quick shift or immediate change in the way in which we view situations and events. This attitude "adjustment" is gradual, iterative, and a journey.

While grace, gratitude, and greatness are prerequisites for this training, it is also the case that as individuals engage in this transitions practice, these three attitudes will continue to oscillate, grow, and develop until individuals internalize these attitudes as features of an emerging mindset. It is with this mindset that individuals, groups, and organizations will be able to notice, name, mark, and embrace the transitions moments and experience the benefits therein.

CHECKPOINT:
- What would happen if you named your own greatness?
- What obstacles do you need to overcome to name this greatness?
- How would it feel to name your own greatness?

In this next chapter, I will discuss one of many reasons to adopt the three "Gr's." I will explore the meaning of discomfort, sources of these feelings of uncertainty, and why it is important, and how to normalize the discomfort of our transitions.

CHAPTER 5: NORMALIZE THE DISCOMFORT

"What happens when we're willing to feel bad is that, sure enough, we often feel bad but without the stress of futile avoidance. Emotional discomfort, when accepted, rises, crests, and falls in a series of waves. Each wave washes parts of us away and deposits treasures we never imagined." – Martha Beck

In the spring of 2008, my wife, Susan, and I found out that I was pregnant with our first child. We had already decided to take a trip to Europe, my first, and so it became a celebration trip. We kept the big news between us during our trips and the weeks that followed waiting for our 12-week appointment with our doctor. When we returned from Paris, we went for that checkup. All was good and we were on schedule to welcome a little boy sometime in March of 2009.

It was a relatively smooth pregnancy—a little morning sickness, several cravings, and lots of joy and anticipation. We painted his nursery, our family hosted a huge baby shower, and we continued to prepare and excitedly wait. Then, on November 14, 2008, something was not right, I was not feeling well, I called my wife who was on her way home, and I shared that something was off, and I did not know what to think. I rested on the couch and initially assumed this was all a part of pregnancy. By the time Susan got home, I really was not feeling well and told her that we should go to the hospital. I went upstairs to get my shoes and coat and, standing in our bedroom, my water broke. It was too soon, he was not ready, and yet I was going to have this baby.

Susan called 911, they sent an ambulance and, as they arrived, I gave birth on the floor of our living room to this tiny baby boy. They rushed us to the hospital, Tyler, as he was soon named, was taken to the neonatal unit and I was taken to another room for an examination. Doctors and nurses kept watch and showed great care for Tyler and my family. The specialists explained that it was just too soon to tell, Tyler was small, underdeveloped, and arrived too early. Over the next few days, Susan and I read Tyler books, held his tiny hand through the isolette, and talked to him long into the nights. Even with all of the expertise, care, kindness, and medical attention, Tyler left this world in the early morning of November 17, 2008, just three days after arriving at the hospital. Susan and I rocked him in a chair as he took his last breath and, to this day, it is still the hardest moment of our lives together.

Before that morning, I had never really known loss, not anything like it. Susan and I sat alone but together in a small family/visitor room while we waited for the nurses. In that instant, we experienced an immediate and tragic change. We also, unknown to us at the time, started a transition that Schlossberg (1984) reminds us can be unexpected and emerge from *not* receiving or earning something, the absence of a previously anticipated moment. In that room, together in our grief but also alone in our own, unique sorrow, Susan and I turned to each other, and with no knowledge of the future, we said, "We will not let this break us apart." I really do not know why we said that. What I do know is that our relationship, from the beginning, had been built on being intentional and communicating those intentions. We were always aware and clear that being together, committing to each other, and loving one another was a choice and we made this choice every day.

This transition, the associated emotional discomfort, and the intense grief presented us with a choice. We could choose to bury the discomfort deep, avoid the moment, and push those around us away. Instead, we chose to let the discomfort wash over us and at times consume us. The sadness would rise, crest, and fall and then repeat the cycle. We, of course, had no sense of what could possibly follow. The only thing we were certain of was that there was no avoiding this discomfort, neither of us had enough willpower or fortitude to push these strong feelings of loss down, and thank goodness for that. We really had no choice but to let the discomfort come and go as needed and all I could do was stay in these moments and make the daily choice to get out of bed, put one foot in front of another, and feel whatever it was that I would feel on that day.

I would love to tell you that I had done the work to open up to those feelings and had learned how to walk in and through this grief, mourning, and mud to get to a better place. This loss and terrible transition happened well before I found Brene Brown, Nancy Schlossberg, and other influential researchers and writers. At this moment, I also was unable to employ my old tactics—it was too much discomfort to avoid, ignore, or run the other way. Luckily for me and Susan, we faced this terrible tragedy head on.

This kind of pain and grief needs time to heal. Yet, when faced with the most difficult and tragic moment of my life, I had a choice. I could return to my go-to strategy of pushing people away, using my sadness and anger to separate myself from others and mask my true feelings about the moment and the discomfort, or I could engage in an attitude of grace and kindness with myself and Susan and make space for this transitional moment. This journey that had no clear ending and no certain destinations, I could lean into this pain.

It took over a year to garner the energy to really reengage with our lives, our friends, and routines and traditions and when we emerged, the world looked different, we looked different, and our lives as individuals and as a couple was forever changed. As Martha Beck (2012) noted in the quote at the beginning of this chapter, this emotional discomfort acts like waves washing over us and, if we pay attention, adopt an attitude of grace and gratitude, there may be treasures left behind.

At that moment, we still did not know what we might face or build together, and yet, we also knew that we had noticed, named, and started to navigate this transition. Whether transitions continue for a few years or just a few moments, they are never easy. Walking in and staying present for the pain was never about trying to make this loss easier or coming up with a solution to the pain. The goal of normalizing the discomfort is just to know that difficult, uncertain, and sometimes tragic moments happen, of that we can be sure. We must practice, prepare, and train in and for these transitions. As Dr. Susan David (2016) suggests, we need to learn emotional agility, individually and collectively, so that our moments of discomfort are no longer a surprise and we no longer try to run from them. She suggests that we must be intentional, mindful, and employ productive ways to notice and engage in our emotions. In these transitional moments, we should learn to stare down, lean in, listen, and learn from the discomfort.

CHECKPOINT:
Learning from our discomfort requires us to name and navigate it. Use the following map to "dance" with your own discomfort.

DANCING WITH DISCOMFORT MAP

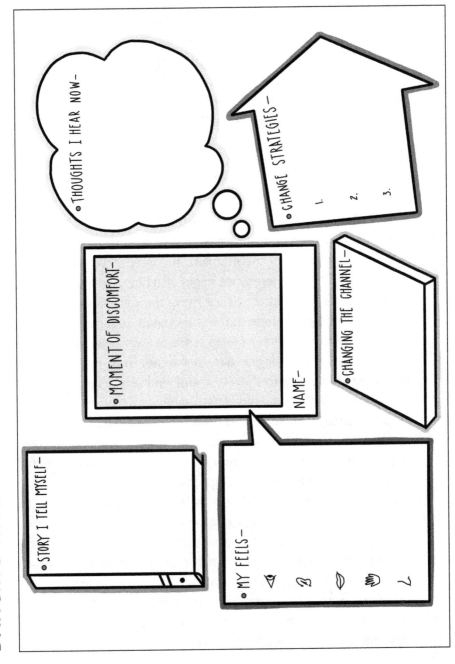

THOUGHTS I HEAR NOW—

CHANGE STRATEGIES—

1.

2.

3.

MOMENT OF DISCOMFORT—

NAME—

CHANGING THE CHANNEL—

STORY I TELL MYSELF—

MY FEELS—

But what about these deposits of treasure mentioned earlier? There is no easy answer, and everyone's response and experience will be different. This is when I return to the real and personal struggle of expressing an attitude of gratitude. How could I be thankful for anything in any part of this tragedy? This transition?

I believe, from my own transitions and walking with others in their moments, gratitude is harder and takes longer to find with higher degrees of dissonance. The ability to find gratitude also emerges from a mindset that will be discussed in the next chapter, a learning or beginner mindset. The ability to hold two conflicting ideas, in this case, grief and gratitude requires a "yes-and" mindset or approach to navigating our transitions. The more uncomfortable, uncertain, and muddier the moment, the deeper we must search for gratitude. This is where grace might also help. We must be kind, compassionate, and patient as we move through these moments. Moreover, finding gratitude in these moments requires each of us to be present and maintain a keen sense of awareness for even the smallest detail. Authentic gratitude for me came from my connection with Susan, her ability to show love and kindness to me, our ability to communicate that we needed help helping each other and having the patience to let ourselves feel however we felt in those moments.

Keep in mind, authentic gratitude in this moment is not pleasure or happiness in the dissonance or the event that initiated the transition. In fact, if I am being honest, I hate the idea of finding a silver lining in a tragedy. Gratitude is not that! In fact, Dr. Susan David, in a recent podcast episode with Dr. Brene Brown described the idea of toxic positivity. The ideas that we *should* find the positive in any tragedy does us more harm. It prohibits us from being seen by ourselves and others and can create more discomfort and isolation. Paradox or a "yes, and" mindset calls for integration of the dissonance and the discovery, the grief and the gratitude. In this case, gratitude is acknowledging our willingness and ability to do the work required to keep our heads up, to keep moving, and to stay connected, present, and open to the needs of ourselves and those around us. So, to recap:

- Acknowledge the direct relationship between the depth of discomfort and the work required to find gratitude.
- Apply grace and patience to find the treasures in the moment.
- Focus on small words and actions because they matter.
- Remember that gratitude is not a reaction to or feelings about the dissonance, it is a response to the work we do individually and collectively in the transition.

Transitions are difficult for all kinds of reasons and they are also opportunities to receive treasures. Even in the most difficult and tragic of moments, there are treasures to find.

Lastly, finding gratitude in these moments does lead to treasures that might be useful in future transitional moments. Staying aware and present can help us notice connections, love, and strength in these difficult moments, may offer new experiences and actions that may contribute to developing a mindset of openness, and might represent useful tools to help navigate future transitions.

DISCOMFORT

The discomfort of which I speak in this book is the uncertainty, dissonance, and self-doubt we have all experienced during our lives. It involves wrestling with unpleasant realities that often conflict with our perceptions of what should be or our prior assumptions about what is. It also includes feelings of friction and disequilibrium created by moments of transition.

Like discomfort, safety is in the eye of the beholder. These perceptions are personal and are often based on our own beliefs, thoughts, and experiences. Being unsafe or expressing feeling unsafe is not the same as discomfort. In fact, it has been my experience that individuals especially those with power and privilege express feeling unsafe when they are actually looking for refuge from a moment of discomfort. While this topic requires a comprehensive discussion, this is well beyond my own expertise, and many experts have written and spoken about this important distinction (Brown, 2020; Saad, 2020). This is to acknowledge that if anyone feels unsafe, targeted, or at risk for any reason, this is not the discomfort of which I speak in this book and it is not a moment to navigate and learn from or be present in at any time. Safety is a baseline requirement for everyone's well-being and if you ever feel unsafe, it is important to remove yourself from that moment, create space so everyone feels safe, or cease the moment or experience until everyone can feel safe. While everyone should wrestle with discomfort, *no* one should be put in positions of feeling unsafe. Discomfort must be noticed, named, and addressed sometimes gradually and over time. Low or no safety is not a process or a journey, it is an unacceptable outcome that requires immediate attention and must be ended. No one can successfully navigate any level of discomfort if they are also unsafe.

Leading, building, creating, and learning are all uncomfortable. "Leadership is scarce because few people are willing to go through the discomfort required to lead" (Godin, 2008). Merriam (2005) also reminds us that "for learning to occur, an experience needs to be discomforting, disquieting, or puzzling enough for us not to reject or ignore it, but to attend to it and reflect on it. It is then that learning takes place." Transitions include varying intensity, duration, and frequency of discomfort. Normalizing this discomfort requires us to acknowledge these feelings and learn how to navigate this discomfort and one important step to getting comfortable with discomfort is increasing our awareness of why we feel this dissonance.

SOURCES OF DISCOMFORT

Normalizing discomfort or dancing with discomfort involves learning to face moments of uncertainty, self-doubt, confusion. Discomfort arises from a variety of sources and I have tried to organize them into a few categories below.

Discomfort also emerges from the higher relative value placed on outcomes as compared to process by individuals, teams, and organizations which is too often reinforced by institutional structures and standards. The following offers a brief discussion and a few examples of possible sources.

FEAR OF FAILURE

Unfortunately, many of us are all too familiar with fearing failure. According to Theo Tsaousides (2018) in an article in *Psychology Today*, fear of failure describes this intense worry or anxiety associated with considering all of the bad things that *might* happen if we fail to achieve a defined goal. For some, it is a fleeting moment that can be managed while for others, it is so paralyzing that they would rather avoid or quit some event or transition than face the risk of failure.

Martin and Marsh (2003) offer three different typologies for motivation to achieve related to failure: success-oriented, failure-avoidant, and failure-accepting. Success-oriented individuals embrace an attitude of optimism towards achievement and maintain this positivity even in the face of setbacks. Those who are failure avoidant—approach achievement, tasks, and goals with anxiety and worry motivated by fear of failure and self-doubt about their own ability. Individuals with this mindset are often adversely affected by failure. This reaction to failure then confirms their fear and creates a reinforcing cycle of anxiety over the possibility of failing. Individuals classified as failure accepting have all but given in to the failure and are no longer motivated or resilient in the face of challenges.

Fear of failure arises as a source of discomfort most often for those individuals who identify as failure avoidant. They (and I) worry about the imagined outcomes of a failure that might include embarrassment, self-doubt, shame, feeling less than adequate, or not well-liked. As I mentioned earlier, much of my early life was spent minimizing the chance of failure. I chose events, situations, tasks, and challenges that I was almost certain I could achieve. I worried a lot about failing, so much so that I just did not try many new things for fear of looking ridiculous, not being able to accomplish a task, and not making the cut.

I remember starting middle school and sitting in class, nervous, worried, and unsure of myself. While elementary school had its share of worry and anxiety, middle school brought new kids from different schools together in one classroom. In many ways, it felt like starting over, transitioning from the comfort and familiarity of elementary school to a new, unfamiliar, and intimidating space of the middle school. My fear of failure and looking ridiculous or being wrong in front of my classmates was, in a word, terrifying.

Yet, I was a good student, studied hard, turned in all of my assignments, followed the rules, and succeeded, and still I sat in class with so much worry and stress over my fear of giving the wrong answer when called on in class. This transition included a renewed fear of failure that was compounded by the unfamiliar context and individuals with whom I was now learning.

Why do I describe my transition to middle school? Because it is important to remember that students regardless of age, outward demeanor, and performance may be nervous, worried, and feel self-doubt during these significant transitions. Moreover, even as we look back and think the stakes may have been lower, failing a math test or giving a wrong answer, the fear of failure is still paralyzing and terrifying to some students. In hindsight, I realize how long I had been trying to manage the feelings in all of my transitions, middle school included!

Imagine how my experience might have been different if a teacher had been aware of my fear of failure. How might my experiences in class have changed with awareness, guidance, and support? I often knew the right answer or understood the next step of a problem or process but remained quiet—too worried about failing in front of my class. This fear of failure is real.

It is not enough to tell someone just to try and get over it, or not to worry no one will laugh. This fear of failure must be acknowledged, and individuals must be given space to notice, name, and walk through this uncomfortable mud. We cannot will these fears away or hope an individual will grow out of them. This is usually not the case. It is not something to grow out of. It is something that needs to be faced, talked about, and students, employees, and others need to practice wrestling with these feelings and reflecting on these moments. Acknowledging and having a willingness to sit in this fear, represents an important step to managing the discomfort.

Several years ago, while running a race, I remember coming upon one of the obstacles on the course. Imagine a twenty-foot-high climbing structure made of wood and a series of ropes shaped as ladders. To enter the obstacle, our team first had to jump into the cold, small pond, swim to the other side where this climbing wall awaited us. It was already a cold and windy day and we were more than halfway through this five-hour day of racing so, you can imagine, I was a little tired. I started to climb this twenty-foot wall and was doing okay until I reached the top. There are many people around me, crowding me in, stepping on my fingers, and hurrying me along. As I approached the top, I realized that to get to the other side and work my way down, I would need to swing one leg over this long piece of wood, followed by the rest of my body, and begin my descent. It was at that moment, looking around, contemplating my next move, I realized I was tired, cold, wet, and twenty feet above the ground. I looked over on the other side of the wall at my Marine buddy who was about halfway down the other side. As I made a first attempt to swing my leg over the wall, I was awash with fear.

I looked at my buddy with tears in my eyes and said that I was not sure I could make it. I was paralyzed with a fear of going over the side but also of failing. I gathered myself, looked at my friend who was being incredibly supportive, and I stood there—holding the ropes, shaking from the cold and dampness—in my fear, my worry of not making it over, of looking like a fool. I owned the moment, took a deep breath and tossed my leg over again, then my body, and before I knew it, I was making my way down the last half of this huge climbing wall. Of course, some of the fear in this story came from the fatigue, cold day, and height of the climbing wall. The reason, however, that I share this story is because, I also believe that my willingness to show my vulnerability and share with him that I was scared and worried both about the actual wall and what not climbing over meant for the race, made it possible for me to get over the hurdle.

I am not saying that everyone can or should overcome their fear of failing by climbing over a giant wall but what I am saying is that fear of failure, worry of not succeeding in a new professional role, as a new student in a new school, or even as a parent, is real and often feels like a twenty-foot climbing wall. Like yelling down to my buddy on the other side of the wall, it is critical to acknowledge that fear, notice, name it, and let it happen. This is the first step to working through the dissonance, feeling the fear, and being okay that you are worried about not succeeding. It is okay and what is the worst that can happen? You might fail and you might not—it is what is and that is the point of being in and embracing our transitions. They are full of possibilities even in the most hidden places.

BINARY THINKING

A leader at a fairly large organization was invited to participate in a year-long, leadership academy. He was honored to be asked and very excited to start the work. This leader believed, based on some feedback from those who nominated him, that this was a great opportunity to grow into a high-profile leadership position at the organization. One of the first steps of the academy involved identifying colleagues, employees, and current and past supervisors to participate in a 360-evaluation process. This is an opportunity for an emerging leader to receive authentic feedback from trusted individuals and with the support of a coach, use this feedback to inform some of the work that they do during his year in the academy.

After collecting the data, facilitators met with each academy participant. This leader received feedback showing that he excelled in his ability to design and implement programs, establish goals for teams, and follow through on commitments. The data also revealed that this emerging leader needed to work on communication skills and improve on his ability to cultivate trust with and among colleagues and direct reports. This leader was devastated. For him the data represented failure. This perception and interpretation of the data created a mental spiral for this emerging leader. In this moment, he was no longer able to see an opportunity, this once hopeful transition to a new role disappeared. The "mixed" results of the data, in his mind, were not mixed at all. It was clear to him that he was a failure. This inability to see and embrace a reality that includes multiple outcomes, gray areas, and "yes-and" versus "either-or" approaches leads him to conclude that he failed, he did not have what it takes to lead or take on the next opportunity. For us to authentically wrestle with dissonance, to stand in our truth, and experience all that this involves requires us to see all the data, all the aspects of the evidence, and celebrate the bright spots and the spots in need of growth and attention.

Binary thinking is one of the quickest ways to arrive at failure. If there is no in-between, no focus on progress, it is next to impossible to succeed in anything. It is a limiting way of thinking that amplifies our falling short of some defined outcome or timeline. The perception of this data as proof of failure feeds our self-doubt and prevents individuals and this leader from being in the moment, having awareness of the possibilities, effectively leveraging and navigating this transition. As previously discussed, data can serve as an important element of information or feedback to move us forward but this data should empower and motivate us not control us or lead us to avoid trying to achieve something.

Binary thinking—this polarity of thinking—is an all-or-none approach that contributes to our fear of failure and to the associated struggle and discomfort of our transitions. Fear of failure and binary thinking often make it difficult to honor, appreciate, and leverage the opportunities during our transition journeys.

CONCEPTION OF A ROLE AND IMPOSTER SYNDROME

As individuals transition to new professional roles, academic situations, attend different schools, leave an organization, and move to a new location, there is self-doubt and uncertainty. I vividly remember the first time I stood up in front of a group of students to teach statistics. I had just graduated with a master's in economics and was asked by the department chair to stay on to teach in their business school. I spent hours upon hours, preparing my lectures, planning the assignments and class activities, and trying to anticipate every question that might arise. I had a serious case of imposter syndrome. Imposter syndrome refers to times when an individual feels less competent than people believe they are. As I was gradually transitioning out of graduate school into a teaching role, I had lots of self-doubt and worry. To anyone on the outside who reviewed my CV, my academic record, or talked to me, the evidence would suggest I was prepared and ready and more than capable. To me and my imposter syndrome, this could not be further from the truth.

While worries around failure represent an impediment to normalizing dissonance, it is also true that our conception of our own identity development and our growth and development during transitional moments can also impede our ability to dance with discomfort. Imposter syndrome often emerges and definitely did for me as a result of an image, a picture I had of what a statistics professor at a business school would look like or do and how they act or respond to their students. My conception of a professor in academia was of an expert, someone with all the answers, unrattled by student comments and questions, and prepared for any situations that might emerge. I also believed this was not me.

Sure, I studied, trained, and did well in school, but I still had a lot to learn. Looking back, I also recognize I had created and established some measure, a non-existent and unrealistic bar of this identity. One of the roadblocks during this transition was the mismatch between my conception of a professor and the reality of being a professor. No one is talking to anyone about this imposter syndrome and no one, especially academics, is admitting that they mess up, feel nervous, or do not always have the answers.

Employees, leaders, and students also experience these feelings of self-doubt and imposter syndrome. For example, early on in a student's doctoral training, they often confide in me about their worries related to whether or not they will ever write like an academic or be seen as a scholar. They often wonder out loud and express doubt about what it takes to be a researcher, to engage in this scholarly work, and complete a doctoral degree. Their concept and prior beliefs and assumptions about these new identities whether trying on a new identity, taking on a new professional role, becoming a parent, or playing guard on a basketball team feeds self-doubt and uncertainty.

Our ability to normalize the discomfort in these imposter syndrome moments as students, professors, leaders, sisters, daughters, and parents is partly dependent on our ability to name and notice these moments and then figure out how to define, create, and design our evolving identity for ourselves. If we only focus on what we should think, say, act, or wear, it is difficult to thrive in this uncertainty and discomfort. If, on the other hand, we can let go of the should and consider how we might imagine, design, and build our own path by shining a light on the shame and uncertainty, it may alleviate some of the distress, anxiety, and discomfort in these transitions.

Fear of failure and binary thinking each represent roadblocks to leaning into and standing in our discomfort. It is also true that this misalignment of who we should be how we should feel or act and the reality of those transitional moments also prevent our acceptance of the discomfort. Transitions practice requires us to be present, focus on the moment, the "is" rather than the "should."

SETBACKS = FAILURES, VALUING OUTCOMES OVER PROCESS
Another source of the discomfort during transitions has to do with our perception of setbacks and challenges, all the telltale signs of an incoming transition. It is also true that individually and collectively we tend to value outcomes over the process. Moreover, if we hold on to a fear of failure—our binary thinking—as we move into a transition and encounter bumps, bruises, and challenges, our reaction and evaluation of the moment will be failure (du Plessis, 2015). Defining the transition journey as smooth or bumpy, a success or a failure, makes it almost impossible to fruitfully engage in these often rough and unpredictable transitions.

When I was in third grade, I started taking golf lessons. I loved the lessons, the work, the attention to detail, and everything about the game of golf. I spent my summer days, morning till evening at our local golf course moving from driving range to putting green and then out on the actual course and back again. I took every lesson I could, entered all of the summer tournaments, and even traveled for a few others. I was pretty good, won several championships, and was even invited to play in some of the boys' tournaments, and a travel team because there just were not enough girls playing at my level.

When the competition got tougher and the matches got tighter, I struggled. When I was good, I was unstoppable but when I made a bad shot, missed a putt, or got stuck in a sand trap or water hazard, I did not do well (remember the field hockey game). Eventually, I backed away from golf and turned to other team sports. I still occasionally play but just on and off with friends where the stakes are very low and the risk or consequences of making a mistake are also low.

Looking back on my golf days, I originally believed that my interests just changed, and I often explained the exit from golf as me just wanting to join a sport, a team with other high school kids. Let's be honest, being on the golf team was not the coolest and this high school kid wanted to be liked and included but, upon closer examination and honest reflection, I realized that the actual reason I stopped playing golf had more to do with the fact that I just could not handle the competitive pressure. As a young person, I had a fear of failure, struggled with perfectionism, and binary thinking. I also spent a lot of time repeating "should" statements about myself and my golf game. When I missed a putt, I did not have the knowledge, skills, or experiences to navigate these moments, to stay in the feeling of missing a putt and work in and through these experiences.

It is hard to admit this, but I would often fall apart, crumble, with tears, frustration, and anger. This was not really about the missed putt as much as it was about feeling embarrassed for what I thought was an epic failure. While I am still a work-in-progress recovering from this fear, binary thinking, and an inability to focus on the journey rather than outcomes, I have gained an awareness of these moments, learned how to show myself some care and consideration, and slowly navigate my thoughts in these transitions.

Learning to normalize discomfort is not easy and even as we learn to focus on these transitional moments and be present, in the here and now, these instances probably will not feel less challenging. What changes is our ability to name where we are, describe and see the now, the is, and cease worrying so much about what was or should be. Learning to normalize the discomfort just means that we learn how to walk in the mud, admit that it is muddy, and maybe put on some boots and just keep walking through it until we can walk into a more sturdy and less muddy place.

LEARNING TO NORMALIZE THE DISCOMFORT

Like transitions practice, learning to normalize the discomfort takes commitment, preparation, time, and practice. It includes working on our attitude (see Chapter 4), adopting an awareness about our own struggles with wrestling with discomfort (Chapter 5), developing a learner identity (see Chapter 6), and while it is difficult to stay uncomfortable, it is important to start this work, these transitions before you are ready. Walking right into the discomfort is sometimes the only way to begin and, if we wait until we think we are ready, we may never pay attention enough to do the work required.

These transitions are not easy, none of this work is, and no transitions will ever be but that is the point. It is important to remember what Brene Brown said during her About Campus interview (2016): "failure is not learning gone bad, it is not the opposite of learning. Failure is part of the learning process."

I played softball, tennis, golf, basketball, field hockey, and even tried women's rugby. On the off-season from field hockey, I stayed in shape by running, biking, and lifting weights. I eventually tried my hand at a few road races, a triathlon, and even a marathon. I just loved and still love staying active and being fit. Here is the thing, my younger self did love the competition and being fit but training and competing were hard. Team sports, competition, training, and preparation, looking back, were hard in ways they did not need to be.

Simon Sinek and Aiko Bethea talk about aligning your what and your why. I think this was part of my issue. It is true that I did love to compete but my "why" for competing was more about perception, weight loss, and being liked. I am not saying I did not enjoy the work. I did but I also knew that "being fit and healthy" was admired and appreciated. I also wanted to stay fit, stay slim, and this was a great way to do this. The problem with this why is that my struggles with fear of failure, perfectionism, and binary thinking made the journey, the process of training, learning, improving, and growing so much harder for the wrong reasons. I still want to run and train and initially struggled with these same fears and worries. Then, I was invited to participate in an adventure race.

A friend of mine had organized a team to run a Ragnar Relay, a relay-style set-up that requires teams of twelve to run over 300 miles in 72 hours. They needed another person and I said sure. I did not know what I was getting myself into, but I was already training and the legs of the race were well within my own endurance training. While I would love to share all of the adventures of this amazing weekend, the bottom line is that that race started to change my mind, my perception of what competition is. Then, several from the same group decided to complete a Tough Mudder.

This is the race I mentioned earlier, remember the twenty-foot climbing obstacle? It is a race across rough terrain that includes about 12 or 14 obstacles ranging from crawling under electrified wires, climbing through and over mud (mudslides), to large climbing and rope walls. The day of our race was cold, windy, and rainy and it took us over five hours to complete this grueling race and it was *amazing*. The Ragnar Relay and the Tough Mudder, together, put me on a journey, a transition where I began to realize that training, racing, and competing is not about binary outcomes, or avoiding bumps and challenges, or even winning. These races helped me to recognize that competing and participating in these races are exhilarating and worthwhile because we will fail, we will have setbacks and we need to learn to expect all of it.

The exciting part of these competitions is how individuals respond to these setbacks. This realization was never truer when I signed up for my first 50K ultramarathon. This is a 31-mile running race on a pretty rough series of trails. As I prepared and trained for this race, it was not just about putting in the miles but fueling, wearing the right equipment, and practicing for setbacks. What I realized is that I love competing now because it is about problem-solving, figuring out a puzzle in the middle of this competition being present for the discomfort, the fatigue, the pain, and the joy. That first ultramarathon pushed me beyond any limit I had ever imagined for myself. It was hard, it hurt, I was uncomfortable, and yet, I was exhilarated, excited, and thrilled at competing and completing that race. I did another one but this time, a 50-miler. I also did an adventure race that included canoeing, mountain biking, and running.

The point is that my younger self enjoyed competing and I was never the best or even planned to try to be the best. I just loved to compete but my fears and focus on outcomes got in my way. I gave up on a few races, backed out of others, and often made excuses for why I could not participate.

As I got older, I still struggled with this attitude and mindset until a friend invited me to try. What happens if you get curious about your own greatness? Well, you might succeed or you might fail and so what? It is about getting into the game, the competition, our lives, and trying. That invitation represented a start of a transition for me. I am still on that journey and moving towards an attitude of grace, gratitude, and greatness. I no longer believe that smooth sailing or feeling good is a sign of a victory or success. Instead, I recognize that we need resistance, setbacks, and failures to grow. Working hard and being out of breath is not a sign of weakness, it means that you are present, doing the work, following through on a commitment. This transitions practice will help each of us to start this work and continue to do this work. We need to adopt attitudes that support this work so that we can cultivate a mindset that embraces dissonance, can stand in the mud, and be present for the discomfort.

One of my favorite US Presidents offered one of my most favorite quotes where he is frustrated with individuals who criticize and find fault with those trying to make a difference or change the world.

> "It is not the critic who counts; not the man who points out how the strong man stumbles, or where the doer of deeds could have done them better. The credit belongs to the man who is actually in the arena, whose face is marred by dust and sweat and blood; who strives valiantly; who errs, who comes short again and again, because there is no effort without error and shortcoming; but who does actually strive to do the deeds; who knows great enthusiasms, the great devotions; who spends himself in a worthy cause; who at the best knows in the end the triumph of high achievement, and who at the worst, if he fails, at least fails while daring greatly, so that his place shall never be with those cold and timid souls who neither know victory nor defeat."
> – Theodore Roosevelt (April 23, 1910)

I was a timid soul for a long time and still battle with that voice on a regular basis. Like Roosevelt, I believe that life and growth require us to be in the mud, get messy, feel uncertain, and express doubt and struggle—this is life, this is work, and this is how we continue to develop our personal and professional identities. Roosevelt was not speaking about trying to have a baby, playing golf, entering middle school, or teaching statistics but all of these transitional moments include trying valiantly, coming up short again and again, but daring greatly. Transitions training asks each of us to do the work, stumble in the dirt, get up again, and never be with "those cold and timid souls who neither know victory or defeat."

So far, we have discussed the meaning of transitions, who experiences them, what they look like, and how they feel. We have also explored the attitude equipment needed to do this training and the importance of learning to dance with dissonance in this work. The next two chapters introduce two additional accessories needed to do the work: a learning identity and tools of reflection. Like grace, gratitude, greatness and learning to dance with dissonance, learning identity and reflection will develop during the transitions training but it is also important to start this process before beginning the training.

CHAPTER 6: LEARNING IDENTITY

"In times of change, learners inherit the earth while the learned find themselves beautifully equipped to deal with a world that no longer exists." – Eric Hoffer

As I mentioned at the start of this book, I love all things outdoors. I enjoy running, biking, swimming, snowboarding, hiking, adventure races, kayaking, camping, and any other activity I could find. I also always wanted to learn to climb but I was too afraid, I did not think I could do it well, or would do it right, and would look foolish participating. One summer, I spent a month in Vermont and finally built up enough courage to do it. I put on the harness, my friends anchored the appropriate ropes, and up I went. I was scared, nervous, and worried but as I listened to my friend's instruction and shared my own nervousness, I started to feel invigorated, excited, and proud of myself. I also realized that this courage I expressed was also my willingness to be vulnerable and honest about my uncertainty. While climbing may not be a typical transition, the experiences, thoughts, and feelings are exactly like a typical transitional moment. The sources of discomfort include uncertainty, fear of failure, binary thinking around success, and concern over possible setbacks. What might seem ironic is that the *sources* of discomfort are actually *avenues* to managing transitions.

Remember, I like a good paradox. The paradox is this: situations that cause us discomfort can actually relieve us from our discomfort. However, this can only happen if we become attuned to the learning in the experience. The key to managing transitions lies in our ability to adopt a learner identity. In her writings about adult transition and learning, Sharan Merriam (2005) poses the following question: "How is it that we learn from some life events and not others?" I would say that it all comes down to whether or not we take on the persona of a learner.

The term life-long learner is often used to describe individuals who, throughout their lives, actively and outwardly pursue the acquisition of knowledge. For example, given my track record for obtaining degrees or trying new sports, my persona might convey that I am a life-long learner. But what does it really mean to assume a learner identity? What is the end goal for individuals who approach experiences with the mentality of a learner? And, of course, why is having a learner identity important, especially for those of us seeking to learn in moments of transition?

I think the importance of understanding the value of assuming a learner identity is illustrated in the conceptual framework by Bierly, Kessler, and Christensen (2000) differentiating between the pursuit of knowledge versus the pursuit of wisdom. In the framework, the authors suggest a hierarchy of outcomes associated with acts of cognition. As you listen to the outcomes, see if you can pinpoint where the learner would stand: (1) knowing data results in memorization, (2) having information leads to comprehension, (3) gaining knowledge develops understanding, and (4) possessing wisdom leads to better living and success (Bierly et al, 2000). I might suggest that unlike the external behaviors we typically associate with life-long learners, assuming a learner identity is an internal process. It is a decision we make to gain wisdom from experience. In fact, I once heard learning defined as *profiting* from experience.

If you are anything like me, you may be waiting for the *how*. How do we create this shift in our identities and become learners of our experiences? Actually, just as with physical activities such as running, it all comes down to training and accessorizing. While runners have training equipment, clothing, and footwear that assist in their training, learners have resources that assist in the pursuit of wisdom.

MINDSET

Thomas Edison is credited with the saying "genius is one percent inspiration and ninety-nine percent perspiration." This motto has been used by trainers, teachers, and leaders alike to kindle a spirit of motivation in their players, students, and employees. What Edison recognized is that important work is hard. Important work takes perseverance, determination, fortitude, and of course, the willingness to put in the work. I think that what it comes down to is having the right mental outlook, the right mindset.

Managing transitions is hard work. Just as an athlete prepares to face a tough competitor, or a doctoral student prepares for a dissertation defense, or a business executive prepares for a crucial presentation, managing transitions sometimes requires ninety-nine percent perspiration. What makes these tasks just a bit easier, just a bit more manageable, is having the appropriate mindset. For myself, I know that when I head out for a run, or even if I prepare to sit down with my son to help him complete his homework, having the right mindset sets the tone for a positive experience.

The right mindset, according to Carol Dweck (2008) is a growth mindset. As my friends in education circles know, mindsets can be categorized as fixed or growth. Having a fixed mindset means focusing on outcomes; I won or I lost, I succeeded or I failed or I am talented or I am not talented. Having a growth mindset, however, means focusing on processes: I tried and now I need to try something different, I completed the race and now I need to work on my pace, and yes, I tried to block the goal and will continue to work on my agility. Although much of Dweck's work is centered in educational settings, Dweck maintains that having a growth mindset is important for developing talent across settings. "A growth mindset allows each individual to embrace learning, to welcome challenges, mistakes, and feedback, and to understand the role of effort in creating talent" (Dweck, 2009). A growth mindset is the pillar supporting our work as learners.

Recently, I read an interesting take on mindset that translates nicely to the work involved in managing transitions. In his book, *Beginners: The Joy and Transformative Power of Lifelong Learning*, Tom Vanderbilt extols the power of experiencing life with a beginner's mindset. In an article about Vanderbilt's book, Jen Rose Smith (2021) writes that the concept of a beginner's mindset finds its roots in Zen Buddhism. She goes on to share that individuals who embody a beginner's mindset hold wonder, curiosity, and purity and are not tarnished by experience (Smith, 2021). As we have discussed earlier, transitions represent new beginnings, and what better way to face transitions than with a beginner's mindset.

CHECKPOINT:
Smith (2021) recognizes that "perspective and mindset are powerful factors in how we cope with the challenges we... face." Think about a current or recent transition.
- How will a change in mindset impact your experience?
- What small steps can you take to change your mindset?

MISTAKES AS OPPORTUNITIES

As bears repeating, transitions put us in unfamiliar situations. Think of this concrete example. Imagine that you are in an unfamiliar room. Maybe you are in a new location or just experiencing the popularity of an escape room. In the room you are faced with several doors. You are unsure which is the door leading to the outside versus a closet or second room. What do you do? You try all the doors until you find the one that leads you out of the room. Did you make mistakes? Of course! You simply learned that a particular door did not lead where you wanted to go and tried another. Imagine if after opening the first door you gave up? What would you have learned from this mistake? Most assuredly, doors can be barriers, but they can also open us up to new opportunities. The same is true for mistakes.

Some of our best transition moments hinge on our ability to make mistakes. And, if you think about it, there is so much more to making mistakes than the act itself. In and of itself, it is the prep work (are we prepared to make a mistake, to be wrong), our attitude (have we learned to accept the good with the bad, the negative with the positive, live in the discomfort), and the courage and vulnerability needed to take a risk. If we dismiss, ignore, or brush aside mistakes, we never learn. In fact, making mistakes is a part of our DNA. In *How We Learn* (Dehaene, 2020), French neuroscientist Stanislas Dehaene credits mistakes as a form of natural learning. Dehaene states that "our brain can adjust its models only when it discovers a discrepancy between what it envisioned and reality." From a misstep when we are learning to walk to formulating research hypotheses we anticipate and learn from mistakes.

Making mistakes is the work of learners, with one caveat. We have to approach mistakes with a learner identity. And, as I have said before, this work is not easy. Even if my middle school self would have been armed with a learner identity, with the mindset that making mistakes means learning and feelings of discomfort and the fear of failure would be lurking. I would argue though that the anticipation, the experience, would have been quite different. Stanislas Dehaene suggests that we are natural mistake makers yet somewhere along the line we learn to fear rather than embrace mistakes. I think of my own children. As youngsters, they do not carry with them the same fear of failure as we adults do. In fact, they would likely storm into a room filled with doors and open every door possible!

I like to examine dictionary definitions as they provide food for thought. Merriam-Webster defines a mistake as a wrong action or statement proceeding from faulty judgment, inadequate knowledge, or inattention. *Aha...* there it is! How different would it be if we defined mistakes as *not having enough knowledge* or *not paying attention?* Talk about learning and intentionality. As a runner, we might not have enough information about the terrain we are stepping into and we might slip and fall. Or, we might not be paying attention and we might run into a tree (a story for another time). What have we learned from those mistakes? If mistakes are part of the accessories we carry with us, I would suggest we learn a lot!

However, recognizing that mistakes are learning opportunities does not give us a free pass to behave without accepting responsibility. Remember the story of my behavior when I missed blocking the goal in the state championship? In this instance, I was wrong. However, I (hopefully) used these experiences to transition into being a different person.

CHECKPOINT:

In Japan, children are allowed, and expected, to work out a problem in front of the class for ten minutes or more. Even if the student is wrong, there is no shame. In these classrooms, mistakes are an indication not of failure but what still needs to be learned. (Tugend, 2011)
- What routine or tasks could you include in your daily life to normalize this work of making mistakes?

NOVICE *AND* EXPERT

Early in my life I may have considered expertise as a goalie, runner, student, and, more recently, as a professor to be the ultimate outcome. I thought that knowing it all and having the "right" answers was the goal. After all, I am a recovering perfectionist! Now, I shy away from describing myself as an expert in these arenas. I do know a bit about field hockey, golf, running, teaching. Yet, I am not really a novice either. Think about your own context. In what roles are you hovering toward being an expert? Being a novice? Recently, I'm attached to the idea that the path, or continuum on the novice to expert spectrum is both cyclical and context-dependent. Remember, there are dangers and limitations to binary thinking, in having to be a novice or an expert. Rather, what if we think of these identities as fluid? I might suggest that having a learner identity involves toggling between being a novice, an expert, and back again.

I love the image painted by Ericsson, Prietula, and Cokely (2007), who note that "consistently and over-whelming, the evidence show(s) that experts are always made, not born." And, while I agree with this premise, I would venture to add one more qualifier to this proposition: experts are, like me, a continuous work in progress. Or, better yet, an expert is someone who recognizes when they are a novice. Having a learner identity, whether it be for a sport, a new hobby, a new job, or simply learning more about the people in your life, means that you recognize your *noviceness* in any situation. And, yes, we can be a novice in situations that are very familiar to us. When we approach new and novel tasks, we are more open to admitting we are not an expert. We may even be more open to making mistakes. But once we, or others, have deemed that we have become experts, we cease from approaching experiences with a beginner's mindset and we perceive mistakes as errors.

Ericsson and colleagues define experts as "motivated students." Ponder that for a minute. What if we approached experiences and, yes, transitions as motivated students? Reflect on a recent experience, or anticipate an upcoming experience, in your professional context. There are many tasks and responsibilities that become second nature to us. We accomplish these daily tasks and projects with ease. We might even venture to say that we are experts in performing these tasks. But what if we entered these experiences, these familiar tasks, as motivated students? Making the leap between novice and expert, recognizing that we always have something to learn, takes deliberate practice (Ericsson, 2006). The more we practice putting on our learner identity, the more we deliberate practice living in the discomfort, the more we deliberately and intentionally question what the moment is teaching, how experiences are changing us. We are becoming experts and dealing with transitions.

Think about this. How would the situation have turned out for me in golf if I had recognized that each new competition, each new level of play, each different course or terrain forced me to once again become a novice? How would the situation have changed if I did not declare myself an expert but continued the deliberate practice with which I played in the beginning?

CHECKPOINT:

I recently stumbled upon this quote attributed to Harry S. Truman: "It's what you learn after you know it all that counts." Projecting a learner identity involves unearthing opportunities from both familiar and novel tasks. Consider your role in your professional context.

- What are some of the ways you can open yourself up to learning that "counts"?

DELIBERATE PRACTICE

We have all faced transitions ubiquitous to human experiences such as births, deaths, aging, and transitions unique to our lived experiences. However, for me, only recently have I been intentional about paying attention to the transitions in my own life and practicing being present in the transition moments. Before we proceed, let's return to that image of a door for a moment. While the door can present a barrier, the hinge presents an opportunity. Frequently, I find myself thinking about what I call "hinge moments" and how hinge moments create the change within transition spaces.

Think of an athlete opening their locker to don their transition equipment. What makes the locker door open? An opening mechanism is a hinge. I believe deliberate practice is a type of repetitive hinge moment that is part of the training equipment we need to grow and positively change as a result of transitions. Certainly, the transition toward becoming a seasoned athlete becomes easier each time we deliberately open the locker door. Similarly, approaching any transition in our lives becomes easier when we deliberately choose to don our learner identity.

In their book, *Make it Stick*, authors Brown, Roediger, and McDaniel (2014) remind us that deliberate practice is effortful, targeted focus on work that leads to new learning. Deliberate practice engaging in reflection, metacognition, thinking about our thinking, and self-evaluation helps us embed new learning into our habits of thinking and acting (Brown et al, 2014). Deliberate practice, adopting the habit of being intentional and present in transition spaces, requires cognitive effort to slow down in the moment and attend to the learning opportunities. Too often, individuals in schools, communities, businesses, and other organizations are enslaved by the tyranny of the urgent. Little or no time is provided to deliberately practice critical reflection and self-evaluation about our thinking habits, biases, assumptions, and default ways of responding. The destination overshadows the beauty, challenge, and potential of being in the moments associated with the transition. Stated another way, we focus on the product more than the process.

Deliberate practice is the repetitive hinge moments that allow us to immerse ourselves in the mess, uncertainties, and potential of the transition. In application, it's the CEO who intentionally practices a learner identity, being a life-long learner willing to learn, unlearn, and relearn based on the needs of internal and external constituents/stakeholders and the organization's mission. American moral and social philosopher Eric Hoffer (1902-1983) spoke about the value of having a learner identity resulting in life-long learning stating, "In times of change, learners inherit the earth while the learned find themselves beautifully equipped to deal with a world that no longer exists." Individuals, groups, and organizations manage what they monitor by naming the transition moments and repeatedly engaging in deliberate practice that results in a productive struggle with the learning associated with transitions. Educators modeling deliberate practice for their students verbalize the covert thoughts and critical reflections that demonstrate how to learn while engaging with the content being learned. In my opinion, one of the greatest returns on investment related to deliberate practice is becoming someone who is learning how to learn in any context, with any content or skill, and in and through transitions.

CHECKPOINT:

As you ponder the concept of deliberate practice being a hinge moment, how would you answer this question, "What is the role of a hinge moment in accessing a new pathway during a transition?"

TRANSPARENCY

Take a moment to observe the hinges in the room you find yourself in right now. As we have seen already, hinges actually can carry a lot of symbolism and I do not think it's too much of a stretch to imagine a hinge when we think of transparency. I recall reading about exterior doors in Sweden and I think there is a lesson to be learned here. Exterior doors in Sweden open out for practical reasons. Living spaces are generally smaller and the outward opening door creates more room in the living space. Outward opening doors also keep cold breezes out by pushing the cold away when opening a door. Symbolically, outward opening doors create warmth and space. However, the warmth and space does come at a cost. Outward opening doors have hinges on the exterior. These hinges can be removed and permit unwanted guests from entering our space. *Aha!* Creating warmth and space opens us up to the unknown. Transparency!

Imagine this. I am getting ready to go out for a run. I announce to my spouse that I will be leaving shortly. I put on my running shoes, my running gear, and grab my earbuds. Anyone looking at me would know for certain that I am going for a run. My outward appearance would reflect this. But what about when our training becomes less overt? What about when we are training to be a learner, training for the transitions in our lives? Although often invisible, transparency is an important piece of training equipment we must include. We have to make our learning, our training, and yes, even our struggles known. In many ways, transparency is a gift we give ourselves. By being transparent, we give ourselves permission to announce that we are on a learning journey, to attend to the feelings of doubt, shame, and isolation that emerge. Most importantly, we are honest and open about our imperfect journey.

We can learn a lot about transparency from our children. As I watch our children, I realize that they almost never worry about presenting their true selves to others. They laugh out loud when they are happy, they cry when they are hurt or sad, and much to my and Susan's chagrin, they are sometimes painfully honest in social situations. Compared to children, as adults we put on our professional hats and shroud ourselves in opaqueness. We become teachers, executives, directors, and administrators and instantly we become experts who find it difficult to present our true selves.

Remember my middle school experience? Think about this. How would things have changed if everyone in the class, including the teacher, were open and transparent about their personal discomfort? It is transparency that helps us to become comfortable in the discomfort. Knowing that someone is experiencing similar feelings or, at a minimum, knowing that someone else is attuned to our discomfort makes the transition more manageable. In fact, transparency allows us to be models for others.

CHECKPOINT:
I hesitate to apply the term "silver lining" to anything related to the 2020 pandemic. Rather, keeping a learner mindset, I would rather think about the lessons this pandemic has taught. In a sense, the pandemic is a hinge point for us as we transition through life. As we have talked about, transitions are uncomfortable, messy, and disorienting but with our newly discovered tools, we can learn from these experiences. So what does this have to do with transparency? Well, for almost a year now, we have learned that wearing facial coverings and maintaining distance can protect us from this virus. But imagine how it will feel when we can remove our masks and close the distance between ourselves and others. Sit with that feeling for a minute.

- Will it feel liberating?
- Will it feel awkward?
- Will we be nervous?
- Will it take bravery?

Of course, but isn't this what it means to be transparent?

VULNERABILITY AND COURAGE

Whether we are educators, business leaders, employees, or individuals in various life stages, the universality of transitions is an expected human experience. This chapter has highlighted the training equipment that enables us to don our superhero capes—our learner identities—and manage transitions more effectively. And, let's face it, who doesn't need more equipment? I for one am always looking for an excuse to purchase the latest gadget on the market that promises to make me a better runner. I think what is still missing in our learner identity toolkit are two traits that some may view as diametrically opposed: vulnerability and courage.

Now, you know I love a good paradox and, at first glance, vulnerability and courage seem to be at odds. Instead, I would argue that vulnerability and courage, woven together, are complementary, propelling the individual toward a readiness for and acceptance of the great good that can come from transitions.

Vulnerability, as Brené Brown (2018) describes, is not synonymous with being weak. Instead, vulnerability is having the courage to be present and stay in the "mess" even if you cannot control the outcome. For teacher-scholars, that means shedding the notion that we only impart our wisdom and knowledge but are not learners ourselves on our own learning journey. One of my educator friends, let's call her Kelly, offers us a powerful example of being intentionally vulnerable during her interactions with adult learners. Kelly is aware that her students observe and internalize how she acts and reacts to moments of vulnerability and failure. Kelly's internal dialogue about the power of a good mistake is an intentional action leading to learning that helps her to reframe the power of vulnerability for herself and her students. Rather than trying to cover up her mistakes or not knowing the answer to a student's question, Kelly opens herself to be vulnerable with her students. Kelly realizes that we don't want students to get upset, feel embarrassed, or even shut down when they fail and that she is able to model a positive response for her students. By demonstrating our own vulnerability, we can model the power of an imperfect journey that includes viewing mistakes and corrections as good teachers. These steps take vulnerability and courage, bravery to show our mistakes, admit our failures, and say we just do not know.

As many of my educator friends admit, we often focus on perfection—being totally prepared, having all the answers, and anticipating student questions, missteps, and needs. But, being hyper-focused on performance and perfection, getting it "right," which seems to be the impossible gold standard we strive to achieve, means that we are unable or unwilling to show vulnerability. Vulnerability is the training equipment of champions who stand firm in the transition, so they don't miss out on many opportunities to learn along with their students.

Learning alongside others in the dynamic and active spaces of transition takes courage. Being a "student of our students," whether the student is a new employee, a first-time high-school student, or a non-profit executive director helping a volunteer transition to an employee, requires us to engage and know each other, and the knowing takes courage.

Parker Palmer (2007), in his book *Courage to Teach*, suggests that knowing our students is deeply rooted in self-knowledge and a well-examined life. Holding a mirror to our thoughts, actions, and words takes courage and intentional inner dialogue to promote learning and change. Philip Dow (2013) describes courage as an intellectual character trait that shapes our lives, influencing our thinking habits as we seek and use knowledge. Courage enables the athlete to face an opponent with hope and optimism and the business leader to view change with the lens of potential and grit. Interweaving vulnerability and courage can fill the educator with persistence and empathy to cultivate belonging as a means to enlarge their engagement with students. Courage and vulnerability practiced together are effective training equipment that can open us up to others and enable us to gain confidence in growing, developing, and learning in and through transitions.

CHECKPOINT:
I hope you are seeing how many of these tools or pieces of training equipment work in concert with one another. Think about it, being vulnerable, courageous, transparent, making mistakes, and having a beginner mindset work together to polish our learner identity and make us more comfortable in the discomfort accompanying transitions. Take a moment to reflect on how these tools work in concert in your professional context.

COMMUNITY

For as long as I can remember, I have participated in team sports. Those who have played team sports realize the importance of relying on your team (your community) during training and competition. But what about sports that are generally more individualistic? What about running, playing a singles match in tennis, or even golf? We might think of these as individual sports, but there are plenty of team members that make our transition to athletes easier. In fact, in most facets of life, training and transitions become easier when we rely on others for help. Everyone, from independent contractors, to freelance writers, to self-contained teachers, benefits from the expertise of others who have successfully navigated transitions.

Human beings living in the 21st century may have experienced the transition from a post-industrial age to functioning in a global knowledge economy. The knowledge economy is fueled by technological advances, evolving social media influences, and diminishing insular geographical borders. And yet, humans exist in a myriad of communities including social, educational, athletic, organizational, religious, and political communities just to name a few. Conducting our daily activities and respective work within the context of the global knowledge economy leads us to conclude that further acceleration of access to information through technology, advances in sciences, and modes of communication means that knowledge will grow increasingly more perishable (Toffler, 1970). Today's facts become tomorrow's misinformation. Think of neuromyths about learning like individuals are either right- or left-brain processers. So, while I have no argument against learning facts or data, in societies where people regularly change jobs, residences, social ties, etc., these transitions place a premium on learning efficiency and learning in communities.

A final, and perhaps most important piece of training equipment in our transformation toward learning is our participation in communities of practice. We are social creatures. We encounter communities of practice in all aspects of our lives: our families, church groups, sports teams, clubs, and work teams. It is in these communities that we engage in learning through experience.

A community of practice is a group of people who intentionally engage in collective learning focusing their activities and discussions around a common interest for something they do to learn how to do it better (Wenger, 1998). Those who embrace a learner identity also embrace a community of practice. Members of a community of practice build a repertoire of resources such as lived experiences, tools, knowledge, and approaches to addressing problems (Wenger-Trayner and Wenger-Trayner, 2015). This community of practice collective approach to learning in transition spaces can occur in classrooms, teams, training for a race or competition, or completing a work project.

Continuing with our analogy of hinge moments creating the meaningful change in transition spaces, imagine the locker door again. How many hinges does it have? Most locker doors and other types of doors have more than one hinge. Individuals in our communities of practice can offer hinge moments, acting as the opening mechanisms to new pathways, understanding, and knowledge as we leverage their repertoire of resources to navigate transitions. Let's take this image of a locker one step further.

Think of the locker room itself. Most locker rooms have a multitude of lockers. Each one represents another individual training for, usually, some type of physical transition. The locker room itself can represent, then a transitional space, that we enter with a community of others.

Now, some of you may be thinking, what is the benefit of a collective approach to navigating transitions? Maybe you are a self-described individualist, and "shared thinking" is a foreign transaction to you or an activity that you have never cultivated, let alone enjoyed.

Author John Maxwell in his book, *Thinking for a Change*, shares an experience he had with the late, great basketball coach, Pat Summit of the University of Tennessee's Lady Vols. John spent time with Pat, her assistant coaches, and the players observing their interactions in the locker room and on the court. From his observations and interactions, John's takeaways are that Pat was a warm, intense, and exemplary leader. These traits, intentionally cultivated, propelled her to be one of the most acclaimed and successful basketball coaches to date. But he shares that his most noteworthy finding is that Pat chose to practice shared thinking. John describes a pivotal yet regular "hinge moment" locker room interaction as the team transitions from the first half to the second half of the game. During half-time, players spend the first ten minutes doing a collective review and analysis of the game without the coaches' input. They share their observations and solutions for weaknesses with the coaches. Pat and the assistant coaches engage in active listening, accepting input from the players about their findings and tentative adjustments, which are then shaped and adapted by the coaches. Under Pat Summit's leadership, the Lady Vols accomplished eight national championships. Valuing people, their experiences and ideas, and the interactive process is a model of shared thinking in the athletic domain that can be used in corporations, classrooms, and communities of practice experiencing transitions.

There is a synergy that comes into play when people think together (Maxwell, 2003), yielding a higher return on investment in the community of practice as we actively engage in challenges and opportunities transitions present us. Just as an athlete feels supported by their coaches and trainers, learners with a learner identity in communities of practice face life transitions with feelings of wonder and curiosity rather than dread (Bussolari and Goodell, 2009).

CHECKPOINT:
- What does it mean to you to stand and face the transition moments in a community of practice?
- Do you have a community of practice and if not, how could you cultivate one?

As we conclude our discussion of what it means to embrace a learner identity, let's take a moment to recap the training equipment that helps us transition to our role as learner:

- Mindset
- Mistakes as opportunities
- Novice and expert
- Deliberate practice
- Transparency
- Vulnerability and courage
- Community

For those of you out there who are like me, a self-proclaimed Type-A personality, this can seem like a long, daunting list of changes we have to make. Just remember, this is not a checklist of items to accomplish. I know we Type-As like to envision the finish line. This work is not about finishing the run. It is about experiencing the run.

The very serious work that occurs in 12-step programs helps those suffering from addiction on their transition toward recovery. The 12-step program emphasizes the importance of courage, vulnerability, admitting faults, improving consciousness, and an opening of self. In this program, members learn, in the midst of communities, to manage the transition space and move toward healthier versions of self. Just like the pieces of training equipment outlined here, the steps are not linear, but cyclical. One additional step members take on their journey is to take an inventory of self. Now that we have transformed our identities and become learners, we need to engage in critical reflection to propel ourselves forward.

CHAPTER 7: CRITICAL REFLECTION AND TRACKING YOUR PROGRESS

"Do not dwell in the past, do not dream of the future,
concentrate the mind on the present moment." – the Buddha

I remember learning to drive and coming home from driver's education and being exhausted. My arms were sore, my neck hurt, and I was emotionally and mentally tired. Learning to drive is overwhelming because, young drivers especially, are constantly watching the road, checking the side mirrors, looking in our rearview mirrors, and making sure we maintain the appropriate speed all at the same time. The process felt clumsy and awkward, and the stakes were high once you ventured out of the safety of the big empty parking lot. Eventually, though, I became less aware of the quick shifts in attention from the road to the mirrors, and the process of orienting myself to the other cars around me started to feel comfortable and became a routinized part of driving. Checking our mirrors on the road lets us know where we are relative to traffic and gives us quick glimpses behind and to the side as we charge forward. We do the same riding a bike and I have even seen music instructors playing the piano and choreographers teaching a new dance move glance in a mirror to keep an eye on people, places, and things behind them.

Like my young driving self, critical reflection often feels tiring and awkward at first but, with practice, it becomes part of a routine that informs how we stay present in, learn from, and navigate our transitional moments. Critical reflection can happen in different ways and at different times. Sometimes it happens in real time when we are in the middle of an activity or action and we take a moment to look around and take stock of the situation. During these moments of pause, we often ask questions about and notice what people are saying, how, they are behaving, and in what ways we are reacting and feeling in the situation. We are also exploring the moment for context clues that can inform our next steps. Drs. Nagoski and Nagoski call this practice a form of monitoring and Donald Schon (1991) in his books about reflective practitioners refers to this as in-action reflection. When I was in the field hockey goal, my success depended on my ability to monitor a game situation, check in with myself regarding my positioning and preparation for a shot, and then relay information to my teammates, accordingly. In this monitoring or in-action reflection, I tried to make sure that the defenders were in position and I constantly analyzed the moves of the offense.

Becoming a better and stronger goalie, effectively navigating a new professional role, and successfully starting a new academic program also requires time to pause and rest, time to critically review and ask questions *after* a moment in the transition has passed. Schon (1991) refers to this kind of critical reflection *on-action* reflection. After a field hockey game, win or lose, Coach Shelton would often have us review the video and, like my team, individuals also conduct after-action reflection about their performance using various tools including fitness tracker apps. Just as we monitor during live reflection, we might check our progress through engagement in post-event reflection.

CRITICAL REFLECTION

Critical reflection involves more than looking back at a replay or straight recall of the events of the day, more than a series of plays in a game or repetitions in a workout. For example, when my field hockey team reviewed film from games, we stopped and started, slowed down the footage to notice and name certain plays and positions. We reflected on particular moments, talked about what happened, considered ways to make adjustments, and planned for future scenarios. Similarly, when I review my own workouts, I recall the terrain, my speed, the duration, how I was feeling, and what I was thinking throughout the race or workout. Reflection, a way of tracking my progress, represents another important tool for learning to notice and name our transitions and also inform how to adjust and act during subsequent transitional moments.

The usefulness of critical reflection as a tool for navigating reflections depends on our ability to notice what is going on around us, or our *presence*. When we check our mirrors or monitor a moment, we pause briefly, in the action, to literally or figuratively step back to notice and sometimes assess how things are going. For example, when students start their first day of school or a new academic program or individuals take on a new role at work, they often, with the help of a teacher or mentor, pause briefly during the transition to share how they are feeling, to talk about the nervousness, and consider ways to manage the stress. In other instances, we might review our progress after the day is concluded. After that first day of school or the new professional role, we return to our thoughts, feelings, and actions of the day and event. Our ability to intentionally pause and pay attention to these moments can contribute to our ability to better navigate transitional moments.

Making reflection a habit can have significant and positive effects. Mezirow (1997) suggests that critical reflection is powerful enough to change *what* we think and also *how* we think. There is a difference between *what we know*, which is called informational learning, and *how we learn*, or transformational learning. Think about learning facts or just rote recall of memories, versus looking back at circumstances, experiences, and even relationships critically. Those reflections can change how we think, our habits of mind, and our points of view (Mezirow, 2000).

I was teaching a college course that I had taught many times before, but one semester the students were not responding in the same way as previous students had. This particular class seemed less engaged and did not participate as much but we moved forward anyway. We had a lot to cover and this was an upper-level course so I charged ahead with content, failing to touch base with the students to inquire about the low engagement. In a way, I was driving without checking my mirrors or running without my fitness tracker. A few classes later, I finally took a moment to orient myself to the students and shared my own observations, and invited their feedback. I shared that I believed they were bright and interested students and I did not know why they were not participating in this course. The students were honest with me and shared that they were seniors, the class was first thing in the morning, and the content was hard. They said, "it's like we need a warm-up or something."

This purposeful moment of critical reflection contributed to my learning and lead to implementing a *brain stretch* warm-up at the beginning of each class. The slides were bright pink, with an image of a brain doing a workout, and it included asking relatively easy recall review questions to start the class. This minor adjustment made all of the difference and helped my students reengage in the class material. I had to pause and reflect to recognize that the students were not engaged and ask them about what I noticed. Interestingly enough, the resultant warm-up is something I will revisit later in the book as it seems we all need to ease into this work.

IMPLEMENTING A REFLECTION PRACTICE

Learning the definition of critical reflection and the different approaches to this practice is important. Critical reflection, however, is only useful in our transitions when we are able to adopt a reflection practice that suits our needs, personalities, and experiences. While each of us should practice a combination of in-action and on-action reflection, the details of our approaches will vary. There are many, many ways to engage in reflective practices and this section offers just a couple of approaches to the work including appreciative inquiry and a simple three-step process.

APPRECIATIVE INQUIRY

Appreciative inquiry uses a strengths-based approach that involves the explicit identification of a person's or organization's strengths to promote individualized growth and success (Cooperrider and Whitney, 2000). Appreciative inquiry originated in business, as struggling companies engaged in identifying and leveraging their strengths, rather than focusing on their areas of relative weakness. It was often used as a means to develop leaders and organizations but as this approach became more successful, it was generalized to education and other sectors. Appreciative inquiry might feel like a counterintuitive approach to improvement because the approach focuses on existing strengths rather than what is going wrong, but there is evidence to suggest that strengths-based inquiry and reflection have positive effects.

For example, Bandura (1997) writes that the examination of strengths increases self-efficacy or one's belief that one can do something. Focus on strengths also promotes growth mindset (Dweck, 2016). When students view themselves as people who can learn and get smarter, they are willing to put in the work to learn, which leads to higher achievement. Moreover, utilizing a perspective that values openness and a willingness to ask questions may contribute to our ability to notice and stay in the difficult transitional moments as they come up.

Above, I shared a story of my students and their low engagement. Remember, I had taught them before, knew they were bright students, and needed help to figure out how to bring those strengths to the forefront. As we engaged in a group reflection of the moment, I started from "you are bright and I know you have great ideas, I want to hear them" rather than "nobody participates." Earlier in this part of the book, I discussed the importance of grace, gratitude, and greatness and learning to normalize the discomfort of these transitions. Appreciative inquiry offers another means to be present and focus on our strengths and the opportunities they present. Noticing and naming that my students were strong and talented and acknowledging the importance of their participation to our class community contributed to our ability to collectively navigate this momentary transition from low to higher engagement.

Appreciative inquiry, like critical reflection, depends on presence and intentionality. We can also rely on grace, gratitude, and greatness to work on appreciative inquiry. During the 2020 pandemic, a group of faculty members engaged in some post-reflection regarding teaching through COVID-19, and, unfortunately, the conversation quickly became a venting session that shifted from healthy dialogue to unkind blaming and comparisons. Sensing that things were moving in an undesirable direction, I stopped the conversation and tried to take an appreciative inquiry approach to our group reflection.

In this moment, I practiced grace by acknowledging how our circumstances were unbelievably challenging. I asked my colleagues to take some time and consider their best moments of teaching since the pandemic started. Everyone shared and their stories were more about human connection than any failed zoom call or technology glitch. Our most memorable and positive moments were not about teaching, but connecting with our students and each other as people. Critical reflection using an appreciative lens opened us up to sharing laughs about technology fails, discussions about managing fear, and mutual questions about our uncertain future. Critical reflection with gratitude and an appreciative inquiry may contribute to our ability to embrace and normalize the discomfort of our transitions.

Reflection, in and on-action, offers another tool for us to practice being present, giving grace and gratitude, and finding ways to stay in and navigate our transitions. Appreciate inquiry offers one way to go about this work and Kolb (1984) provided another approach that includes a process of inquiry, "what, so what, now what" to guide reflection.

WHAT, SO WHAT, NOW WHAT

Let's consider the what, so what, now what sequence in the context of a medical diagnosis. The *what* is the problem, let's say it's a torn hamstring. When I went to see the trainers in college, I explained what was happening with my leg and they were able to diagnose the problem and figure out that the muscle was torn. That was the *what*. The *so what* came next. The so what of a torn hamstring meant that I could not practice with my team, had to sit out of competitions, and that if I chose to do those things anyway, I could make the problem worse. The situation now includes an athlete who has an injury (the *what*) and the information about the implications of the injury (the *so what*). The other aspect of the moment to consider, according to Kolb (1984) is *now what*. The trainers knew what I could not do, but what could I do to rehabilitate and heal? What exercises would be helpful? How could I support my team without being able to practice and compete? *Now what* included a plan for me to continue to contribute to my team, apply the knowledge I had gained on my current situation and adjust to the moment.

Like my athlete self, we can also apply this three-step reflection process during moments of transitions that might include taking on new professional roles, a first day of school, becoming a parent, or getting a new job. *What, so what, and now what* offers another way to structure our practice of being present in the moments, and learning to apply this presence to future settings and experiences.

Melinda Gates shares her "what, so what, now what" story in her book *The Moment of Lift*. Most of us know Melinda Gates as a wealthy philanthropist married to Bill Gates (currently separated at the time of writing) but she is also a person with a story of her own. She shares that when she first started working at Microsoft, she felt like she had to act like someone other than herself to be successful. She was a girl from Texas, thrown into life on the West coast. Her first business trip took her East, to New York City, and she felt terribly uncomfortable and out of place, remarking that she had never hailed a cab in her life. She felt like the only way to succeed in her new role and new context was to be less herself and more like the person she thought would be successful, someone who was more aggressive and maybe less kind than she was before taking the Microsoft position. Acting like someone else, someone she thought would be successful, was the *what*. The *so what* was that she didn't like the person she was becoming. She was aggressive at work, and she found that when she left work, the gruff mentality and way of being persisted, and she didn't like herself. She felt exhausted and defeated. She decided that her last resort was to stop acting and start just being herself. And if that didn't work, she would head back to Texas. Her *now what* was that she decided to act like Melinda. I think we all know how the story ends. She attributes her success to realizing that she was trying to be someone other than herself, and her last ditch *now what* effort ended up being her best move yet. Melinda's true strengths, not the unnaturally aggressive and cold traits that she associated with strength, ended up being the catalysts for her success and the keys to many years of sustained work.

Kolb's three-step process of the "what, so what, now what" represents another approach to critical reflection and, like Melinda Gates illustrated, is an effective way to stay present and remain an active participant in the moments as they happen.

Taking a new job and feeling insecure about the skills that you bring to the position. Figuring out how to raise children and pursue career aspirations. Deciding if a promotion is what you truly want, and weighing all of the real factors in life before moving forward. All of these transitions can be examined, considered, and paths determined by designing and implementing a practice of critical reflection. We have the opportunity to carve our paths thoughtfully, we can check our mirrors and look at our surroundings (e.g., family, friends, coworkers, our own feelings and instincts) as we move forward. We can also stop and look back as we review our progress, taking a moment to think about what happened at work, home, or school. What was the best part? What made it so good? How can we leverage those positive elements for the next time?

Holocaust survivor Dr. Edith Eger says that we always have a choice in how we move through our days. Things happen to us that we cannot control, and her experiences at Auschwitz were the most horrific we could imagine, and yet she believed she still had a choice. Similarly, the 2020 pandemic contributed to us feeling out of control, and going to school, walking around unmasked, and existing with the fear of contracting and spreading the virus changed us and our surroundings. At the same time, however, we had choices in those moments, to look critically at our days, identify the good, own the discomfort and uncertainty and hold onto being present and staying in the moment to get to and through the next day. This is not a rose-colored glasses or silver lining approach to hard situations, but rather staying present, being in the moment, and adopting a constructive way to move through our days and lives with intention.

BARRIERS

Making a habit of critical reflection, of checking our mirrors and reviewing our progress, can be difficult. Our days are busy and our downtime is sacred, and adding something else to the list may seem unreasonable. Finding time in the moment and at the end of the day or week to think back about our experiences might not feel productive.

TIME

Whether we are teaching, leading non-profits, running our families, and managing our professional teams and organizations, we are all expected to meet some type of productivity standard. This means we are required to account for what we do during the day, and, for some of us, it also means we are rewarded based on success and outcomes earned. For teachers, it could include student test scores or evaluations, for leaders it might mean reaching an expected sales figure or earning a particular profit margin, and for families, these measures might be more about getting kids out the door on time, dinner on the table, and toys picked up before the day is over. No matter the expectations and success measures, we do what we can to please and achieve our "numbers." No matter the context, this pace can be grueling and simultaneous we feel like we are doing the best we can, that we are not enough, while under tremendous pressure to achieve. These time constraints are real and pressure-filled and yet, they are also one of the reasons we need to pause, make time to be present, and reflect in and after these transitional moments.

Dr. Ronald Epstein's (2017) book *Attending* describes the healthcare environment from a physician's perspective, and he notes that many physicians enter medicine to heal and connect with people, but patient billing and rigid insurance standards often get in the way of healing processes. Dr. Epstein focuses on mindfulness, and he suggests that even in the busiest hospitals, there is a way to find the time to slow down, be present, and carefully think about each patient. He creates time for reflection.

In his practice, he makes time, prior to meeting patients, to breathe, review their charts, and ready himself for the work ahead. He then enters the room, finds a place to sit down, and works to cultivate an environment of healing and connection.

Dr. Epstein then engages in a collective sort of reflection where he inquires as to the patient's most difficult aspect of this health condition. While listening, he is essentially checking his own mirrors and paying attention to his own assumptions and their reality. In these moments, these reflections help to bring him back into the actual reality of the moment to learn that the patient is not worried about the prognosis but actually concerned about falling. The moment of reflection allows him to shift priorities and, oftentimes, leads to a manageable course of care like writing a referral for physical therapy to help the patient feel steadier on her feet. Dr. Epstein's question helps him to align his plan of care with the patient's goals, but unless he asks, he cannot know if they are the same. The brief moments spent taking a breath, centering oneself to be present in the moment. Sitting down and asking a reflective question do not take much time on the clock, but they are arguably the most productive minutes of the day.

Teachers, leaders, and students also worry over not having enough time and while the academic environment is different than a hospital, teachers, leaders, faculty, staff, and administrators are charged with moving forward and valuing progress measured by assessment results. Jensen (et al, 2016) describes how schools around the world whose leaders prioritize professional learning to include action-reflection cycles also offer teachers reduced teaching loads, time to collaborate and observe one another, and reflect and share on their work. The professional learning is as integral to their work as their teaching. This reflective practice contributes to improving their teaching, well-being, and promotes an atmosphere that values improvement and learning.

Dr. Epstein (2017) and Jensen (2016) offer ways to carve out time for reflection in busy contexts. It is critical that we make time for reflection in and after transitional moments. It is also evident that we must be intentional in carving out the time to practice these skills and reflect on our feelings, thoughts, and actions in these experiences. Whether that time is a few minutes to take a deep breath or hours in a week to dedicate to professional learning and reflection, time for reflection is valuable.

NOVICE EXPERT PARADOX

Discomfort is the hallmark of transitional moments. You have lived in and through these moments and felt the associated emotions countless times in your life. Being comfortable with an environment or a practice or a set of skills usually feels much better than the unknown and unfamiliar. But everyone who is comfortable now once went through those stages of learning. Adopting a practice of reflection is no different. It requires intention, practice, and more intention to integrate critical reflection into your own method for managing transitions.

Reflection and vulnerability go hand in hand. It takes courage and openness to check your mirrors and to review your progress. You may see things that suggest you should consider making a change and the status quo could be improved. Confronting those realities head-on, rather than driving right past them without checking mirrors, is hard. Looking back and noticing and naming strengths and areas for improvement takes dedication and persistence through the discomfort. In the context of a busy and stressful world, avoiding vulnerability may seem more appealing than walking into discomfort. But allowing yourself the grace to overcome the barriers of being short on time (consider adding reflection to your calendar) and a novice at reflection (consider inviting a friend or trusted colleague to join you) to step back and check your mirrors and review the app may have profoundly positive effects.

RETURN ON INVESTMENT

A friend of mine who works in the education non-profit world always listens to my thoughts and ideas with openness and curiosity, and then she kindly asks about the *why*, or the return on investment. This discussion about reflection makes sense, but is it worth changing current habits, carving out time from an already busy schedule, and learning a new practice that might unearth hard truths about our work and relationships? The answer from my experience is yes, and ample research supports the practices also. Reflection is not about rebuilding or reinventing ourselves. It involves amending, adopting, and building on our current strengths and creativity to better navigate our transitional moments. The tools and resources we need to engage with, stay present in, and manage these challenging moments are in us, and critical reflection contributes to our ability to see our strengths and leverage those possibilities.

Whether we wanted to or not, we had to creatively figure out how to operate in the long, unknown moments of the 2020 pandemic. In many ways, the pandemic represented a series of transitions that included quickly pivoting to this new norm, to eventually and gradually finding our way through and staying in these often-long moments of the pandemic. Our trusted systems of going to work and school, communicating face-to-face, and operating in a world without pandemics were no longer the reality and we had to adapt. In many ways, this global crisis awakened us all to each moment of our days. We had to strategize ways to survive and thrive with kids at home, friends, and family out of work, and health worries abound. Each of us identified the most important priorities in the moment of the day and then figured out how to attend to those priorities or do those tasks using different skills and tools. Reflection offers a way to foster the ability to think beyond what we do as a matter of routine. It offers a way to step outside of ourselves, even for just a moment, and check our mirrors. We are able to notice the moment, surveil the landscape, and take in the thoughts and feelings and then act as needed. Reflection is a tool that facilitates such creative and nimble thinking and action.

While the 2020 pandemic imposed an urgency to reflect and repurpose, the need has always been here. Every individual, team, group, and organization experiences transitions regularly and these moments require creative thinking and openness to assessing the situation and making changes. Learning and practicing the ability to identify one's strengths and using those strengths in a variety of situations with an emphasis on the process of learning versus the facts of learning will help to equip each of us for more manageable and successful transitional moments. Imagine if schools valued the process just as much as—if not more than—the outcome. The grade did not ride on the tests, but on your learning along the way and the final product. And what if the "along the way" took different forms? What if you were given different ways to learn and part of the process was figuring out which you liked the best, which worked well for you? Embedding and valuing critical reflection fosters transformational learning, and when we know *how* to learn, then *what* we learn can change because the fundamental skills are not tied to specific content or subject matter, but to the process that can be applied in different contexts.

REFLECTING ON REFLECTION

I hope that you feel able to answer my friend's question about the return on investment of critical reflection. Making a habit of checking our mirrors and reviewing our progress or reflecting in-action and reflecting on-action, gives us the opportunity to regularly check in and be present with ourselves, our work, and our relationships. A deep breath and centering thoughts, a critical look at a classroom, retrospective processing of a job, these actions help us to learn from our experiences and identify our strengths to leverage and improve the next time. As we will discuss in the next few chapters, critical reflection like dancing with dissonance and adopting attitudes of grace, gratitude, and greatness will play a critical role in the transitions training.

CHAPTER 8: TRANSITIONS TRAINING

As I mentioned earlier and discussed throughout the book, I love sports, exercise, competing, fitness, projects, and anything in that neighborhood. I also love the planning involved in the preparation for a race, competition, exercise, or any other goal. I like reading about and experimenting with possible equipment, researching training plans, reviewing information about the event, and just anticipating the start. I also work with doctoral students, listen to their stories, observe their progress, and participate in their journeys. The more I listened to my students, the more I realized training for events like a running or adventure race is not all that different than preparing for a new academic journey, program, or event.

Starting any new event, like running, biking, or adventure racing, a new job, marriage, parenting, kindergarten, graduate school, or any other transition, as varied as they are, also have so much in common. Individuals, teams, and organizations, during these moments, feel nervous, uncertain, anxious, excited, and thrilled. These transitional periods, regardless of duration, intensity, and frequency represent shifts, adjustments, and an evolution within us and our learning, abilities, identity, and knowledge (Bridges, 2009). This training program offers a structure, approach, and strategies to learn how to effectively navigate our transitions. Benefiting during and from transitional periods requires individuals to notice and mark the moments, wrestle with and lean into the associated discomfort, and quiet the voices of self-doubt. To do these things requires attending to the moments, embracing discomfort, interrupting the voices, adjusting focus and attitudes, and a beginner mindset and learning identity.

When I was a senior in college, I trained and ran my first half marathon. At the time, I was excited and motivated but also very nervous and worried about whether or not I could finish this race. I followed a training schedule, had the right equipment, and a semblance of a plan. I arrived at the race, met up with some friends who were also running, stepped up to the line, no warm-up, no mental preparation, and very little practice. I just started to run. Like many of our transitions, anticipated or not, I had the shoulds, coulds, and self-doubt playing in my head as loud as the spectators cheering on the runners. I arrived at the infamous hill at around mile seven and, halfway to the top, I stopped. I was hurting, tired, defeated, and just done. The doubt, uncertainty, and dissonance were just too much for me. I did end up finishing the race, but it was terrible. In fact, I barely remember the second half of the race because I was just trying to get through it.

Compare that first experience to a few years ago, when I signed up and ran a marathon—all 26.2 miles. By now, I had finished a few half marathons and done some of my own work with this transitions training. I was learning how to focus, be present, and work in and through the mud and discomfort of these moments. At around mile 21 of the race, my legs cramped up, I hit that infamous wall that everyone describes during these long races. I struggled for a few moments and those voices of self-doubt were increasing in volume, instead of stopping, shutting down to try and avoid the moment, I gathered myself and my thoughts. I did not try to escape, and I certainly could not avoid the moment. I needed to get to the finish line one way or another. I realized that I had to be in it, the misery and dissonance of mile 21, and instead of worrying about mile 23, 24, or even 26, I stayed at mile 21, one step at a time. I remember running through the final neighborhood of the race, adjusting my gait to manage the discomfort in my legs, and eventually crossing the finish line, one mile at a time. I also distinctly remember going home and finding another marathon that would happen a month later because I was determined to apply what I had learned that day. While I had not yet formulated this transitions training, I was able to manage this transition because I had been practicing and learning to notice, name, and navigate these moments of discomfort. I was figuring out how to stay in and even embrace the muddiness of the moment, one step and one mile at a time.

Through my own transitions and opportunities to observe, engage with, and support others in their journeys, I have noticed that we benefit from a training schedule, scaffolding, and strategies to effectively navigate these moments. While exercise plans, running and project schedules, routines, and training regiments vary, most include some form of preparation, practice, performance, and pause. In my experiences with transitions and these in-between moments, it has become clear that intentional practice for and in these transitions represent tremendous opportunities if we just pay attention.

Thus far, we have talked a lot about the different types and durations of transitions. We have explored the myriad feelings of doubt and uncertainty and the multitude of events and moments that catalyze and represent transitions. Part III of this book invites you to consider a practice to effectively navigate these transitions and this training includes different kinds of work. The program features and sequencing are designed for use during transitional and non-transitional moments. Individuals, groups, and organizations can implement this practice as a way to simulate transitions or experiences that recreate the emotions and behaviors associated with transitions but also intended as a structure and approach to executing, experiencing, and examining transitions in the moment.

As you will read later in the chapter, the program includes warm-up, practice, performance, and reflection so that we can learn to notice, name, and mark these moments, gain awareness of our own self-doubt, and adopt attitudes and strategies to effectively navigate these moments. We can learn to quiet the voice in our head that tells us we cannot and should not and trains us to refocus and reset with a learning mindset. Even though our transitions come in all shapes and sizes with a high degree of uncertainty, it is possible to prepare and practice. Moreover, I am convinced that participating in and adopting strategies from this training program will make for better transitional experiences.

This training program represents intentional choices and actions to create space and flexibility that can be molded and shaped to fit individual needs, experiences, and circumstances. Even with infinite configurations of the sequence and duration of training, the practice represents a strong foundation for and a way to think about approaches for doing the work of transitions.

Lastly, this program will not eliminate doubt, fear, worry, or dissonance and we do not want it to—that is not the point of the practice. Remember, discomfort contributes to our learning and growth (Merriam, 2005). This practice will help each of us to be more present, aware, and ready to take on these transitions and support and guide others in their journey. In some ways, this practice represents a healing process. As we notice, name, and mark our discomfort in the transitions, it also awakens us to the possibilities in these moments. This practice aims to convince individuals and organizations to embrace the dissonance, to walk into it knowing you can manage whatever emerges in the moment, and to find real, authentic, true gratitude in this messy, muddy, and hard work.

THE PROGRAM

"What we are waiting for is not as important as what happens to us while we are waiting. Trust the process." – Mandy Hale from The Single Woman: Life, Love, and a Dash of Sass

A student shared with me that she remembers starting her first days of doctoral studies and having no idea what to expect, expressing worry about her own knowledge and abilities, and questioning whether she deserved to be in the program. She admitted to me that as she looked around the room at all of her new peers she wondered, "Why me? All of these students are so accomplished and so smart. What am I doing here?" She doubted her ability to be a doctoral student, to do the work required, and to ever write a whole dissertation.

Like this doctoral student, I remember arriving at my first triathlon event. I dragged my little brother along just so I would have someone with me. I walked into the gymnasium to register, got my race packet, and listened to the race director share the instructions for the day's events. I remember looking around the space realizing I had no idea what to expect, worrying that I did not have enough ability or training to do this race, and questioning whether or not I should have signed up for the race in the first place. I thought, "Why am I here? Do I belong?" We often spend so much mental and physical energy clinging to a future outcome, waiting for what is next and thinking about the "should." Mandy Hale, in her quote, reminds us to wake up, focus attention, and be present in this moment, right now. This training program aims to help individuals find, see, and be in these transitional or in-between moments.

CHECKPOINT:
- What is here right now?
- What is occupying your thoughts?
- How are you feeling in this moment?

While two very different experiences, the feelings expressed in these stories are almost identical. Starting a new academic program, competing for the first time (i.e., running, biking, dancing), starting a new class, walking into a new school, or a new job are different experiences, but our thoughts, emotions, and the stories we tell ourselves are often the same across these different contexts. Entering *new and different* circumstances, no matter how many we have navigated and regardless of personal or professional status and level of experience, engender feelings of anxiety, uncertainty, discomfort, and stress. These moments also bring excitement and the possibility to listen, learn, and develop alongside others in this new community.

The benefits of preparing and practicing for transitions also bring awareness, increased confidence, attention, and focus to the moment and a way to focus on the benefits of current opportunities. Imagine if individuals paid close attention to these moments. Imagine even further that their peers, employers, and teachers could recognize these transitional moments. Now imagine facilitating check-in moments, space, and time to talk about feeling vulnerable and uncertain. If individuals and groups facing new and unfamiliar moments (like doctoral studies, triathlons, or the 2020 pandemic) engage in this training they may feel more prepared to stay in these moments, support others with their own discomfort, and effectively navigate these transitions. It is also possible that *newness* of the situation might become familiar—uncomfortable but familiar. The idea behind this framework is not to dodge the dissonance. It cannot be done. It is to anticipate, notice, practice, and prepare, and notice for the inevitable transition, pivot, or bump that will come.

Organizations and individuals use words like introductions, welcome sessions, orientations, first-year seminars, human resource meetings, onboarding, employee relations, and many other labels. While these events and supports are important, they do not sufficiently address the anxiety, worry, and uncertainty individuals feel and experience as they move into these transitions. Starting college represents a significant milestone and transition. New students often attend some kind of welcome or orientation session. While these events are effective in introducing a campus, orienting students to a place, they are not always effective in getting to know the individual student and integrating them or acknowledging the transition and the associated discomfort.

Many individuals and teams do not have the opportunity to engage in long-term, ongoing programs or even episodic and temporary orientations. Without attention to these pivotal moments, organizations, their members, and newcomers miss out on opportunities to learn about and from each other, identify areas for possible integration of needs and talents, and cultivate an organizational culture that promotes inclusion, belonging, an authentic valuing of each individual member of the community, and providing opportunities for individual growth and development in these transitions.

The transitions program represents a design, plan, and example for how to cultivate intentional time, space, and activities to help individuals and groups switch their attention from the outcomes to the process, the journey, and those waiting moments.

Imagine, for example, a transition where you had someone or some group, perhaps a coach or community identifying, naming, and creating space, place, and time to examine, reflect on, and learn about these moments of dissonance. Imagine even further, that this coach or community, offered structured time to learn and prepare for these moments or even scaffolding in the moment. Picture students or personnel spending time together calling attention to transitions, sharing their experiences with the self-doubt, and learning together that these thoughts and feelings are part of the journey.

The extent to which individuals, groups, and organizations learn from and develop in these moments is, in part, a function of how we do or do not leverage these transitional moments. The intentional investment of time and resources in transitions training contributes to an ability to create places and spaces in our personal lives, classrooms, boardrooms, and athletic fields for preparation and practice before and during these transitions contributes to an individual's learning in and about these unfamiliar spaces.

FOUR STAGES OF THE PROGRAM

This training program represents a process for designing and implementing places, spaces, and activities to navigate these transitions. Whether training for a running or bike race, competing in a golf or baseball tournament, participating in a friendly competition in your hobby of choice, or preparing to begin a new school, graduate program, or job, individuals establish routines and schedules for achieving their goals. Just as a personal coach might design a plan for an individual to prepare for race day or the big event, this book offers a training plan to prepare, practice, and successfully navigate personal and professional transitions.

Table 1 presents key principles of this training program. Within and across the stages of this training program. Individuals learn to attend to the moment and discomfort, change our attitudes and voice in our heads, and adopt a learning mindset. This work leads to better focus and an ability to do the important work of now.

Table 1: Key principles of the training

Key principle	Features of each principle
Moment	attend, try, reclaim, and reflect
Discomfort	dance, reach, own, and learn
Voice	interrupt, interrogate, frame, and learn
Focus	narrow, adjust, practice presence, and stay
Attitude	reset, negotiate, release grace and gratitude, mark greatness, and thank yourself
Learning identity	engage, stay curious, question, reflect, and learn

No matter the transition, this training plan can be personalized to match individual needs and appropriate intensity and duration to match unique individual, team, group, and organizational in-between moments. The subsequent sections offer a discussion of the stages of this training program. Figure 1 provides a depiction and overview of the program stages. It is worth noting that while each step in the sequence is critical, it is also reasonable to expect that different contexts might stretch or compress the sequencing to suit their needs.

Figure 1: Training program

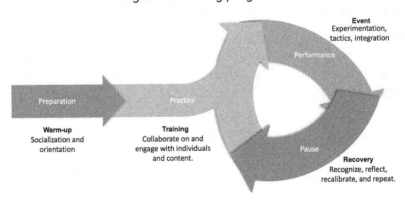

For example, new employees or students participate in activities to build community, orientations, and other practices and strategies towards entering a new role and it may be possible to mark the performance and represent the first day of school or official work. On the other hand, as I have learned from public school teachers and small organizations, the linear nature of warm-up, training, and performance are often condensed into one or several back-and-forth activities, so while they are all important and do not happen in a particular sequence, they also occur, often, on the *same* day.

In one instance, a middle school teacher recounted when a new student joined her class. In this moment, she recognized this student's transition and did practice the features of this transition framework and, yet, all of these steps could not happen in a linear sequencing over a period of time. She engaged in these practices within a period of days of the student joining this new setting. Regardless of the context, the framework for monitoring and managing transitions can be pulled or pushed to meet the needs of students, employees, leaders, and others in these novel situations. Moreover, while preparation and practice are critical, the sequencing is not what matters, what matters is using this program to raise our awareness and notice, name, and mark a state of here and now. Engaging in warm-up, practice, performance, and pause means we have a better chance to embrace these challenging moments. Table 2 offers a brief overview of the features of each stage of the framework.

The subsequent sections describe each stage and in subsequent chapters, I will share more details about each, along with possible approaches, strategies, and activities.

Table 2: Training phases

Phases		
Warm-up	Readiness	Reset, engage your learning identity, attend to the moment, dance with discomfort, interrupt the should, narrow your focus, execute a plan, share your story, stay present
Practice/training	Trains	Try the moment, reach for the dissonance, adjust your focus, interrogate the voice, negotiate through the transition, stay curious
Performance	Perform	Practice presence, establish time and space, reclaim the moment, frame your questions, own the dissonance, release grace and gratitude, mark greatness
Pause	Rest	Reflect the moment, educate yourself, stay focused, thank yourself for the work

WARM-UP

In Chapter 7, I recounted a story about my students engaging in a brain warm-up. In this case, student engagement was low and all that was required was a way to switch on students' attention to the course, their readiness for learning. Facilitating a brief question and answer review of previous materials gave students space to gradually warm-up, collaborate with peers, and set their intentions for this class period. Like beginning a class, a project, or any transition, warm-up and preparation are critical first steps in this training program. Whether working alone or in a group, team, or organization, preparation is required.

Readiness for change is important for successfully navigating these transitions. It permits individuals and groups to switch gears into the present moment and focus and pay attention to feelings, thoughts, and actions associated with these transitions. A warm-up offers a way to intentionally start the process, warm up the body and mind, and prepare for the work ahead. In breathing meditation and prayer rituals, this is referred to as centering. Similar to beginning an exercise routine, playing an instrument, performing in a play, or any other activity, starting should be slow and gradual.

As noted in the table, warm-up is readiness. It is the moment in the training where individuals reset and gradually and intentionally wrestle with discomfort, stay present, and share the experience as it unfolds. Starting this process, instead of ignoring, avoiding, or just rolling with it, means individuals or groups in these transitions may adjust and thrive rather than suffer through the opportunity.

McGowan, Pyne, Thomson, and Rattray (2015) in discussing the benefits of athletic warm-up, suggested that even a five to ten-minute warm-up activity contributes to increased preparation for the subsequent activity or exercise and also improves mental preparation through increased concentration and self-confidence, and a narrowing of attention towards the tasks at hand. Like McGowan et al (2015), Dr. Mary Radnofsky (1988) discussed the importance of warm-up in her classes. She suggested that students need time in warm-up stage before the start of class to turn on their system and ready themselves and the class to learn. This warm-up might include a combination of small tasks, questions, and learning to cultivate self-confidence, trust, and connections. It could also include community building, check-ins, sharing of ideas, and small preparatory tasks and learning moments.

This warm-up represents a way to mark an intentional period of time or a short moment for quiet, individual preparation and self-checks, meetings, consultations, and group or one-on-one sessions. During this warm-up phase, individuals or teams aim to get ready, shift mindsets and attitudes towards this work, this moment and do the work, some work that resembles the transition, "transition-lite" or quick, easy bouts of simulated transitional periods. Getting ready means mentally and physically preparing, warming up. It also includes changing the channel in our minds and dampening the fear and self-doubt. This might happen by shutting that voice in a metaphorical box, switching the station in our heads, or finding supportive ways to cultivate grace and gratitude for and in ourselves.

As much as I love running, exercising, and participating in new experiences, I notice that I still need a warm-up period, an adjustment that moves me from a previous moment. It represents a hinge moment as discussed in Chapter 6. This is a switch, opening a door to welcome in the unknown and discomfort ahead. The warm-up includes a slow, gradual mental and physical progression (i.e., a light jog, pre-meeting conversation, a quick review of a presentation, or a slow, easy spin on a bike). Even with experience and training, I must work, intentionally and purposefully, to change the channel and shut down the voice in my head that questions my ability, intelligence, and belonging.

These warm-ups can happen alone, in pairs, or groups, and represents a getting-to-know-you moment, a reacquaintance with yourself or the group and these warm-ups can happen at a new event, a recurring meeting, as part of a relationship, in a project or during some kind of activity. Regardless, each moment of transition requires a warm-up session. The length and sequencing of this first stage depend on the organization's need, structure, and resources. However, the success of this training program hinges on spending even just a small amount of time and effort on this early stage of the program. During the warm-up, coaches, teachers, and participants listen and learn, make tentative plans/ schedules, spend time answering and asking questions, and building connections and relationships.

Warm-up activities cultivate familiarity and connection between and among individuals, groups, and organizations (Blatner, 2005). For example, our school began a mentorship program that paired faculty with one or two at-risk students to improve student behavior, attendance, and ultimately academic outcomes. The purpose was to support faculty in developing relationships with the students and improving their sense of belonging. Prior to this program, faculty had varied levels of comfort regarding connecting with students outside of classroom interactions. Many teachers admitted that they did not know how to start non-instructional conversations with students and were not sure how to engage with students outside of the classroom. Faculty needed a way to ease into this work, they required support, a sense of confidence, and time to prepare. Faculty, with time, found ways to connect with students including inquiring about extracurricular activities, joining students in the cafeteria for lunch, and attending students' sporting and music competitions.

These faculty discussions were a source of necessary training for teachers. While faculty competently engage in a classroom setting about subject matter topics, they recognized a transitional point that included the addition to their role and identity as faculty and teachers. Doing this work required a warm-up and time to start the work. In this example, it is evident that individuals—even faculty considered experts in their field—need practice, conversations, and community to fine-tune their plan. After even a few moments or short periods of warm-up, individuals may be ready to train, attentive to the moment, able to interrogate that doubtful voice, and execute a plan in the next phase of the program.

PRACTICE/TRAINING

As individuals, teams, classes, project groups, and organizations move out of the warm-up phase of this transitions practice, there should be a sense of readiness to engage, learn, and be present in these difficult moments. It is likely that from this warm-up leaders, teachers, coaches, and individuals can switch their attention, gain awareness, and attend to and act in this moment. The practice stage of the transitions training includes actively trying the moment and reaching for the discomfort. It also requires individuals, leaders, and others to interrogate the voice and tamp down the fears and the "shoulds," to do the work required to navigate a transition. Additionally, individuals need to adopt a curiosity about the work. This plan might include a conversation, mindfulness practice, a series of workshops, or another mix of activities for any individuals including teachers, students, employees, or leaders.

This stage of the training program includes a series of intervals with high and low-intensity training. The intensity of the training sessions varies according to the level of what I call transitional intensity (TI). Transitional intensity includes some combination and level of discomfort, anxiety, stress, the unknown, and self-doubt. Low-intensity training includes low-impact sessions as well as recovery intervals and sessions. A low intensity or active recovery segment of an interval involves less relative TI. A low-impact session or recovery "day" refers to a session of low-impact training separate and apart from an interval sequence. As we will discuss in Chapter 10, individuals will engage in a mix of high-intensity intervals, low-impact sessions, and recovery. While the low-impact and recovery sessions represent relatively lower levels of intensity, this is still work but is less taxing than the high-intensity interval. The design of this practice with a variety of discomfort, uncertainty, stress, and worry contributes to individuals', teams', and organizations' abilities to notice and navigate our transitional periods.

Intervals vary as much as the transitions we have been discussing and may include high-intensity intervals and can be long or short bouts of intensity. The other variable open to adjustment is the ratio of high to low intensity. For example, an interval could include 60 seconds of high intensity followed by 60 seconds low intensity, 30-60 seconds, or other variations. Regardless of the plan, it is meant to simulate the physical, emotional, and cognitive aspects of any approaching transition. A sample training plan for a transition interval might include a series of intensity and active recovery. For example, it might look like:

- Instruction, building new knowledge, learning, and new skill or task.
- Recovery might look like a conversation with a new peer or colleague, a short moment of individual reflection, consideration, and breathing in the moment.
- Second interval: doing the work, practice a new skill, try out the skill in a new context, rehearse it for someone else.
- Recovery: feedback, reflection, and considerations for next time.

The activities in the high-intensity interval and recovery are less important than being in the activity, present in the moment. Everyone needs to figure out what high intensity looks like for them and get into those moments with eyes wide open and with some frequency.

Interval training and this practice aim to simulate transitions, feelings, attention, attitudes, and dissonance. These bursts of training will prepare individuals for actual moments of transition and also teach us to notice, name, and mark how we feel and behave in order to iterate and adapt to improve our effectiveness and efficiency in our transitions. A student walks into a new space, a third-grade classroom, and while looking around, he thinks to himself that there is a familiarity here. Something about this moment is recognizable but he is still nervous, worried, and unsure that he should even be in this room, wondering if he belongs. He then realizes that he was in this space earlier in the summer with these same students. His parents were here and so were the other parents and teachers.

Orientation, onboarding, and other visits sometimes offer a way to practice the moments—short bursts of anxiety, scaffolded by parents and mitigated by the fun and comfortable atmosphere of the afternoon. While individuals, groups or teams, and organizations may not actually engage in intervals like exercising, the idea is to create intentional and intermittent moments that recreate the stress and self-doubt of an actual transition with some structure, support, and control.

Relationships established in the warm-up phase offer individuals a lifeline and some confidence to engage in this new practice. For example, in speaking with a faculty member at a local university and my own experiences with doctoral students, it is evident that our students have a lot to learn in this first year of study. Being a doctoral student is a lot of work and can be quite overwhelming. Moreover, students enter these spaces with a well-developed professional identity, so, when they start this new adventure, the "not knowing" creates quite a bit of dissonance. Our work together, over the summer, getting to know each other, sharing research ideas and plans, and talking a little about the academic program and expectations represents a way to prepare them for the work ahead. The workshops and group sessions we do after the community building are so much more productive because they have already had quite a bit of time and space to express their nervousness and to ask questions about the unknown. And, when they bump into an unknown in these workshops, students are *much* more likely to ask questions because they feel like they already know me and their peers from the community building we have already done. The time spent on the community building and warm-up kind of exercise pays huge dividends when it comes to starting academic work. The interval training in the workshops includes short simulations of academically rigorous activities, questions, and tasks. The combination of warm-up and training means students are more ready for these fall transitions to classes and dissertation work.

Personal and professional training includes physical, cognitive, social, and emotional development. The warm-up phase initiated the gradual awakening and work and this phase continues this work with simulated and scaffolded purposeful transitions practice. Even with these two categories, the training could take myriad forms. This practice may look like a scrimmage, dress rehearsal, tune-up run, or any other kind of activity that replicates these transitional moments with perhaps less at stake or risk. Practice stages include scaffolding where individuals use guideposts or support to practice these transitional moments. Those might include expected or unexpected in-between moments that are supported by guideposts, coaches, experienced teachers, or leaders, or other facilitators. Regardless of the type of practice, these training and practice periods are selected and devised to give individuals and groups real-time, actual time in the mud. Rather than talk about what has or might happen, how or what it feels like during simulated transitions, this practice creates a structure, schedule or game plan to support individuals in their transitions.

The instruction, individual practice, and feedback in this phase represent scaffolding and support for the practice and future performances, the change event for which individuals are training. These first two stages help individuals narrow their focus, mark the moments, and lean into the emotional worry and discomfort often related to the new space, their new peers, and the novel experiences with supports and scaffolding from trusted others. Now, I would imagine that employing interval training to prepare for a foot or bike race might make sense to most readers. What might this look like, however, in a classroom, boardroom, organization, or project team?

Recall, transitions are full of self-doubt, uncertainty, worry, and—if we are paying attention—learning. Simulating this requires putting ourselves and the team in a similar space to do this work. Watching my twin five-year-old children go to kindergarten is a perfect example of a transitions journey. Attending a new school and going to elementary school for the first time is definitely a kind of transition. It evokes a healthy dose of anxiety, worry, and self-doubt but also anticipation and excitement.

As I have been writing this book, I realized that in many ways, we, as parents, usually unconsciously or unintentionally engage in a type of transitions training and stage two of the work. It is not possible to practice sending kids to kindergarten but what we can do is engage in activities that provide short, manageable intervals of the feelings and experiences of a transition. This might include attending a summer day camp, enrolling in three days a week of pre-school, or spending time with a friend (without their parent present). These experiences represent an interval session of sorts where kids practice, slowly, gradually, and with guidance, the moments of transitions. We do not often, purposefully, go through this same process with older kids or adults. Imagine if we did these transitions training ourselves, with our kids, colleagues, and other individuals and teams.

As an educator, I often try to place my students in simulations that mimic transitions. These activities might include short check-ins to reset, an activity where students practice a skill or share new knowledge, and some time and attention to the moment. In these training sessions, we work together to make the doubt and nervousness visible. It is critical to support and guide these moments, to offer a way to talk about and mark the associated feelings. Doing this work, learning to wrestle with the discomfort builds our capacity for transitions. Scaffolded simulations are meant to gently and carefully induce some of the nervousness and self-doubt while simultaneously bringing awareness to the moment. Having students share what is in the space, how they feel right now, supports their own skills and knowledge, to navigate these transitions. Later in the book, I will provide much more detail on different ways to engage in this training.

CHECKPOINT:
Think about a transitional moment you recently experienced:
- How did you feel?
- What strategies did you use to navigate this experience?
- What do you wish you knew or had practiced before this transition?

Warming up, readying ourselves for the work and building relationships with other participants/peers/students/colleagues, and then practicing *prior* to the performance phase means individuals can reflect, problem solve, and adapt as they approach hills, bump up against obstacles, and just do not feel as well as they anticipated they might during their version of race day.

PERFORMANCE: "RACE" DAY

To this point, the program focused on simulation and moments that mimic the emotions and thoughts associated with transitions. Warm-up and training stages offer individuals, groups, and organizations opportunities to gradually move into and practice with simulated transitions or experiences that elicit worry, discomfort, self-doubt, and uncertainty. While transitions can be expected like a school bell, start of a race, or a date on the calendar, they can also be unexpected or unanticipated: job relocation, physical injury, becoming a parent, and other surprising transitional moments. Regardless of the shape, size, and type, the warm-up and practice phases aim to prepare each of us for these moments, these in-between times in our lives—the important and valuable waiting period that happens before some desirable outcome is achieved.

As individuals engage in this transitions practice, it should be the case that by the time a real transition occurs, these events should feel and look familiar. Although individuals and groups will start to recognize transitions and the related feelings as familiar, there is still work to do. This phase requires individuals to practice presence, build in intentional time and space to own the dissonance. This phase is marked by important questions and during the performance phase, we practice our hand at this skill. Most of what happens in the actual transition is calling on the practice and learning from those training days. Practicing, reviewing feedback, and making adjustments to effectively navigate the transitional period.

During this training stage, individuals continue to focus on seven key principles including practicing presence, establishing time and space for the work, reclaiming this moment, framing important questions, owning the dissonance, and releasing grace and gratitude. In a subsequent chapter, I will unpack these concepts in much more detail and offer strategies to honor and cultivate each of these important principles.

The dissonance continues as these are also new experiences, but a community has been established *and* you have done the work to prepare for these days—problem-solving with information from previous sessions. Attending regular check-ins to report and reflect on the dissonance, name and describe those moments that are really new, and figure out strategies to move forward (now what?) Returning to the pre-work as needed (community established and available during and after the race begins). Integrate—individuals start to identify their place of belonging within the organizations, and reciprocity results in better systems, processes, and use of talents, time, and resources.

Even as individuals enter new programs, positions, and organizations with appropriate credentials and experiences, there is still a period of transition into the culture, context, and processes of this new place and their particular role. Graduate students must navigate the processes and culture of a university, employees must learn the who and what to complete tasks and engage in their work, and young children must learn the routines and expectations of their new classrooms. Race day—whether it is an hour, a day, or longer—marks the moment of the transition for which individuals have been preparing. While race day often signals the end of the training phase, it does *not* mean that individuals, teams, groups, or organizations should not continue to use or make available some forms of scaffolding and support to help individuals navigate their new context. It also means that individuals continue to stay in the moment, present for whatever comes, ready to embrace the uncertainty and discomfort.

PAUSE AND REST

The pause stage of the program is the last and first step of transition training. Monitoring and evaluating progress happen after the training and performance but it also useful for thinking and engaging in subsequent work. The pause or rest stage includes reflecting, learning, continuing to focus, and expressing gratitude for the work done and the work to come. This pause phase might include conversations with students, teachers, colleagues, and others. It might also involve journaling, sharing our story, and considering what we might do as we continue the training program. Reflection is certainly fundamental to this phase but also requires focus and gratitude. We will discuss all of this in greater detail in the next chapter.

Eccles and Kazmier (2019) suggest that rest is essential to skills learning and expertise development. They also note that rest includes much more than inactivity. Kaplan (1995) argues that sleep is important but not sufficient in reaching a resting state or reducing attention fatigue. Eccles and Kazmier, like Kaplan, include both sleep and wakeful rest or recovery in their consideration of a resting process. Although much of this research is situated in the context of exercise and athletics, these concepts can be applied to other contexts including school, work, and family-related transitions.

SUPPORT FOR OUR TRANSITIONS

Transitions are successful when individuals, groups, and organizations engage in training and practice to listen and learn from themselves and each other, make attempts to identify and value the contributions of each individual, align the interests and needs of individuals and organizations, and engage in ongoing check-ins and reflection. This program of guided transition offers an effective means to support and develop individuals, students, colleagues, teachers, leaders, employees, and many others as they move in and through critical personal and professional transitions. This program of warm-up, training, performance, and recovery includes intentional time and strategies for individuals to name, attend to, and prepare for these transitions. It offers a way to focus on the moments, discomfort, practice our attitudes of grace, gratitude, and greatness, and practice a learning identity. Relationships, connections, skills building, and practice, together, contribute to more effective and manageable transitions into new spaces and places.

CHAPTER 9: WARM-UP AND REST

"It is very important that we re-learn the art of resting and relaxing… it allows us to clear our minds, focus, and find creative solutions to problems." – Thich Nhat Hanh

One definition of work refers to a discontented state that requires effort to engage in activities and plan and participate in leisure. Although not usually called work, leisure is another kind of effort that, like training, requires intentionality and discipline. Prior to engaging in this transitions training, it is important to both warm-up and plan for and consider the role of rest in our training. Just as physical and mental efforts are required for learning to navigate these transitions, it is also critical to make time for resetting to initiate training and pausing to reflect and learn from the training and associated experiences (Ericsson, 2006).

In this chapter, I discuss the role of warm-up and pause in transitions training and examples of strategies to engage in this work. Warm-up and rest represent aspects of this practice where individuals engage in slow and gradual increases or decreases in work. As we explore these stages of the framework and review examples of how to do this work, keep in mind the idea of *readiness*. Reset, engage in learning, attend to the moment, dance with discomfort, interrupt the should in our head, narrow our focus, execute a plan, share our story, and stay present. These themes emerge in multiple stages of the framework but should be prominently represented during warm-up and rest.

Warm-ups and rest are opportunities to reset and focus. Warm-ups bring us into a moment of readiness for awareness and rest contributes to resetting to a moment to calmly reflect on the work and consider what we learned and can use during subsequent transitions. These bookends of the training are critical to our ability to manage these developmental moments. When I first started running races, I would show up, sign in, and honestly, just hope for the best. I felt worry, nervousness, and self-doubt and, at the time, my strategy was to push down the feelings, ignore this worry, and just hurry to the start line.

Looking back, I think this hurrying was my way to try and avoid the emotions and thoughts in the moment. This meant, I started the actual race cold, unadjusted, full of doubt, and just mentally and physically unready and unprepared. As you might imagine, my performance was less than optimal but equally important, I was not fully present to appreciate and enjoy any moments nor did I take the time to reflect on the experiences or apply the learning to future transitional moments.

As I have competed in more races, I recognized and learned the importance of a warm-up. I arrive at races much earlier, I fuel up, stretch out, and even chat with fellow runners about the day and the race. By the time the race starts, I am warmed up, mentally more at ease, and focused and present at the start line. I am definitely still nervous and doubtful. Those feelings never disappear. But now, with a warm-up and this training, I am able to recognize, name, and own those feelings. I can check in with myself about the feelings, be in and move through them. As you might imagine, the race is still hard, challenging, and bumpy but it is also enjoyable, exciting, and full of possibilities. I perform better, cheer for myself and my fellow runners, and am present in the day.

Running may not be the transition you imagined as you read this book, but running, like transitions, often represent a new, unfamiliar, and uncertain experience. We can mitigate related feelings and improve our navigation of our transitional moments by including a warm-up in our routines. A warm-up represents intentionality in transitions work and creates space for a readiness for change, to learn, and prepare for any transition. In previous chapters, we talked about readiness for change and the idea that preparing for and raising awareness of these moments of transition happen with warm-up and practice for educators, leaders, students, and athletes.

Wingate (2007), for example, describes a pre-induction framework for transitions that includes supporting individuals in their learning to learn. Pre-induction represents one kind of onboarding or warming up for entry into a new program, role, or other transitional moment. Warm-ups or a pre-induction time is critical to engaging early in related activities and can also reduce anxiety around transitions. Radnofsky's (1988) research into warm-up before engaging in learning also described the tremendous benefits of this process. She notes the importance of preparing students for the day's topic and turning "on" their system for learning. In order to do the focused work of transitions and navigate these moments effectively, individuals must purposefully move into these warm-ups to begin a practice of staying and being in these important periods.

Preparation, resetting, and narrowing focus on a particular moment resonated with me as I thought about exercise warm-ups. I could imagine feeling the increased body temperature, muscles loosening, and mentally getting into the workout, all of which helped set my mind with intention to focus on the workout. Now, imagine warming up, turning on our system before or in the early moment of a transition. How might that work? How might the warm-up and preparation, contribute to our transitional moments?

As the warm-up turns on the students' systems, this creates space for students to intentionally be present and can contribute to their ability to productively engage in this work and what might follow. Teachers, leaders, and individuals are able to initiate and exercise students' and colleagues' thought processes, discuss and consider the what and why of the coming transition, and perhaps devise and synthesize a plan for engaging in this transitional period. This warm-up prepares us mentally and physically and represents a space to surface our thoughts and honestly communicate what we are feeling and where we are in that moment. It also invites us to share our own vulnerability and admit to feeling uncomfortable and worried. A simple five to ten-minute warm-up can help us to begin to see and talk about a plan to navigate the discomfort.

As previously noted, the training program includes a combination of preparation, practice, performance, and pause. Preparation and pause include low-intensity work and ways to engage in this work. At first glance, it may seem that these stages of rest, pause, and not engaging in active work are somehow less important than practice and performance. This is not the case. Without a moment to intentionally center the work and focus our attention, we risk relying on old habits of avoidance or running away. Adopting a routine of warm-up and noticing the moments may increase the likelihood that individuals, groups, teachers, and leaders are able to stay in the experiences, feelings, and thoughts and better manage the transitions.

WARM-UP

According to Merriam-Webster, a warm-up refers to an activity, mental or physical, that prepares an individual, team, class, or group for the demands of another identified activity or goal. Warm-ups and this preparation contribute to our readiness for transitions and change. I often arrive at meetings, classes, conferences, and even my Peloton ride, early. I appreciate the opportunity to engage with individuals before the event, set myself and the space for work, and listen to my Peloton instructor describe the workout ahead, what I might expect, and what might be coming. This information, time, and space contribute to my awareness and narrows my focus to the task or moment at hand.

Like exercise and working out, preparing for and being in transitions require us to get ready. For example, a few weeks ago, I was asked to present to a group as the expert on this particular topic and I needed and wanted to get ready. Shifting into this new and unfamiliar role requires a warm-up, which includes physical set-up like computers, space, and required equipment, as well as file organization and requests for other important tools or resources. Often this readying also involves a mental shift or change in mindset. For example, prior to this presentation, I was engaging in a lively conversation with my students, laughing, talking, and casually interacting about class topics and upcoming events. During my preparation, I work to shift into an appropriate mindset and narrow my focus to the relevant knowledge and topics for the presentation. This mental reset might include arriving early to engage with the audience, ask questions of the group, review notes, and just take purposeful time to move into this role. These warm-up moments gradually move us into the physical and mental space prepared for the work ahead.

A warm-up routine like the one described offers an opportunity to raise our awareness of the previous grogginess and fog we may have experienced during a transition. This fog, like operating on autopilot, prohibits us from being fully present. Engaging in warm-up activities may contribute to our ability to intentionally pay attention, dance with discomfort, and devise a plan. The shifting helps to interrupt the voices of self-doubt and bravely share our stories, worries, and doubts with others. Warm-up may also contribute to building trust and connection with others and prepare us to enter into the work that follows. Skar (2004) stresses the importance of this mental readiness, "one must be prepared to go into the suffering and chaos of life's transitions in order to continue to be fully alive, and to come out the other side with a new attitude and perhaps a new self-organization." These warm-ups need not be longer than five to ten-minutes, but they should be included in our practice and training.

During this warm-up individuals and teams can share and play with ideas and offer encouragement and feedback. It also offers a way for the group to appreciate what Radnofsky calls the "published" work of others. The collective work means individuals see and hear that others have similar thoughts and feelings which, like our focused attention, can contribute to lower anxiety and stress and the possibility of embracing the uncomfortable moments. These pre-work warm-ups that include sharing ideas and putting yourself out there may contribute to building trust among individuals which also helps individuals integrate into new contexts and challenging transitions.

These short preparatory sessions are as different as our myriad transitions. They may be solo efforts, dyad teams, or group sessions. They might also include connection, community, collaboration, or independent efforts and regardless of the shape and size, warm-ups matter to our experiences in the actual transitions. Warm-ups should be designed and executed to suit the needs of each individual, team, and group. The following offers just a few examples of ways you might engage in this important work.

CHECK-IN

Before starting any work, individuals, and groups should engage in something as simple as check-in activities. Individuals, classes, teams, and organizations can use preparation and warm-ups to shift, reset, and ready themselves for transitional moments. Check-ins serve to help us mentally shift to a state of readiness and shake loose the nervousness, worry, and uncertainty.

For example, whether engaging in solo or collective preparations and warm-up, individuals can engage in a meet and greet. This could mean reaching out to others on your team and in your group or organization in the space. Group check-ins could be brief introductory conversations where they introduce each other to the group. An individual going it alone could execute a meet and greet by gradually reaching out to others in the common spaces and places of the transitions. Sharing names and nuggets of information like reason for being here or where you are coming from and listening and telling stories can contribute to needed preparation for a transition. Meet and greets serve as a warm-up where individuals and groups shift into a moment, bring attention to their experiences and feelings, and begin a practice of focus and presence on the matters at hand. This work helps prepare each of us for staying present in our transitional moments.

As an example, I recently worked with an organization that designed and implemented a series of warm-up sessions with their clients in order to help the clients effectively pivot to virtual environments. A colleague who serves as the executive director for this non-profit shared how her team supported the transitions of team leaders to serving and supporting clients in 100% online programming. She shared that leadership provided support for team leaders and their clients which included Sunday meet and greet sessions to introduce, welcome, and get to know each other. Participants were also assigned a mentor who provided job-embedded coaching throughout the year. The non-profit also provided tech-checks to ensure familiarity with technology tools, requirements, and expectations which sounds very similar to the organize yourself and group activity discussed in a subsequent section. Warm-up activities, like transitions, take a variety of forms including physical and mental efforts and can be designed to meet the needs of different individuals and groups.

Another form of check-in might start with powerful questions or discussion prompts directed toward individuals, pairs, groups, or organizations. This offers another way to talk about and surface our intentions, goals, worries, excitement, or celebration. A discussion prompt offers an effective resource to mentally reset towards the impending work. Examples of prompts might include:

- What brings you to this space?
- What are you excited to do?
- What is worrying you?
- What is one goal for our time together today?
- How are you feeling about this work?

Again, these questions apply to solo pursuits, dyads, and group discussions. Powerful questions represent an easy and accessible tool to reset, focus, and learn to stay in the moment and be with whatever comes up. Warm-ups and check-ins, more specifically, contribute to our ability to shift our attention and be present and focused and simultaneously may also cultivate a trusting and connected community to initiate the work of the transitions training (Allen et al, 2017). Even if you participate in a solo warm-up, it is possible to seek out and identify trusted people and places to provide support and feedback in these important moments.

After graduate school and a short tenure as a lecturer at my alma mater, I took a faculty position at a local community college. Part of being a first-year faculty member at this institution included a one-year onboarding program. This brought all new faculty from around the campus together in a space to share with and learn from each other. I recall several meetings where we were placed in dyads with other new faculty and part of the warm-up process included responding to and sharing about a discussion prompt the facilitator shared with us. These were often anxiety-inducing moments because we did not know each other and were never certain that we would be able to respond to the question. The point of the warm-up, however, was to engage in conversation, to find an entry point using the prompt, and focus our attention on the work and day ahead of us. In a short five to ten-minutes, I got to know a new colleague, was able to shake off a bit of my own nervousness, and ready myself for the day ahead.

CHECKPOINT:
- As you think about the purpose of check-ins during transitions training, what approach or strategy might you implement to engage your community in a warm-up?

GROUP NORMS AND DESIGNING RELATIONSHIPS

Like check-ins and discussion prompts, norms and attention to relationships may contribute to setting our intention and focusing our work. Remember, transitions are often full of uncertainty, doubt, and worry. Transitions work is also hard and if we follow our instincts, we often prefer to circumvent the bad thoughts and feelings, avoid the moment, or push it down and get through the transition quickly.

Group norms, collectively creating a set of guidelines or rules for talking, interacting, and navigating discussions, contribute to mitigating the associated discomfort of the transition. Similarly, designing relationships represents another example of articulating guidelines or parameters for participating in connections with others. Both methods of warm-up offer ways to ask for what is needed, create a climate of support and authenticity, and effectively navigate and experience times when the work gets harder. As individuals or groups engage in this work and form new habits around experiencing transitions, it is important to provide scaffolding and the needed supports to practice in these moments of transition. These norms and relationship guidelines vocalize and publicize the tools needed and those available to contribute to our transition work.

Marriage and parenting represent significant and sometimes difficult transitions for most everyone. Difficult does not mean bad or that these should be avoided but that these milestones take work, practice, and support. When I got married and we started having children, there were lots of thoughts, feelings, and emotions swirling around our heads and our home. Are we doing this "right?" Am I a good parent? Am I making the right decision? These questions reflected our uncertainty and worry about how we were doing in this new role. Group norms and designing relationships played an important role in helping us to learn to better navigate these transitional moments.

Through a bumpy and sometimes challenging transition, we created norms and guidelines for our parenting and marital work together. We designed ways to talk with each other, hear and provide messages of support, made suggestions for what we needed, and devised a way to go about our parenting and relationship. It is not a perfect process, and it may seem odd to design guidelines and norms for something so personal, but these short warm-ups can bring attention and focus to our transition moments. Participating in these activities helped us to recognize what we were feeling during these periods, how we were acting and interacting, and what we could do to be better for ourselves, each other, and our family.

Group norms and designing relationships makes support, resources, and the process visible. It focuses our attention on the present and the ways in which we can voice our need for help during these moments of uncertainty. These activities also provide a roadmap for moving in and through these transitions rather than avoiding and can contribute to our ability to stay in the present and take on whatever surfaces. Both of these activities offer a means to share and determine expectations, establish trust, and plan for future interactions. It offers a way to set up and make available resources that might be needed later and this is another way to strengthen our readiness.

CHECKPOINT:
- If you could design norms or expectations into a significant relationship, what would you need?
- What would you add to the list of norms?

LESSON WARM-UP

Lesson warm-ups represent another opportunity to increase interest in the moment and work to be done. These activities may also increase our comfort in the space and with each other. These also represent an initial orientation to the transition moments. Examples of lesson warm-ups include organize yourself, visual/picture warm-up, chalk talk, and study guides. In all of these activities, individuals, groups, teams, leaders, and teachers have opportunities to collaborate, participate, and engage in the work, review topics, and discuss concepts. This work contributes to our ability to focus attention, be present, and start to notice, name, and lean into the dissonance of the transitional moments slowly and gradually.

Organizing yourself is an activity that can be done independently or in a group and the goal is to ready your mind and your space for the work. It is a way to center ourselves, the space, our minds, and the work—organizing in the present and cultivating a readiness to change and transition. In sports and exercise, this might be referred to as a mental rehearsal or visualization to generate attentional focus and concentration for a task or game plan (McGowan, Pyne, Thompson and Rattray, 2015). For an individual, it could be literally organizing physical and mental accessories like our attitudes and mindset but also supports, people, and equipment or tools that we might need. The act of organizing may contribute to connection and building trust and creating spaces to do the work and practicing authenticity and honesty about our experiences in these transitional moments. For example, as students enter a new grade, school, or program and individuals start new jobs or roles, it is important to take time to initiate intentional connections among peers, create buddy systems, study groups, and organize touch points for when support is needed or required.

Here again, like check-ins and other warm-ups, this work identifies equipment needed but also unearths and shines a light on the transition, the associated feelings, and their importance to our development. A colleague who is a leader and teacher in a local high school shared that her district has a long-standing practice to begin the school year presenting students with an overview of course content and a list of class expectations. The purpose is to acclimate students to class routines, homework procedures, and behavioral expectations. At the high-school level, students proceed through their schedule and receive a list of dos and don'ts from six or seven teachers. Their first day of school experience also represents time to share ideas about tools, resources, and other supports to effectively be present and navigate their transitions. Recently, her administrator moved to change this practice, or at least, the timing of these necessary discussions. Her administrator noticed the value of these warm-ups and teachers were encouraged to forgo content-related activities and engage students in team building, relationship building, and warm-up activities instead. Throughout the day, students could be seen collaborating on building structures, interviewing classmates about personal interests, and taking part in games to learn from and about their teachers. Both practices, reviewing course expectations and building community, prepared students for the school year and their gradual transition. It is true that context expectations relay valuable information, but it is also the case that students will never be able to relive their first day of school. This kind of school warm-up sets the tone for the entire year as well as future transitions they will experience. Taking the time to establish relationships, connect students, and connect with students is an important part of the warm-up activities.

Another warm-up activity that may offer an entry way and easing into these transitions involves using some kind of digital multimedia as part of the warm-up. I refer to this type of warm-up as bridging media. It usually includes a tool or resource that serves as a bridge to connect students to students, students to teachers, and students to content (Borkoski and Donaldson, 2020). It is a way to bring relevance to the space and the moment and serve as a possible way to mitigate anxious transitions by making connections between familiar resources like TED Talks and podcasts and unfamiliar content including new readings, knowledge, or project information.

Visuals, podcasts, or videos offer a means or a bridge for a group or team to discuss an unfamiliar or uncomfortable topic through an examination or review of images where they can write and share their thoughts. For example, individuals might review a video to understand new content that aims to connect familiar experiences and knowledge to novel content and skills. Using visuals provides a means to focus, create presence, and engage in conversations that might help to reset our minds and bring us to a place of readiness for the work. As we initiate a transition, we enter these spaces with myriad thoughts, expectations, and perceptions. These bridging media may help to unlock some of these thoughts and feelings and invite us to bring them out into the open, to the forefront of our own minds, and/or share with others.

I teach a first-year doctoral leadership course and these students, in the midst of becoming doctoral students and scholars, often express trepidation regarding their own ability to do this work, write as an academic, and apply these skills and knowledge to their own professional endeavors. Over the past several years, I have implemented podcasts and other artifacts as bridging media to try and open up individuals and groups to talk about this work. I have found that individuals are more easily able to connect to these shared experiences, they can better see themselves in these podcast stories, and are then able to manage and talk about their own related experiences, worry, and self-doubt. This kind of a warm-up is supportive, familiar, and effective in opening students to exploring their own discomfort and uncertainty. During these in-between moments, individuals wade through the discomfort of the unfamiliar with doubt and concern. Using visuals and other bridging media offers a way to see and hear the experiences of others, relate to their own journey, and use these resources to purposefully focus on personal thoughts and feelings.

Chalk talk, where teams or individuals find associations between ideas, words, and/or phrases, and study guide where leaders, students, teachers, and others respond to review questions and write as much as they can remember on the topic, concept, or procedures are also great methods of warm-up. Both of these activities are meant to stimulate thinking, prepare individuals for the coming work, and represent slow and gradual work towards more intense activities.

During the 2020 pandemic teachers, students, and parents had to pivot and transition quickly to remote learning. Our five-year-old twins started kindergarten on Zoom so not only were they shifting to full-time school, now they were learning online. Early in the school journey and throughout the fall, their teacher used a form of chalk talk—minus the chalk—to start their days. She would point to a day of the week, the weather, or some other word and ask the students to share something in their own experiences that related to the word or phrase selected. From this warm-up, students reset and got ready for their virtual class, built a connection and trust with their teacher and peers, and practiced sharing their own ideas. At the same time, this warm-up offered time to orient towards the technology, the video app, and the new virtual classroom.

Chalk talk and study guides may seem most appropriate in a classroom or work setting but it is entirely possible to adapt these kinds of activities to parenting, marriage, playing the piano, and other transitions. A study guide outside of a classroom setting may be useful as a springboard for organizing a new work group, engaging with a new project team, or hosting a meeting of new employees. Transitions often involve shifting or adding roles, responsibilities, and projects. Engaging with the change may require a gradual entry and something like a prompt or study-guide-like activity may prime the pump for a great and productive discussion and introduce new colleagues, employees, and teams to one another. The point is to create space and time for preparation, warming the engine, review and consideration of next steps.

As previously discussed, these examples are just a few possibilities. I would encourage you to create, adjust, and augment your activities to fit your needs. What is important about these warm-up activities is that the activity represents a means to reset, cultivate openness, and attention to the moment, and bring focus to the work. These activities should also start our dance with discomfort and quiet the voice of self-doubt. This work helps us to intentionally shift gears, gradually move into a space that ready us for the work ahead. It is a space to call out that we are doing this and prepares us for the challenges ahead.

PAUSE AND REST

As previously noted, work includes activity and effort often associated with physical and mental exertion. It is also true, however, that even as leisure represents a ceasing of physical activity, it is classified as work. Leisure involves enjoying the present reality, not resignation or complacency but a "consider[ation of] things with an accepting spirit" (Dewey in Breunig, 2017). It is categorized as work because it requires purposeful intention and discipline to take a break and do something differently (Pieper, 1999). Like physical activity, rest and sleep are also required to restore ourselves and improve cognitive performance and mental health (Sonnentag and Zijlstra, 2006).

Rest is often associated with physical inactivity, ceasing to practice or train related to athletics, musical instruments, and other physical endeavors. Eccles and Kazmier (2019) argued that while individuals or teams may stop to rest from physical activity, mental or psychological activity usually continues. For this reason, they suggest that a more comprehensive and accurate conception of rest includes both physical and psychological inactivity. Sonnentag and Zijlstra (2006) suggest that *recovering* from job demands is equally important as *attending* to our job demands. There is a need to detach from work, refill energy reserves, attend to gratitude, and focus on leisure.

Eccles and Kazmier (2019) suggest that rest is essential to skills learning and expertise development and they note that rest includes much more than inactivity. Kaplan (1995) argues that sleep is important but not sufficient in reaching a resting state or reducing attention fatigue. Eccles and Kazmier, like Kaplan, include both sleep and wakeful rest in their consideration of a resting process. Ericsson (2006) even refers to this deliberate practice of rest as "recuperative naps" where rest and sleep offer restoration, a return to equilibrium, and a way to avoid burnout. Although much of this research is situated in the context of athletes' performance in their chosen sport, these ideas could be applied in a multitude of circumstances. It should be no surprise that the transitions model presented in this book includes a pause or resting stage. Moreover, as we will discuss in the next chapter, rest and recovery are also integral to any practice or routine that includes interval training.

Learning to stay in a moment, being present, and navigating transitions is hard work. I have established the need for a training schedule that includes warm-up, practice, and performance. Equally important to our ability to do this work, is the work of rest. Individuals, teams, and organization need to routinize a resting process into their transition process. These moments of rest, sleep and wakeful rest should be included during our practice, performance, and reflection stages of this training. While I will examine the role of rest in practice and performance later in the book, this chapter reviews the features of rest as well as possible activities to engage in rest.

Intention, attention, and focus during transitions only work and yield positive outcomes when we also purposefully include a resting process in our routine. Being well-rested refers to a psychological state of feeling fresh and motivated while low levels of rest may contribute to emotional exhaustion, burnout, and low motivation. Incorporating resting experiences means that individuals need to reduce thinking about goals and engage in activities that require low or minimal demand. It also means finding variety in our routines to avoid what Eccles and Kazmier refer to as tedium and the sameness in our training. Just as warm-ups work to switch "on" our minds and focus, rest works to reduce our mental demands and facilitates a switching "off" of our attention and focus.

I remember transitioning into my first leadership role in my professional context and feeling the need to work, stay ahead, learn, and figure out all I could about whatever was going on in the moment. This consistent and constant focus on tasks, projects, to-do lists as well as battling my own uncertainty, self-doubt, and worry about whether or not I could become this leader, contributed to tremendous fatigue. After running myself crazy and simultaneously battling my own feelings of not being enough, I crashed. While I would not have described it in this way, I believe I was emotionally exhausted and nearing burnout and I had only been at this work for a few months. A mentor suggested to me that I really needed to learn to set boundaries and purposefully schedule time for lunch and downtime. I needed to integrate a resting process into my regular work routine.

Like our professional work and other performances, transitions must include a pause. It is critical to reduce our thinking and total focus on the event, the goal, the work of the transitions. Our transitions practice must include intentional reduction in effortful thinking and make attempts to regain internal control of your own schedule and tasks. All of these tasks, whether efforts towards physical and mental activity or inactivity and rest, require intention. There are numerous ways to reduce our mental and physical activity and refocus on wakeful rest and the following offers just a few examples of how individuals, groups, and organizations might do this restful work.

CHECKPOINT:
- How do you incorporate rest?
- What does it look like?

ACTIVITIES

The warm-up will teach and help normalize switching on our focus and preparing for the work ahead. We also need to spend time and use to learn to switch off the activity, physically and mentally. The research is clear that getting enough sleep is important for mental acuity, health, and productivity. The Center for Disease Control (CDC, 2017) suggests that adults get at least seven hours while children and teens require anywhere between eight and twelve depending on their age. The kind and amount of wakeful rest is less clear or prescriptive than sleep. This part of the resting process could include activities outside of a primary-focus activities like athletics, music, academics, professional roles, and many other activities. It is also possible that taking time to listen to music, reading a book unrelated to the primary activity, brisk walking or light jogging are just a few of the long list of possibilities.

In the case of wakeful rest, the process of this work is not so much about the task, it is about the intentionality of the action to engage in rest. Rest *is* work because it requires effort, discipline, focus, and commitment. Incorporating a resting process requires an authentic willingness to do the work of rest, to engage in tasks that allow our bodies and minds to disengage, to take a pause. It is hard and the voices of doubt and worry can be loud but, at some point, we each need to trust this process and believe that the stages of preparation, practice, performance, and pause all contribute to our ability to notice, name, and navigate these transitions.

Phil Maffetone, a researcher, educator, and clinician, in his training regimen for athletes suggests that to speed up, individuals must slow down. In short, he suggests that athletes focus on an individualized target heart rate in the early stages of training. What this often means is that strong, accomplished athletes used to training at much higher rates and faster paces, must slow down to stay in this target heart rate. His work provides evidence that it works, and his athletes do get stronger and faster and experience fewer injuries. While this transitions training may not use a heart rate monitor or even include aerobic and anaerobic training, the idea of slowing down to speed up can be applied here. Slowing down and incorporating a warm-up and resting process may increase the likelihood that individuals, groups, and organizations notice, name, and stay in the transitional moment no matter the discomfort.

Research shows that sleep plus wakeful rest contributes to lower anxiety and improved performance and concentration for tasks at hand (McGowan et al, 2015). With even small doses of a resting process incorporated into the transitions training, it is possible to build strong connections, increase feelings of belonging, and improve our ability to reset and adopt a mindset of focused preparedness.

The stage of pause in the transitions training, like the warm-up, is associated with key features of the acronym REST. Reflect on the moment, Educate yourself on the previous training sessions, Stay focused on the moment to pause, and Thank yourself for the work already completed. Designing and implementing this kind of practice may decrease information overload, reduce confusion and uncertainty, and invite more meaningful activities, connections, and decisions during our transitional moments (Wingate, 2007).

Warm-up and pauses are critical. Without time to set and reset or switch on or off, it is difficult for individuals to show up focused and ready for transitions work. Incorporating in five to ten-minutes of warm-up along with adequate sleep and intermittent wakeful rest contributes to more efficient and effective work during our transitional moments. The next chapter provides more evidence of why warm-up and rest matter. It will also introduce concepts and activities relevant to the practice stage of the transitions training. With *readiness* and *rest,* it is possible for individuals to TRAIN(S): Try the moment, Reach for the dissonance, Adjust focus, Interrogate our voice, Negotiate the transition, and Stay curious.

CHAPTER 10: PRACTICE – INTERVALS

*"Do not dwell in the past,
do not dream of the future,
concentrate the mind on the present moment."
– the Buddha*

Effectively navigating our transitions requires preparation and practice in transitions or transition-like moments. With practice, transitions become more familiar, manageable, and something we can notice, name, and lean into as they happen. Each of us becomes able to stay in the moment, to normalize the discomfort, and thrive, grow, and develop during and through these transitions. Discomfort and uncertainty contribute to our growth and change but only when we pay attention. We gain confidence, we interrupt the voices of self-doubt, adjust and narrow our focus on the transitional periods, stay curious and learn, and find grace and gratitude in these difficult and amazing moments. Adopting and routinizing warm-up and practice do not make transitions easier; they are still work, growth hurts, and change requires us to do hard things. With preparation and practice, we notice more often, and with more detail. We can identify and ask for the support, space, and the place we need to navigate, reflect on, and learn from these transitional moments. Preparation and practice contribute to our ability to form new habits to fully experience our transitions with intention and courage.

While warm-up is a slow progression of focusing on the associated discomfort of the in-between moments, practice represents a means to create transition-like situations for individuals, groups, and organizations to learn and rehearse skills. These simulated sessions provide opportunities to gain new knowledge and cultivate attitudes, and behaviors to improve our ability to recognize the attributes of our transitions. During this work we adopt and use strategies to navigate the transitions and generalize these approaches to multiple and varied contexts. Generalization means that individuals and groups have an opportunity to identify the feelings and skills associated with transitions in order to adapt as needed, regardless of the transition duration, intensity, or context. Raising awareness and gaining familiarity with these experiences contribute to our ability to effectively face these transitions.

In this third stage of the framework an individual TRAINS: Tries the moment, Reaches for the dissonance, Adjusts the focus, Interrogates the self-doubt, Negotiates through transitions, and Stays curious. Learning to do the work—to focus, question doubt, and remain curious—contributes to the ability of individuals, teachers, leaders, groups, and organizations to experiment with skills, approaches, and strategies during simulated transitions. Training involves putting ourselves in uncomfortable contexts, situations, or activities in order to start the process of normalizing the discomfort and build habits to effectively navigate transitions. These states of training should not be painful but uncomfortable. Bjork and Bjork (2011) called these desirable difficulties. The difficulty in the work helps individuals identify the skills, attitudes, and knowledge that work for them in their unique transitions.

The practice stage of transitions training includes sessions with a mix of low and high-impact training. Sessions range in effort from steady and challenging to intermittent bouts of maximum effort and recovery. Effort refers to a level of work or exertion required for any given moment. Low-impact sessions include steady, consistent levels of work. Recovery is activity requiring less effort but feels less taxing than low-impact sessions. High-intensity training sessions involve high to maximum level efforts of work where individuals may feel that they have nothing left. Transitions are difficult, uncomfortable, stress-inducing, and often feel like wading through muddy terrain. These moments are intense, rigorous, and require work. There are also times, even during a transitional period, when individuals, teams, and organizations slow down and take time out for rest.

The oscillating nature of transitions calls for training that incorporates sessions of intervals. In this practice stage, individuals, groups, and teams design training that combines recovery, high-intensity work, and low-impact efforts to prepare for our transitions. Bjork and Bjork (2011) suggest the creation of "desirable difficulties" to enhance learning. The researchers recommend varying the conditions of practice, spacing out the effort, and integrating different kinds of learning and practice. With interval training, we can find ways to make situations and conditions hard but—as Bjork and Bjork (2011) remind us—hard in a good way.

As I have mentioned in previous chapters, I love all kinds of athletic events. A few years ago, I trained for a series of five half marathons that took place over the summer. To practice for these events, I considered possible conditions (i.e., temperature, wind, and rain), equipment (i.e., running shoes, watch, clothing, hydration), and my own physical and mental preparedness. With these factors in mind, I designed a training plan that included different terrain (i.e., hills and flats), duration, time of day, and other features. I did the best I could to simulate and replicate what I expected to encounter in these races. Strengthening our adaptability, problem solving, and effective habits and practice for transitions require us to mimic the conditions we expect to encounter and push beyond our ability in order to grow.

CHECKPOINT:

Consider a time when you were planning for an expected transition, a new job, relocation, or something else:

- How did you prepare?
- What strategies did you employ to help you prepare?

Like preparing for running races, interval practice for transitions needs to simulate conditions, feelings, and actions during these in-between moments. These transition intervals need to be designed to include the unfamiliarity, difficulty, discomfort, and worry of transitions to cultivate and strengthen peoples' readiness and ability to navigate these moments. At the same time, even when training for a series of running races or a marathon, individuals engage in recovery activities and take rest days. Similarly, these intervals will include active recovery and rest, time to reflect, and learn from those intense moments of training.

Transitions work requires individuals to set their intention, name their goals, and practice their approaches. We also need to remember that when these intervals get difficult, we must set our intentions and focus on our why. It is also critical to our growth and development that we celebrate our right-now victories. Practice helps individuals to notice the moments of transition, name their intention, and learn to engage, struggle, reflect, and adapt in the moments. While everyone's training will look different and must be designed to suit their needs, everyone's interval sessions should reflect a training routine that mimics the traits of these transitions. It should also offer opportunities to set short-term goals that help individuals stay in the moment focused on the work and why it matters right now.

CHECKPOINT:
Think back to the intentions and goals you set
when you started this book:
- What would you like to change
  about the original intentions?
- What goal did you set?
- What approaches helped you
  to work toward that goal?
- What did you learn from naming these intentions?

When the voices of self-doubt emerge, individuals and teams need to be reminded of their why. Remembering our why may help us to refocus to do the hard work in front of us. While everyone will have particular and unique goals for their own work, transitions training should also focus on some key goals/principles that include attending and reclaiming our transitional moments, dancing and owning the discomfort, interrupting, interrogating, and changing the voice of self-doubt, focus and stay in the moment, find grace and gratitude, and remain curious, reflective, and keep learning from and about the transitional moments.

After saying out loud these key principles and adjusting them to include personalized goals, it is also critical to determine a strategy for achieving the stated goals. For example, when training for a running race, core strength and legs and lung endurance are fundamental to success. For this reason, sessions might involve core work, leg presses, and time on the road to train the lungs. Similarly, in transitions training, individuals design sessions and strategies to achieve articulated goals. In this case it might be that individuals and groups design a session to practice noticing the voice of self-doubt, sharing the stories we are telling ourselves, and devising ways to change the conversation. Strategies might also include mindfulness to train ourselves to attend to moments, stay focused, and find grace. Naming the goals and aligning them with strategies contributes to improving our ability to manage our transitions.

Interval training and practice also require a source of feedback and a means to change contexts to practice these skills. Interval sessions, by design, include moments of wakeful rest or recovery that offer opportunities for in-action reflection. Individuals engage in rigorous activity and, in these moments of steady work, individuals alone or with a team or coach inquire as to how they are feeling, why they are here (now that the discomfort has set in), and what they are proud of in *this* moment. An inquiry-based approach to feedback offers a way for individuals to maintain their focus and learn to stay in the hard moments, the muddy circumstances, longer and stronger.

Intervals take many forms that might include twenty, thirty, or sixty-minute duration of alternating hard and steady work but can also be interval sessions that occur over days. The day includes rigorous activity and the next day might represent a rest day, and this pattern repeats in a sequence most appropriate for different individuals. Where an individual or group needs to start their training depends on their circumstances, transition, and tolerance for change. Too often training is intense, consistent for some period of time and then often we crash in need of rest, unable to effectively navigate or manage these important transitional moments.

Often, individuals, unfamiliar with training routines and schedules, enter into their practice hard and fast. They believe that the only way to get stronger and faster or improve or achieve positive outcomes, in their transitional moments or other circumstances, is to push hard in high-interval training. This may lead some individuals to overtrain or burnout and as discussed in an early chapter, going slow to go fast represents a better way to approach training for our transitions. The practice stage of this framework does just that. Interval training that incorporates high-intensity bouts, low-impact sequences, and wakeful recovery may seem slow, gradual, and less effective when in fact, intervals plus rest often contribute to better performance, improved health, and stronger physical and mental ability.

CHECKPOINT:
- How could you apply the idea of intervals as a practice?
- What type of interval might be relevant to your own transitions?

Like exercising or training as a musician, manager, or parent, learning to go slow to then go fast matters. Slowing down the process, paying attention to our thoughts, feelings, and behaviors in this process of becoming, contributes to improved outcomes. This idea of interval sessions and intermittent intensity and recovery also emerges in the research about effective learning strategies. Roediger and Pyc (2012) suggest that spacing and interleaving offer an inexpensive and efficient set of techniques to improve memory, learning, and educational outcomes. Carpenter (2014) also notes that learning requires repetition, multiple sessions, and different kinds of practice. Similarly, researchers in the field of exercise science point to alternating bouts of high and low-intensity work and intermittent bursts of vigorous activity contribute to improved health, performance, and other markers like cardiovascular adaptation, blood pressure, and muscle capacity. Adopting methods and strategies from both the education and exercise literature, this training framework includes a practice stage that integrates sessions of varying duration, frequency, and intensity.

This transitions practice combines the ideas of spacing, interleaving and low-impact and high-intensity activities to create an effective routine for transitions training. Spacing characterizes an approach to learning that includes a time delay between practice with the same materials (Cepeda et al, 2008). For example, as students learn vocabulary terms, instructors might practice a group of words, move onto math, and then review these same, first set of words later in the day. Spacing offers an opportunity for individuals to consolidate their prior and new knowledge and this process often takes hours or days. Interleaving is another example of how leaders, teachers, and others can practice for their transitions. Interleaving mixes up sequencing of multiple subjects or topics while studying to improve learning. With this approach, individuals engage with different examples and techniques across time.

Varied practices contribute to broadening individual experiences and increase their ability to assess given conditions and adjust as needed. Both spacing and interleaving offer individuals' opportunities to strengthen retrieval practices which contribute to their ability to discriminate between challenges, identify importance nuances, and apply appropriate solutions. Roediger and Pyc (2012) remind us that easy and quick is not better and that fast learning may lead to fast forgetting. It is critical to remember that growth requires work and leaders, teachers, and facilitators need to remember that there is difficulty in the process of learning, effortful practice is required, and wrestling with uncertainty, means setbacks happen and the unknown is an expected part of the work.

Building awareness, naming and noticing the moment, and improving our ability to navigate these transitions is a form of learning. As discussed earlier, our in-between moments, regardless of type and context, include ebbs and flows of dissonance, uncertainty, excitement, and joy. With these ideas in mind, a form of interval training appropriately aligns with practicing for transitions. Like spacing and interleaving, interval training with long and short episodes of work, contribute to positive outcomes. An interval whether in exercise, a classroom, or a boardroom, describes an intervening break in activity that creates space between states of being. In the context of transitions, intervals will include low-impact activities and high-intensity intervals along with sessions of active recovery. As we consider what this training might resemble, it is important to think about the overall training plan, for example, a weekly routine, and the daily sessions both of which include elements of interval training. The subsequent sections describe a discussion of each element of the sessions and examples of each type of activity and sample schedules of the work.

EFFORT LEVELS

"The mind is like a muscle—the more you exercise it, the stronger it gets and the more it can expand."
– Idowu Koyenikan

As previously mentioned, effort refers to work that is determined by duration and intensity. While the measure of duration is the same regardless of who participates in the training, intensity is more complicated. For transitions training, intensity includes levels of work, stress and anxiety, uncertainty and self-doubt, dissonance and discomfort, and the general unknown. These measures of intensity will vary by person, context, transition, and supports. The different types of training are meant to simulate different combinations and levels of something I referred to earlier as the transitions intensity (TI). TI represents the combined feeling and experiences of stress, self-doubt, and discomfort felt during the different sessions of training and during these training experiences, individuals learn and practice how to notice, name, and pay attention to these moments. Eventually, with time and practice, individuals are able to effectively wrestle with their self-doubt, embrace the dissonance they are feeling in the moment, and learn from each interval sequence and training session. Together, these approaches represent opportunities to notice, stay fully present in the experience, and navigate the transitions.

LOW-IMPACT

Low-impact training represents a sequence of activities with mostly familiar, steady bouts of TI. This means that individuals train at levels that, for most of the duration, are recognizable, have been felt, and are tolerable. This work is not a no-sweat session and it is also not aggressive. These sessions are disciplined, focused, and individuals must work to hold back. There are very short moments of new work, increased TI, but they are short-lived and induce almost no stress to the mind or body. These sessions of training may be best suited for individuals starting or returning to their training or younger kids, students, and leaders who are beginners in their roles and current transitional period. This work is also important for those engaging in high-intensity and interval work. A way to continue to work and train but also give the body and mind a break of sorts, a way to actively slow down.

Low-impact training is work but gradual, familiar, and less stressful which increases the chance of right-now victories, self-confidence, and comfort with discomfort. Individuals train in familiar situations and learn to use their skills and attitudes but also strengthen these resources to help navigate future, more difficult training sessions. The first time I ran a marathon, I required a lot of practice and support. I engaged in low-impact activities to slowly and gradually build up the endurance and knowledge to effectively manage and run a 26.2 mile race. Like running your first race, transitions training may be unfamiliar and require slow, steady, and rigorous training. Practice is about mimicking the feelings and thoughts associated with transitions, but low-impact training means that individuals find ways to ease into this training with engagement and exposure to the discomfort, the focused time, and change of attitudes. Low-impact activities offer opportunities to do work that contributes to our awareness of and skills for managing transitions but in a slightly less stressful and anxiety-inducing way.

Low-impact sessions allow individuals to build on current knowledge, experiences, and prepare for more difficult work of transitions. For example, when beginning my marathon training, rather than jump right into a race or even a long run, my training built on my current level of fitness. I was already able to comfortably run five to six miles, so the first few weeks of my marathon training included four to six miles each of five days. This work was already familiar and provided opportunities to practice in the discomfort, stress, and self-doubt. It helped me to practice recognizing and staying in the moments, my thoughts, and prepared me for tougher, high-intensity training sessions.

This low-impact kind of work could also take the form of work-related projects, study/review sessions, and orientation. When leaders, teachers, or other facilitators create time and space for individuals to connect prior and current knowledge and experiences to an already familiar task, it continues to build foundations and prepare for what might come next. Teachers might ask students to engage in review activities related to concepts learned over the last several weeks. They could also ask groups of students to discuss and practice classroom protocols and norms together to both reinforce their understanding and comfort with the plans but also leave time for reflection and questions for learning. Similarly, project managers and leaders might engage their team in a kick-off meeting or session to engage in activities related to this *new* endeavor but also already familiar to the team. Low-impact sessions act as a sort of bridge from previous and familiar moments to newer experiences.

Low-impact sequencing of training sessions are also critical for those engaging in regular workouts with higher fitness levels. Even seasoned athletes, experienced leaders, and other experts benefit from low-impact training. These sessions offer opportunities to continue the transitions training, benefit from high quality effortful work with purpose and intention. These types of sessions, however, come with the added benefit of taxing and stressing our bodies and minds less. The TI exists, we experience it, feel it, and name it but it does not push us to the point that leads to more self-doubt and more dissonance. It creates moments of manageable intensity where, like a pot of water on a stove, we warm-up, reach a comfortable simmer but never boil.

RECOVERY

Like low-impact training sessions, recovery offers a way to wade into the dissonance and mud of our transitions, slowly and gradually. Recovery is more than a warm-up but less than low-impact sessions. As is the case with all stages of transitions training, recovery is also about continuing to focus, staying in the moment, and leaning into whatever comes up. A unique feature of recovery is time to reflect, to practice our grace and gratitude attitudes, and learn from the previous moments of transition and make needed adjustments. Recovery sessions are less about mimicking TI and more about reflecting on the most recent experiences with that intensity. This recovery work can occur immediately following high-intensity work as part of interval training that we will discuss next, or recovery could be its own session of practice, separate, and apart from low or high-impact training.

Recovery, during a session of intervals, gives individuals time to take a break from the TI and reflect on what just happened. For example, several mornings a week I get on my Peloton for bike intervals. These sessions include high-intensity moments of work followed by varying durations of recovery. The recovery gives me a chance to literally catch my breath but also a moment to check-in, be present to notice how I am feeling and what I am thinking. With the support of a virtual coach, the recovery helps me reset, quiet the self-doubt, and intentionally attend to the moment. It gives me a purposeful pause to check in on my why for this work and recommit to staying in the upcoming discomfort. Like the recovery time on the Peloton, we need to integrate these moments into our transitions work. It is impossible and unproductive to just go, to push, to do more and just take the high intensity of a transition. It just does not work. As Roediger and Pyc (2012) remind us, spacing and interleaving are more effective for learning than long blocks of that same learning. No matter an individual's experience level, knowledge, age, or context, we need intentional time for recovery and to pause and reset our focus and intention.

Recovery might also represent a session of work independent of interval training. Active recovery is a form of recovery where individuals, teams, and organizations design, implement, and participate in sessions of work that are effortful but not high-intensity work. These sessions involve light effort and opportunities for after-action reflection as discussed, a few chapters ago. For example, when training for a distance running event, individuals often incorporate swimming or biking as a form of recovery. Individuals still exert effort, see positive outcomes and, simultaneously, are able to also rest and replenish in ways needed for the primary activity, in this case, running. Students, teachers, leaders, and others must remember to integrate moments of active recovery, like swimming, into their transitions work. Staying in transitional moments at high levels of uncertainty, self-doubt, and stress is unsustainable, unproductive, and may contribute to emotional exhaustion and poorer outcomes.

Students, employees, colleagues, and others moving into new roles and positions experience oscillating moments of identity development in the early moments of their transitions. Doctoral student, in particular, go through intense changes, feel high levels of self-doubt, and have to quickly learn how to manage this all while they are enrolled in their first semester of studies. These students often believe that continual and intense work is what will get them successfully to the finish line. They ask for tips, resources, and other ways to get ahead. This is particularly true when students inquire about how they should spend their time over the first winter break. While it is hard for students to hear, I recommend that they read a book, take walks, return to hobbies neglected during the semester and, for those students who trust this process, they return energized and ready for their semester. This momentary period of active recovery contributes to individuals' ability to refresh, rejuvenate, and ready themselves for refocusing on and owning the discomfort of future, uncomfortable transitions.

Recovery during or after transitions practice is critical to our ability to navigate these moments. Recovery requires discipline, focus, and presence. Done consistently and well means individuals are learning to reset and focus in the moment, stay in the discomfort better and longer, and use their attention to and presence in the dissonance and uncertainty to adapt and improve their engagement in the transitional moments. Over time, with work and rest, individuals may notice ways to express authentic gratitude for these difficult moments and learn to normalize the discomfort as part of their journey.

CHECKPOINT:
As you consider low-impact effort, recovery, and rest:
- What kinds of strategies might reflect your experiences with transitions?
- How might you prepare for future transitions using this training?

HIGH-INTENSITY TRAINING

These sessions, unlike low impact and recovery sessions, often take us directly into the unfamiliar and uncertain. The transitions intensity is the highest in these moments. This work pushes beyond what we perceive as our threshold. We are breathless, worried, questioning, doubting, and stressed that we cannot do this task, cannot stay in, or complete this work. In this moment, the training simulates the unknown and discomfort of our transitions. As previously discussed, it is unrealistic and unreasonable to think anyone can stay at this intensity level for very long. Each of us, in our transitions, has tried. We have put in extra hours, read more books, held another meeting, or stayed up all night preparing. We have also lost sleep trying desperately to run away from the discomfort or push down and ignore the self-doubt. The inevitable outcomes are exhaustion, burnout, frustration, and sometimes depression.

Our doctoral students are required to sit for oral comprehensive exams. This milestone is a part of every doctoral student's journey. It is one of those achievements that makes this transition challenging, rewarding, and unique. I often study with students, listen to practice responses, and provide feedback. One of my students asked if I could make time to practice with her. I texted back and said I was actually hopping in the car and had about a 25-minute drive if she wanted to call and practice. She did. When she called, she shared how nervous she was and found it almost impossible to even imagine doing this out loud for a committee. I could feel the angst in her voice, I listened, encouraged her to try and that it would be okay. For the next five or so minutes she provided a scholarly, well-supported response to a practice question. She did the work, she noticed how she was feeling, stayed in the nervousness of the moment, and successfully worked through it. These transitions can be long and full of self-doubt. Short bursts of interval work may help us navigate these moments.

CHECKPOINT:
- What does a high-intensity session look like for you?

For these reasons, high intensity transitions training includes interval sessions. Interval training allows for intermittent moments of high TI interrupted by short recoveries. Participants learn to incorporate in- and after-action reflection so they can be present in the hard work. Individuals no longer use other means for distracting from the transitions. They learn how to stay for whatever comes up in these moments. Interval sessions permit us to practice with the discomfort and wrestle with the unknown. We feel the associated stress and hear the self-doubt. We learn to use the recovery to think about the previous intense work and prepare for the next. In the next interval of work, individuals are able to immediately adjust and perhaps focus on the uncertainty, own and quiet the self-doubt, and attend to the moment. This work provides ways to gain familiarity with transitional moments, be in simulated moments and implement a practice that includes focused attention, naming, noticing, and staying in the moment. Individuals will no longer wish away, walk around, or push down the discomfort. Transitions are normalized and can serve as learning moments rather than moments to avoid.

HOW TO PRACTICE: SAMPLE TRAINING ROUTINES

We have already discussed the different aspects of the practice stage of the training. This section offers a few different schedules and samples of practice sessions and interval segments. Examples of this work include a weekly and daily glimpse of how training could be designed and implemented.

Weekly schedules, like this entire training plan, vary depending on need, context, and goals but any of these weekly practice routines should include a mix of low-impact and interval sessions. While Performance might be high-intensity, consistent, and recurring practice sessions should ebb and flow with the level of transitional intensity (Daly et al, 2007).

Table 1: Sample weekly schedules for the practice stage of the training framework

	Mon	Tue	Wed	Thu	Fri	Sat
1	HITT	HITT	HITT	HITT	Rest/recovery	
2	HITT	LITT	HITT	LImTT	HITT	Rest/recovery
3	HITT (30)	HITT (20)	LITT	HITT (45)	LITT	Rest/recovery
4	LImTT	HITT (45)	LITT	HITT (30)	HITT (20)	Rest/recovery
5	HITT	HITT	Rest/recovery	HITT	HITT	Rest/recovery

Notes: HITT – High-intensity transition training;

LITT – Low-intensity transition training; LImTT – Low-impact transition training

Table 1 provides five different scenarios of transition work. For comparison, rows one and five represent samples of the Performance stage of the framework. Rows two, three, and four offer a few examples of what practice weeks might resemble. It is important to notice that the sequencing of daily work varies by type (intensity level) and duration.

DAILY SCHEDULE

To better understand how this weekly schedule translates, let's take a look at a transition where an individual is taking on a new role and becoming a team leader. The transitional experience of a leader, like all of these in-between moments, involves discomfort, uncertainty, self-doubt, and the unknown. Training might include a session of high intensity work (like row 2, Monday of Table 1). This could include simulating a presentation, a team meeting, or some other activity for which a new leader would be responsible. It is simulated to mimic the feelings of the transition but happens with a coach or a few trusted colleagues.

The recovery period of the same session involves a debrief with the coach, a trusted group of colleagues, or in-action, independent reflection (i.e., How am I feeling? What is my goal? What did I do well?).

The third segment of this high-intensity work could be a repeat of the event (i.e., presentation or facilitation of a meeting) but perhaps the group asked different follow-up questions in this segment. Doing it this way offers a similar experience but also just a little variation to create uncertainty and discomfort. The session ends with a declining recovery where the individual shifts out of the discomfort and uncertainty and into a reflective period of work. While this high-intensity training session is *not* the actual transition, it did include the all too familiar feelings and thoughts included in these moments.

If this schedule is carried out to Thursday of row two, this new leader might engage in a low-impact session which might look like another day of doing something new related to this role, like a budget or market analysis and report. This is low-impact because the individual has engaged in this kind of work in a previous role. It is similar to a prior experience, still effort and work, but the individual is *not* pushing beyond her ability or to a maximum effort. It is low-impact which includes work, practice, reflection, and feedback. The week could end with another high-intensity interval where the individual engages in the work of presenting to the project team, takes questions, and then gets feedback from a coach or spends time reflecting on their own to apply this learning in a subsequent activity.

These training scenarios can take different forms in different contexts (Daly et al, 2007). For example, learning to play a new sport, or an instrument, or sing in a chorus is a different kind of transition.

In these scenarios, participants might practice independently which could represent a warm-up or switching/resetting of sorts. They could shift to high-interval training with skills drills, focused time on game situations, or complicated sections of a piece of music.

This moment mimics a transitional period as it is filled with new experiences, discomfort, and self-doubt. The difference is that this work is guided, structured, and less risky. The participant is purposefully and intentionally practicing these moments for the high-stress transitional moments and taking notice of their own feelings and thoughts throughout. This scenario would also include recovery segments like a brief water break, calling in of the team for a debrief, review of the music with an instructor, or other forms of feedback and reflection. This day might end with a high intensity scrimmage or rehearsal. Regardless of who participates, where the transition occurs, and how long it might take to move through the process, these kinds of practice scenarios help us to stay present, notice, name, and more effectively navigate our transitional moments.

INDIVIDUAL ACTIVITIES

Up to this point, the focus has been on the sequencing of weekly routines and daily sessions. The following section offers some examples of the kinds of activities that you might include as part of your training sessions.

LOW-IMPACT

As previously mentioned, low-impact activities include a sequence of familiar sessions that include moderate training intensity with short moments of higher intensity. Individuals and groups, in these intervals, train in recognizable spaces and places. Low-impact does not mean there's zero-effort. In fact, some individuals find this work difficult as it requires focus and discipline to hold back even when you feel like you could push harder. There are a variety of activities that fall into this category and, like other stages of this framework, will vary by individual experience, need, and interests. In the context of fitness and wellness, low-impact work might include walking, hiking, biking, playing with your pets, kids, or friends. Low-impact activities offer benefits that include lower stress, less impact on our body and minds, and ways to gradually build up strength and endurance for our uncomfortable and uncertainty of our transitions.

To illustrate I recall a recent workout on my Peloton bike. It was nearing the end of the week and I had been training particular hard with high-intensity and hill workouts. With this in mind, I selected a low-impact, 30-minute workout. This work, in the words of the trainer, was comfortably hard. This included a steady pace (i.e., cadence) and moderate resistance interrupted by very short periods of more resistance, a faster cadence, or a combination of the two. This session of low-impact work never pushed me to maximum effort or breathlessness but did offer enough resistance where I did have to put forth effort. My heart rate increased, I broke a sweat, and physically and mentally felt like I had worked out at the end of the session.

In a similar way, we can apply this approach to our transitions. Consider the attributes of that Peloton session:

- Familiar: I have done this kind of work before, bouts of resistance or high cadence.
- Comfortably hard: the short spurts of work required more effort but did not last long enough and was not hard enough to equal maximum effort or discomfort.
- Effort required: low impact does not translate to low work. I still did work, used my energy and strength, and practiced being present for those very short bursts of comfortably hard work.

In the same way, we can practice in and for our transitions. Low-impact activities translates to sessions where, for short periods of time, we engage in uncomfortable, unfamiliar, and uncertain work. For example, imagine that you are training for a 5K, learning to play the piano, or taking on a new role at work. In our haste to achieve our goals, crossing the finish line, playing a song, or succeeding on the important project, we might jump immediately to the high-intensity activities. Instead, we need to stay disciplined, resist the urge to hurry through the process, and stay present in the practice. Low-impact sessions might include familiar running sessions with short durations of work just above our comfortable pace. There is resistance and uncertainty, but it is tolerable. This might also be true of learning to play the piano or taking on a new role at work.

For example, in preparation for a new role, an individual could spend time working alongside the person or team currently responsible for that work. The incoming person might also take on some of the tasks of this new role with the current lead as a support and guide. Comparing this experience to the Peloton example, the individual will continue to do their current role (i.e., familiar and moderate work) and, in short-lived sessions, also assume responsibility for a new task or two (with the support of the current lead). Again, these intervals are comfortably hard, new, and uncomfortable, but temporary. These short-lived opportunities in low-impact sessions offers opportunities to metaphorically dip our toe in the pool. We spend time in these moments, being present, and noticing and staying with whatever feelings, reactions, and thoughts surface.

Low-impact sessions should provide us with opportunities to do some of the hard work of transitions, practice being present, and build up some of the strength and endurance to better navigate these important learning moments.

HIGH-INTENSITY

Sessions of low-impact prepare us well for the high-intensity and most unfamiliar and uncertain points of our transitional moments. This work pushes us beyond what we perceive as our threshold and represent work that is *hardly* comfortable. We will be breathless, filled with uncertainty, and doubting that we cannot do or complete the task. These are the hardest moments that simulate our transitions and offer opportunities for practicing with and learning from being in these moments: naming and noticing what is hard in these transitional periods. During these high-intensity moments it is critical to remember that challenge which results in growth and discomfort is when we learn the most.

Practicing high-intensity work is hard and often requires mental and physical effort. High-intensity work is a combination of maximum effort and discomfort, warm-up, and active recovery. This is important to remember because our inclination is to speed right through at a high rate of effort only to realize that this can result in burnout. The idea of high-intensity work is *not* to remain at maximum effort for the entire duration. In fact, if an individual is operating at maximum effort, he should *not* be able to remain at that level for the whole session. These sessions are characterized by short bursts of difficulty that lead to cognitive strain and frequent errors.

Most doctoral students' journeys include some form of comprehensive exam. These assessments represent a key milestone towards doctoral candidacy and eventual graduation. Navigating this segment of the journey requires high-intensity studying and effort. In some ways, the entire process of preparation is an interval session. In this work, students review literature, discuss in groups topics and questions that might be relevant in the exam. Eventually, they incorporate high-intensity sessions where students are asked practice comprehensive questions and the students respond to these questions. In practice sessions, they receive feedback, cues to move them towards a stronger answer but they are still working at maximum effort, hardly comfortable in the moments that they are responding. Mixing periods of independent study time with simulated practice question sessions represents one example of high-intensity work during a transition.

Kindergarteners, freshman in high school or college, and any other student starting at a new school would also benefit greatly from incorporating high-intensity efforts into their practice. What does maximum effort look like for a kindergartener? To answer this, it is important to review what about the transition is uncertain and stress-inducing. For some students, riding the bus or entering an unfamiliar classroom may be the most difficult part of this transition. In this case, it is important to practice these kinds of sessions. For example, parents might practice walking to the bus stop, or driving to the school. For a five or six-year-old starting a new school this could represent a high-intensity session. This practice walk to the bus might be followed by playing with friends or doing some other, less-intense activity.

Similarly, sending students to extracurricular activities like art, technology, dance, sports, or anything else might also represent a form of high-intensity work. Helping students practice these independent skills, unfamiliar spaces, and hardly comfortable moments, may contribute to being able to better manage these transitions. These sessions of high-intensity work should also include moments of active recovery where individuals or groups have opportunities to stay present, notice how they are feeling, what they are thinking, and share with others.

Another example could include learning to read. Our kindergarteners are experiencing high-intensity work each evening when they try to read a book. They are still learning, sounding out words, learning new words and sounds, and trying to put sentences and ideas together. It recently occurred to me that this work is discomfort, it is maximum effort. I can see, in their expressions and body movement, they are working and hardly comfortable. They make lots of mistakes, share that they do not know the word or sound, and keep trying. This is the definition of high-intensity intervals.

RECOVERY

Like low-impact and high-intensity training, recovery continues our work and intentionality around focusing and staying in these moments of training. It offers another opportunity and way to lean into the thoughts and feelings that surface. Recovery offers a way to wade into the dissonance and mud of our transitions, slowly and gradually. The pace of recovery also permits individuals and groups to reflect on these uncomfortable moments and practice grace and gratitude related to our work. Recovery is critical to our practice as it also represents learning opportunities where we are able to make adjustments to our reactions to these transitions moments and better prepare for the next time. The strategies in the recovery stage of our transitions training will vary depending on the individual or group, contexts, and experience and so individuals and groups should adapt the following to their own needs. Expressive writing and mindfulness practices represent two kinds of strategies that could be employed during the recovery period of our transitions training.

Expressive writing is a form of writing where the audience is the writer. No one is employed to evaluate the narrative other than the person doing the writing. Expressive writing is not creative writing but a way to make our thoughts and feelings visible. When individuals or groups are able to articulate, write, and make their thoughts and actions visible, learning may increase. Our ability to better understand what, how, and why we feel and think in our transitional moments may contribute to our ability to stay in these difficult moments and better engage in the opportunity.

Expressive writing might include observations on a situation, scenario, or experience and how it is affecting you or the work you are trying to do. It could be a list of questions you have about a moment or what to ask after reading a book, listening to a podcast, or attending a meeting. Expressive writing could also be a diagram, picture, or map that contributes to your understanding of otherwise difficult concepts. Emily Dickinson (1890) told us that we should "tell the truth but tell it slant." While there are numerous interpretations of this quote, as I reread this quote and poem, I think that it might apply to our use of expressive writing. Often, these transitional moments, feelings, and voices in our head are confusing, complicated, and even hard to understand. Expressive writing provides one way to tell or describe these moments at a slant. Individuals and groups, through their non-judgmental writing, sketching and questioning may be able to make these uncertain and uncomfortable moments visible.

Expressive writing activities could include a five-minute exercise before and after a high-intensity or low-impact session or practice. In this activity, individuals might start with a series of questions that include: (1) What is here right now? (2) How are you feeling? (3) What are you saying to yourself in this moment? (4) What did you learn? (5) What is still unclear? Again, this writing is *not* for communicating with others, it is a way to make the moment and this process visible. It offers opportunities for us to check-in with ourselves and to, perhaps, look at how our thinking changes from the first to the next writing session.

In groups, expressive writing like the one described above could be done with individuals, and then a facilitator could ask the group to share their responses to some of the prompts. These discussions are *not* evaluative but a way to connect, share, and listen to each other. This provides a means to support each other and recognize how these transitional moments and the associated feelings and thoughts are universal. It is important to also keep in mind that the questions offered for this example can and should be adjusted to the needs of the individual and groups using the strategy.

Another way to implement expressive writing is through the use of a question box or comment/suggestion box. These activities are best used with groups and provides a way for individuals can share what they are thinking, feeling, and wondering about without the worry of judgment or evaluation. The facilitator can use the boxes to better understand an individual's journey and adjust and support as needed.

A common form of expressive writing is journaling. The key to quality journaling is in the prompts. It is not how much you write or how long you sit with the writing but the focus and depth of the work. One way to support good journaling is with high-quality prompts and the good news is that there are lot of sources for this. For example, the New York Times (2019) offered almost 200 examples of all different kinds of discussion prompts. While all of these will not apply to everyone, there *is* something for everyone. When you adopt this practice, I recommend selecting a set of discussion prompts to get started. Here are a few examples that you might consider:

- What am I feeling in this moment?
- How can I express kindness to myself?
- What are things you appreciate about your body?
- How does it serve you?
- One of the things I am proudest of is...
- What is the biggest influence on my day-to-day happiness?
- What values am I honoring today?
- What am I doing to take care of myself?
- What would my 85-year-old self say about today?

CHECKPOINT:
Select one of these questions and
try writing for 10-15 minutes.
- How did you feel?
- What did you learn?

Consider adopting a practice of journal writing,
even for just 15 minutes a day.

Journaling can also take many forms. It can be general expressive writing guided by prompts that you select, questions that are on your mind, or observations and curiosities from the day. Journaling might also be themed. You might start a journal focused on expressing daily gratitude. What are you grateful for today? What mistake or failure are you grateful for today? How do you feel when you are grateful? How do you express your feelings of gratefulness to others? You might also journal in times of uncertainty, difficulty, or transitions. Regardless of the themes and topics, journaling and expressive writing represents intentional practice that may contribute to the ability to notice and name related thoughts and feelings. It makes the process of transition visible so that we can improve our ability to stay with the moment and learn from it.

Research on expressive writing suggests that this practice improves health outcomes like lower blood pressure, improved mood, and a greater sense of well-being. Other researchers also noted improvements in performance, academic outcomes, and connections with others. Psychologists suggest that expressive writing is one strategy to aid in disclosure (Baikie and Wilhelm, 2018). Writing to ourselves for ourselves offers a way to access, express, and visibly process moments. In this case, it permits individuals and groups to process and experience discomfort, uncertainty, and self-doubt rather than avoid or inhibit this unpleasantness (Pennebaker and Beall, 1986). While this activity may not be easy or even pleasant, I am confident that it *is* meaningful to the doer.

Like expressive writing, mindfulness practice offers positive benefits to our health and well-being. Here again, individuals and groups should adopt and adapt strategies that align with their needs and preferences. Regardless of the approach to mindfulness, individuals need to focus on being present and staying in the moment. This often requires paying attention to our sense and leaning in when we are uncomfortable. The following represents a few activities that individuals and groups could use to strengthen their ability to stay in the moment and be present for our transitional journey.

Fleming and Kocovski (2007) developed a plan for addressing social anxiety. One of these activities, the Raisin Exercise is a great place for beginners to start their practice of mindfulness. As Fleming and Kocovski suggest, this strategy can include any type of food, preferable one with unusual shape and texture. Try the following steps to engage in this first step towards a mindfulness practice:

- Select a food and pretend you have never seen the food before.
- Use your senses to explore and be present.
- What does it look like?
- What does it feel in your hands?
- How does the food react when moved and shifted? Does it change shape or size? Does it develop dimples or wrinkles?
- How does it taste and smell?

Focusing on this one object helps us to practice and develop our ability to focus and remain present. To learn to notice and name a process as it unfolds. Even if we are familiar with our selected item of food, I would bet that, after this activity, you have learned something new or noticed a different perspective. If one of these or something else novel is true for you, your practice of mindfulness has begun.

Like the Raisin Exercise, other mindfulness strategies aim to focus our attention on something. Listening and seeing are two opportunities to practice staying present. The listening activity included here is best done in pairs, triads, or other group sizes. For this activity, a facilitator asks everyone to think of a topic on which they are focused, stuck, or have been thinking on for a day or longer. Then, ask participants to pay attention to their own listening and sharing during the activity. Each person takes turn sharing their story. It is also a good idea to set a time limit for each individual, maybe five to eight minutes.

After everyone has had a chance to share and depending on group sizes, create sub-groups with two to three people. In these groups, individuals should respond to some or all of these questions:

- How did you feel when speaking?
- How did you feel when listening?
- Did you notice your mind drifting from the conversation?
- What was the distraction?
- How did you regain attention?
- Did your mind judge while listening to others?
- What did you feel in that moment?
- How did you feel right before speaking? After?
- What are you noticing right now?
- What would happen if you practiced mindful listening with each person that you spoke with?
- What is the impact of setting the intention to stay curious and kind with everything you said and everything you listened to?

Here again, facilitators and participants have options, and the exercise should be adapted to meet the needs of the group. For example, some group members may not feel comfortable or ready to share aloud. In this case, offer an option to record responses in a journal. The goal is not to orally share but to practice noticing and naming your own feelings and thoughts in these moments. How am I responding to myself and others during this activity? Teaching ourselves and practicing being present contributes to our ability to effectively navigate our transitions.

The last strategy, similar to listening, is seeing. This activity could be done as an individual or in different groups. Participants should find a space, inside or out, a window, room, park, car, or other place and sit still. In this place, be an observer without judgment, labels, categories. For example, instead of seeing a car or bike, notice the colors, shapes, sizes, and movement. When participants are distracted (and you will get distracted), notice the distraction, the associated feelings, and the reason for the distraction. Then, walk yourself (literally or metaphorically) back to the space, the colors, shapes, and sizes of the objects in the surrounding.

Whether you hold a piece of food in your hands, listen to yourself and others, see your surroundings and you in them, or engage in some other mindfulness strategy, practice paying attention. Learn to stay in these moments, pay attention to what your senses notice, and show kindness and caring when you are distracted. Recovery, reflection, and mindfulness are not a race, it is not something you win or lose. These are opportunities to rest, to be, and notice and name the moments.

This chapter has offered some insights into what a practice stage of this transitions training should feel and look. I have tried to describe questions that might be asked, voices that might be heard, and feelings that might be experienced and noticed during this training. I also recognize that the variety inherent to these schedules and sessions can be both a benefit and challenge of the work. As I have developed and used this framework, I initially struggled with trying to best articulate, describe, and characterize the sessions and segments of this training. Then I remembered, I *love* music. I do most all of my activities with some sort of music which often reflects the mood and effort for the activity. With this in mind, I decided to create playlists for low impact, high intensity, and recovery efforts. I did my best to represent different eras, types, and artists. Even if you are unfamiliar with a particular artist or song, search on your music app of choice and give it a listen. I trust that it will help center and focus you on the segment of the practice training that is relevant.

Table 2: Transitions training playlist

Low Impact	High Intensity	Recovery
Memories – Maroon 5	So Good – B.o.B	I'm Not the Only One –Sam Smith
I'll Do Anything – Jason Mraz	It's Raining Men – Weather Girls	Take Me to Church – Hozier
Walk Me Home – Pink	Honey – Moby	Collide – Howie Day
Tempted – Squeeze	I Will Wait –Mumford & Sons	After Life – Ingrid Michaelson
How Bizarre – OMC	Mr Brightside – The Killers	Home – Jack Johnson
Cruel To Be Kind – Nick Lowe	Feel So Close – Calvin Harris	Nightswimming – REM
Bad Guy – Billie Eilish	Blinding Lights – The Weeknd	With or Without You – U2
Dance Monkey – Tones & I	Senorita – Justin Timberlake	Worry – Jack Garratt
Why Does My Heart Feel So Bad – Moby	Joker – Steve Miller Band	Brave – Sara Bareilles
Chandelier – Sia	Proud Mary – Tina Turner	Pictures Of You – The Cure
Happier – Marshmello & Bastille	Black Celebration – Depeche Mode	
Waterfalls – TLC	Just Like Heaven – The Cure	
Power or Two – Indigo Girs	Devil Inside – INXS	

CHAPTER 11: PERFORMANCE AND SEEING THE FIELD

"If you hear a voice within you say 'you cannot paint'
then by all means paint and that voice will be silenced."
– Vincent van Gogh

Imagine an emergency room where there are medical students, residents, and experienced trauma physicians. As ambulances arrive, patients walk or roll into and out of the space, it is hectic, emergent, and high risk. For a medical student, this moment looks and feels fast, uncomfortable, and he or she must attempt to manage their swirling thoughts, uncertainty, and self-doubt. It can actually get in the way of an already tense situation.

Contrast this with the perspective of a trauma physician. She also feels the pressure, knows the risk, and yet, because of warm-up and practice-like routines, she can better notice, name, manage, and navigate the swirling thoughts and moments of her performance. The key to a "good" performance in these situations is to learn to wait, lean into the struggle, and attending to what comes up. It is not easy but waiting or slowing down calms the swirling and permits us to do the work required. These performances, like the practice, require discipline, intentionality, and strategies to navigate them effectively.

Performance is not just about measuring outcomes in quantitative measures. In fact, the outcomes are often not the point.

The performance, when best experienced, focuses on the process and the journey. In 2015, Julia Rozovksy conducted a study on what makes a high-performing team at Google. Too often people believe that performance requires the smartest, most experienced, and creative individuals. Project Aristotle, as it was called, discovered that the most productive teams attended to psychological safety and dependability of team members, clarity of roles and norms, personal importance of the work, and the impact of the work on others (Duhigg, 2015; Rozovksy, 2015).

Similarly, leaders of high-performing teams take time to get to know their people, focus on individual development, provide feedback, and lead with vulnerability and communication. It is also true that researchers (Peterson-DeLuca, 2016) identified the top attributes of high-quality teachers as individuals who develop relationships, express patience and kindness, take time to get to know learners, engage these students, and support their success. While these transitional moments occur in diverse spaces in different contexts, the attributes associated with high performance are those which also require time, discipline, and intentionality (Jensen et al, 2016). Performance is and should not be impulsive or hasty. Quality performance is not something we can rush to finish. It is not possible to quickly learn deeply. Roediguer and Pyc (2012) noted that fast learning leads to fast forgetting. In a similar way, a rushed performance leads to a rushed process and lower quality outcomes. We cannot react to our uncertainty and self-doubt with avoidance, sidestepping, or running away. Performance, like warming up and practice, must include a slowing down of the moment in order to see the ER, the field, the team, or the classroom. Slowing down the journey means that individuals are able to notice, name, and monitor these important transitional moments so that each of us can effectively navigate any transition.

PERFORMANCE

I have described the warm-up, rest, and practice stages of this transitions training. It is critically important as we do this work to keep in mind the unique role that each of these stages plays in our growth and development in transitional moments. This entire framework takes work and requires different kinds of effort. Without the discipline, focus, intentionality, and purposeful attention to each of these stages, we would not be able to effectively notice, name, and navigate the transitional moments or performance.

Transitions or what is referred to as the performance stage of this framework requires us to stay present and, even in the face of tremendous discomfort and uncertainty, do the work. Van Gogh reminds us that the voices in our head and the self-doubt act as barriers to engaging in these transitions with our eyes wide open. Our instinct is to sidestep, ignore, or rush through these uncomfortable moments. The transitions training framework offers routine, strategies, and practice so that when the voice tells us we cannot "paint," we respond by painting. This chapter discusses what performances might look like in this framework and strategies for developing ourselves as high performers during these moments.

Merriam-Webster offers numerous definitions of performance that include execution of an action, fulfillment of a request, and the ability to perform. The definition that resonates the most with the performance transitions training framework is "the manner of reacting to stimuli." We have already established that transitions happen to everyone all the time and they look different, vary in duration, and include different levels of uncertainty and discomfort. This training, the warm-up, pause and rest, and practice, together, prepare individuals and teams for how to react to the stimulus. What do we do in these moments? How do we respond and leverage these important learning moments?

This is the performance.

This is why we train.

From our own experiences, it is no surprise that different performances include different levels of success. We sometimes fumble, miss our mark, and just muddle through, waiting for the end to come. At other times, we notice the moment and stay fully present for the duration of that performance. This framework supports our preparation for various journeys and outcomes.

I love teaching but becoming or transitioning to the instructor role takes time, preparation, and practice. Early on in my professional development, I would write out all of my notes, follow a script, panic when students asked unexpected questions, and turn bright red if I made an error on the chalkboard. It was a performance, one step in becoming an educator but I was not truly present in the moment. I worried, doubted, and questioned, and just kept moving until the end of the class trying to just make it through.

With practice and training my performances are now different. At first glance, it might seem they are different because I am through the transition and while I *have* learned a lot and changed, these performances are also different because I am not on autopilot. I still prepare, but now I am present, reclaiming the time and space as moments of learning. I own and lean into the discomfort, and am explicitly grateful, often telling my students so. Becoming a teacher is really a lifelong transition and to grow and develop we must be present in these moments. Transitions, expected and unexpected, will happen and it is our choice whether or not to intentionally decide to show up and stay in these important moments.

The performance stage of this framework does mark the start of a transition, but this commencing is not black and white. Transitions do not always have a clear beginning or end. As we discussed earlier, context and situation contribute to the boundaries of these transitions. For example, new students in a classroom might experience all the stages of the framework within a matter of hours while transitioning to a new graduate program could take months.

Transitioning or becoming a parent, spouse, or leader may also take years. These performances are not marked by a single point in time. They are the culmination of experiences and a set of circumstances, emotions, beliefs, and perceptions. The uniqueness of performance as compared to practice might be that these moments are high intensity similar to our practice sessions but unlike the warm-up and training stages, performance also feels high stakes and high risk. The perception is that in a performance there is little room for mistake, error, and every decision and action matters.

The mark of performance, after engaging in this transitions training, is to be in the moment, present, with an ability to normalize the dissonance. Imagine that in this self-doubt and uncertainty you close your eyes and watch your thoughts pass by. In these moments you might say or think, "I cannot do it, what if I make a mistake" and feel nervous and experience intense self-doubt. Now, as the thoughts and words come into focus and start to pass by, try replacing the self-doubt with confidence, the "I cannot" with "I can, and I will." Performance with preparation means we can change the voices in our heads from self-doubt to self-acceptance. It is possible to embrace the discomfort and stay for what is here and what might come. If the difference between a good teacher and a better teacher is being and staying present then it is important to learn to make time and space for this work and continually revisit how to best engage in these moments.

SLOWING DOWN TO SPEED UP

Athletes—particularly rookie athletes—describe how, after a few years, the game slows down. Kimiecik and Stein (1992) describe this as flow where there is a balance between challenges and individual capabilities. It is a moment when an athlete is able to be present, concentrate on the task, be in the moment, receive feedback, and focus on clear goals. Performance is *not* hasty, impulsive, or reckless. Slowing down to speed up offers both a way of thinking and a way of being where individuals, teams, and organizations dedicate time and focus to move through these transitions effectively.

A Harvard study by Davis and Atkinson (2010) provided evidence that companies and organizations that focused on just going and going had lower average sales and decreased profits. High-performing companies focused on long-term development which allowed for time to share ideas, reflect, and learn. This contributes to fostering a climate of innovative thinking. These companies were able to optimize for speed when the time was right and benefit from increased sales and an improved bottom line. Performance and the transitions training framework seem counter to the fast-paced, driven culture of our current world, but if we learn to notice, name, and trust the process, we might just realize that slowing down now will result in more and better growth in the future.

John Dewey (1897) reminds us that "education is not preparation for life, education is life itself." He suggests further that it is a "process of living…not preparation for future living." Similarly, practice is the process of experiencing and living transitions not readying for future living. In this transitions training framework, practice and performance represent transitions and instances of these in-between moments. One of the differences between the two stages is related to the resources and supports available to navigate the transitions. For example, in practice, individuals rely on scaffolding—what Vygotsky (date?) described as small, manageable steps towards a goal. These supports might include a trusted teacher, leader, colleague, or peer. Performance, on the contrary, involves moments of a transition where the training wheels come off and individuals apply their own learning, development, and practice to effectively engage in the discomfort and uncertainty of these transitions.

In performance, transitions are still difficult, uncomfortable, and uncertain but we have practiced. We have done this work before and are better equipped and more prepared for these in-between moments. Even after scaffolded practice, quality performances require planning and strategy. Navigating these performance moments of transitions leverage our development of training prerequisites discussed early in the book. The following discussion provides examples of a variety of strategies that individuals, teams, and organizations might implement during this stage of the framework.

HIGH-PERFORMING TEAMS

The research on team development and high-performing teams offers evidence of the importance of these attributes. Bush, Abbott, Glover, Goodall, and Smith (2012) suggest that effective and high-performing teams cultivate space for scheduled dialogue. They point to the importance of self-reflection and continual evaluation. Bush et al (2012) also noted that these high-performing teams that are clear on their goals, communicate effectively, and develop shared values and standards, together, contribute to individual and team development, communication, and conflict management. Similarly, Sawa and Swift (2013) agree that improved performance requires a culture of and willingness to learn and open communication. Interestingly, Sawa and Swift also suggested that a challenging work environment contributes to change and growth.

Bush et al and Sawa and Swift also offer recommendations consistent with the work discussed thus far. Inquiry also continues to be critical in these performing moments.

CHECKPOINT:
During your next transition engage in critical reflection and ask yourself:
- What is going well in the role?
- What are you proud of?
- What challenges are you facing?
- Where are you stuck?
- What would you like to do?

Bruce Tuckerman (1965) devised a four-dimension model for high-performing teams and, like his model, this transition model includes a performing stage. In this moment, individuals, teams, and organizations adopt strategies that help them learn to function well, navigate situations and relationships, and work towards goals. For example, I run many miles, learn proper nutrition, and engage in strength training to do the work. At the same time, I am also reviewing what-if scenarios, anticipating challenges, preparing for setbacks, failures, and right-now victories. With approaches and strategies at the ready, individuals and teams feel valued, confident, and prepared for this work, well-equipped to navigate these critical transitions.

STRATEGIES

Viktor Frankel said that "between stimulus and response there is a space. In that space is our power to choose our response. In our response lies our growth and freedom." Our ability to make effective choices relies, in part, on our strategies. Think back to a moment when you were anticipating an upcoming event. Perhaps you were preparing or making a to-do list for an important meeting. Preparation might also include rehearsing speeches or strategies for a presentation or upcoming public event. Even as we warm-up, prepare, and practice for the event, we also implement strategies and approaches to navigate and problem solve our performances. Strategies in the performance stage of this transition build on work completed in the prerequisite and early stages of this framework and integrate tenets of mindfulness and research from Angela Duckworth and Parker Palmer. The following offers examples of strategies to navigate our performances.

GRACE AND GRIT

Recall, that grace is defined as an instance of kindness or courtesy. Even when we are in the middle of a perceived or actual high-risk and pressure-filled moment, we need to grant ourselves some grace. I was speaking to a student about their preparation for an upcoming exam that would be instrumental to their continuing in an academic program. The student expressed stress, worry, and frustration. She also shared how she felt unprepared and in need of more studying, wishing she could absorb more information. Clearly, this was an anxiety-inducing moment that came with great reward or penalty. In this moment, I asked the student to take a pause, to breathe, and try and recognize how far she had progressed in her studies and her work. This is so difficult to do and yet critical to our ability to grow and develop during our transitions.

Learning to give ourselves grace requires individuals to trust the journey and value the process as much as the outcome. It means that we have to give ourselves and the team permission to take a break, set boundaries, and breathe in *this* moment. Achieving this kind of discipline and practice requires strategies that integrate small routines and adjustments in our daily work. For example, one easy way to engage in grace work is to extend this courtesy to others. We have already discussed how much easier it is to be kind to others and so use this natural inclination to develop those skills of grace.

The next time you are at a meeting, teaching or taking a class, or just out for a run with a group, make a point to be kind to someone. Offer grace when the tasks increase in difficulty. When you feel yourself grow impatient with the moment, express courtesy to someone in the meeting or class. This is progress towards giving grace to ourselves. With this foundation, the next step requires individuals to take note of themselves and compare this to what we did or said to someone else. What did we say to ourselves during these performance moments? Is it a voice of self-doubt or one of grace? If it is the latter, practice as if you were speaking to someone else. At first, this feels awkward and uncomfortable but with repetition, it eventually becomes more natural.

Grace also requires us to permit ourselves to be who we are and what we feel in the moment. Giving permission is not easy and, compared to the other strategies, probably requires more time and effort. One way to approach permission is to imagine yourself in a group or with your team. Like giving others grace, permitting yourself to be honest about the difficulty of a moment, share with others what happened or what you are feeling, actually permits others to do the same. If you have difficulty giving yourself the permission to open up and communicate, do not think of it as giving yourself something. Think about how modeling this willingness to be vulnerable and share often results in a collective sigh of relief where everyone in the group meeting or setting has permission to do the same. Learning practices of grace takes time, effort, and intention and I have found that the strategies that initially focus outward on my colleagues, friends, family, or team often lead to my ability to practice grace inward.

Grit refers to power, gumption, and fortitude to stay in these moments. Grit is defined as firmness of mind or spirit and unyielding courage during hardship. Developing grit requires purpose and focus, time in the trenches, feedback, and avoidance of fear-based approaches to our work and play. Strategies to develop grit might include a practice of mindfulness, cultivating intentional time for our transitions practice, reflection, and learning.

MINDFULNESS, TIME, AND PATIENCE

In Leo Tolstoy's book *War and Peace*, General Kutuzov reminds us that "there is nothing stronger than those two: patience and time, the will to do it all." This work and these performances take time. Most individuals, groups, or teams cannot wake one morning and invent a product, shoot a three-point shot, run a marathon, or graduate from high school. This process of becoming requires quantity and quality time.

Our transitions and the performances of becoming can be measured in hours, days, and years. These performances, however, are also measured in the ways we choose to spend this transition time. For example, when I work out on my Peloton, I might have four minutes to go in a very difficult and uncomfortable interval session. I could just wish for it to be over and distract myself with the music, something outside my window, or a thought on my mind. Or, I could focus on every twenty or thirty seconds, one step at a time. Be in the time, patient with the process and focused on the work. I can't wish or rush this work away. What I need to do is use the opportunity to grow and learn.

There are a variety of strategies to train our focus and attention and learn to stay in our moments. Performing at a high level requires us to embrace the time in the discomfort and learn to effectively manage the uncertainty of our transitional moments. Examples of strategies include learning to eliminate distractions, reducing our need to multitask, and being present through mindfulness and breathing practice.

Each of these strategies requires patience and attention to the moment at hand. Whether exercising, studying for an exam, leading a meeting, or planning a team project, each of these transitional moments comes with a certain amount of dissonance, uncertainty, and self-doubt. To address these uncomfortable feelings, we often try to focus our attention *away* from the source of the discomfort. This might include music in our ears, conversations with a colleague at work, or just a focus on other thoughts that come in and out of our heads. With an inclination towards avoidance, sidestepping, or distracting, these strategies aim to improve our ability and willingness to focus on the moment. It offers a way to train our minds to face the discomfort and uncertainty head-on.

Learning to eliminate distractions is one simple step towards focusing on the transitional experience. Each of the avoidance strategies represents a kind of distraction and a way to draw attention away from the matters at hand. Finding places to be alone or remove interruptions will help create a routine or practice of focus. While finding alone time or a quiet place might be difficult at times, what is relatively easy is turning off our smartphones, shutting down our email, iPad, and other devices. This may seem difficult at first so try it for ten or fifteen minutes, stretch that time to an hour or half of a day. Eventually, extend this strategy by building in actual time in your calendar where you have device-free, scheduled time. Now that we have discussed reducing the noise and distractions, and turning off our devices, it might be possible to adopt an intentional practice of mindfulness.

Mindfulness involves a practice of quiet, intentional time to be still. I know that for many of us, including me, this is not always easy. Again, like the device-free moments, ease into this practice. There are a variety of techniques, approaches, and philosophies on how to do this practice. Start with a simple strategy. For example, pick a quiet place, use a timer and set it for five minutes at first, maybe one minute, if you really struggle. Close your eyes and focus on the breath. Mindfulness meditation does not require individuals or groups to have a quiet mind for the whole time. What I have learned is that meditation and mindfulness is about being present, staying in the moment, and noticing what is happening. For example, as thoughts inevitably come into your mind, stay with those thoughts as they enter and also as they exit. How do you feel? What is happening with your breath? What are you thinking now? Mindfulness meditation helps us to notice our state of being, our thoughts, and our feelings. We must try to remain kind, give ourselves the grace we previously discussed, and remain present in our thoughts without judgment or thought towards what might come next.

Breathing is another form of meditation that provides us with a place on which to focus. The breath serves as a focal point and, like meditation, breathing practice comes in all shapes and sizes. For example, diaphragmic breathing requires individuals to pay attention to how they are breathing, practice deep breaths, notice the expanding and contracting of the rib cage, and just stay in the breath. Another breathing practice asks individuals to think about inhaling deeply and then exhaling and imagining stress leave the body. Visualize and try to feel the stress exiting the body with every breath. Again, like meditation, the aim is to stay in the moment, non-judgmental, and engaged in the practice. Mindfulness, like eliminating distractions, requires purposeful choices. Whether individuals, teams, or organizations adopt quiet mediation or some form of a breathing practice, the goals are similar: learning to be present, staying with whatever shows up, being kind, and reserving judgment with ourselves.

Finally, as each of us wrestles with the discomfort and uncertainty of our transitional performances, it is critical to focus in on and remember our "why." We have long-term goals and in these difficult and uncomfortable moments, we have to find the reason we showed up in this moment, not the big, long-term goal but the reason we got out of bed and onto the Peloton. The thing that motivated us or our team to get an early start on this project proposal. In these transitional moments, remind yourself of the purpose: earn a degree, committed to students, be a stronger parent, win the contract, whatever it is, name it, say it out loud or to yourself. Replace self-doubt with purpose.

REFLECTION AND EVALUATION

Similar to training ourselves to focus on the moment, reflection strategies offer us ways to build in intentional time for reflection and evaluation of our transitional moments. As I discussed in Chapter 7, reflection is critical to every stage of this training framework. In warm-up and practice, reflection trains us to pay attention, to notice and name the moment, and to learn from our starts and stops.

Similarly, in performance, reflection is our way to measure our progress, take a temperature of the moment, and learn to adjust and adapt to what we learn in the transition. For example, one mark of a good, novice teacher is the willingness to receive and incorporate feedback (Ericsson et al, 2007). This might mean the teacher checks in with students early and often or asks a mentor or expert teacher to observe a class. Navigating these transitions improves with continual reflection, evaluation, and adjustment. Moving through a transition and integrating these moments of dissonance and discomfort results in us becoming something different and whole.

Mezirow (2000) describes these moments of dissonance as a disorienting dilemma where the dilemma is often an experience that does not fit our current expectations or does not make sense without some change in our own perspectives. In these moments of uncertainty, our instincts are to run, ignore, or push down the feelings and thoughts related to the disorienting experience. Mezirow reminds us that we only benefit from this dissonance when we lean in and reflect on these experiences. He suggests that change and transformative learning require a change in perspective. This happens when we are willing to examine the feelings, assess our own assumptions, recognize the discontent, and explore the options and potential. Through our own intentional practice, willingness to try, and reflection, we learn and integrate this new perspective which leads to our own growth and development during these critical transition periods.

Reflection strategies might include different kinds of journaling like bullets, lists, one-line, or narratives. Individuals, teams, and organizations also implement strategies that enlist a trusted from or group to debrief and share our transitional experiences. The aforementioned strategies represent post-action kinds of reflection. Another form of reflection strategy might happen during the transition or in-action reflection. This might include a think-aloud or taking a time out to examine the moment. Like strategies for cultivating time and patience, reflection practices take a variety of shapes and sizes. The following discussion offers a few examples of how to implement some of these strategies.

Examples of these strategies might include journaling and debriefing with trusted friends in the form of lists, stories, narratives, pictures, portfolios, or videos. If you are just starting out with this strategy, keep it simple. Try a bulleted list or one-line approach to reflection. This means that each day or after critical moments in your day, like meetings, classes, project discussions, or a workout, take time to write down a list of actions, conversations had and thoughts considered. Use bullets to transcribe these moments and examine these lists for takeaways and lessons learned. What did you learn from those moments and what might you adjust to do better next time? If you prefer or as you expand your journaling strategies, try writing a story or narrative after those critical moments. These stories do not need to be long, just enough to recount the event, your feelings, and perspectives, and sufficient content to find lessons learned and evidence you can use to make changes for the next moment of the transition.

If you prefer verbal discussion to making lists or writing narratives try convening with what Brene Brown in her book *Daring Greatly* calls "marble jar friends" (Brown, 2013). These are the friends who, over time and through often small tasks, earn marbles in their jar. These marbles represent the ways in which we cultivate trust. Convening these friends or a trusted group permits us to debrief, articulate the events of the moment, share our feelings, worries, and discomforts in the transition. These groups also offer opportunities for others to notice and name lessons learned and help us brainstorm ways to improve for the next go-around of transitional moments.

CHECKPOINT:
- Who are your marble jar friends?
- How could you integrate their support and conversations into your transitions work?

In addition to the post-reflection strategies, it is possible, with practice, to implement reflection *during* the transitional moment. These might include think-alouds or transition time outs. Think-alouds are like eavesdropping on someone's thinking. Teachers and mentors often use this technique to model ways of approaching a project, an analysis, or other task that might require a specific approach. Think-alouds permits the person doing the transitional work and others in the moment, to hear and see what the individual is doing, the reason for the action, and how they might be feeling in the moment. These moments often support our transitional moments by allowing us to articulate with others our why, admitting to our discomfort, and amplifying the shared uncertainty and self-doubt. These moments may also represent opportunities to learn and grow from each other through this sharing of process and ideas.

Similarly, calling a time out offers an intentional pause *during* the transitional moment. It helps us to slow down the transition process, to stop, recognize, and be present in these moments. Performances require us to pay attention, stay with whatever comes up, and adjust as needed. In-action reflection allows us to do this *while* we are in these critical moments and post-reflection offers a chance to learn and apply these lessons to future transitional moments.

Managing experiences, performances, and transitions contributes tremendously to our successes. An individual's ability to adjust to anticipated and unanticipated hurdles mean successfully navigating transitions. For example, becoming an ultrarunner represents a significant transition even for the fittest of runners. Putting in the miles is certainly a prerequisite but is only the first of many skills to be successful. Running 32, 50, or 100-plus miles means individuals are in a race for sometimes an entire day and night. Ann Trason, one of the most decorated ultrarunners, said that preparation is not just about planning for the possible setbacks but integrating expected setbacks. Ultramarathon runners, regardless of experience level, can be certain that something will go wrong and it is critical to prepare for these moments.

LEARNING IDENTITY

"I have no special talent. I am only passionately curious." – Albert Einstein

Leaning into these moments also requires a beginner mindset, or embracing a learning identity. Even during high-risk and significant moment performances, it is important to admit when we do not know what to do. In fact, entering a performance with a willingness to learn gives each of us permission to engage authentically and be fully present. Sitting at a table during orientation for an academic program, I remember looking around wondering why I was there. I worried I was not ready, the admissions committee made a mistake, and that I was not good enough. Then, the facilitator invited each table to participate in an icebreaker to get to know each other. While I was still nervous, I introduced myself and eventually admitted my concern and my interest in learning. Expressing a willingness to learn, relieves an internal pressure and also welcomes others to admit their own doubt.

CELEBRATE CURIOSITY

During a performance, it is also critical that we bring our curiosity rather than ego to these spaces. All too often in these moments of parenting, promotions, and running events our egos dominate and dictate the journey. It is being proud, loud, and often unwilling to get out of the way even if we might benefit. Ego makes it difficult to ask for what we need, admit how we feel, and even collaborate with others. New students, runners, and leaders often believe they have to act like they are completely prepared, in the know, and unflappable. The ego can prevent us from acting in any other way.

Parker Palmer (2009), in his book *A Hidden Wholeness: The Journey Toward an Undivided Life*, describes how most individuals live divided lives. It is a state of being where inwardly we feel a tendency towards one feeling, belief, or value but outwardly we act in another way. We experience these divided lives when our egos dominate. Our perception of what "should be" dictates our actions and there is a misunderstanding of what it means to identify with a particular role. The reality is that if we bring curiosity to the space, admitting a willingness to learn offers an opportunity to invite open communication and still feel confident and independent. Letting go and staying curious in any performance often helps us to be more present, focused, and in these transitional moments.

CONCLUSION

In this framework, the performance stage relies on PERFORM: Practice presence, Establish time and space, Reclaim the moment, Frame your questions, Own the dissonance, Release grace and gratitude, and Mark greatness. Performances like the other stages of this framework require us to be intentional, disciplined, and focused on the near and long-term goals. As we discussed earlier, goals and achievements are part of this work. It is not the only or most important part, but it is an element of the transitions training. Remember, this training is more than the training itself and we are not defined by outcomes. Goals and our ambition should not get in the way of our daily joy but this does not mean, however, that we do not persevere, we do not work or put in the effort during these transitions.

Performance often represents the goal or approaching the conclusion of the goal and earning an achievement. Even with warm-up, rehearsal and practice, performance is still hard, uncomfortable, and uncertain. The difference between a high and low-quality performance is whether or not we are able to stay when it gets hard, face the fear when it emerges, and celebrate and find gratitude even when the moments turn out in ways we do not expect. These experiences are not about finding a silver lining but learning to use every moment, experience, and setback to our advantage. Recognize that all of these moments make up our journey and that it is not just about the milestones, the achievements that often mark different stops on our path, but the being, staying, and leaning into whatever comes up.

As you have learned throughout this book, I have participated in many, many running races, good and bad. In my recent memory is a marathon that ranks, in terms of outcomes, in the not-so-good category. Interestingly enough, however, as I consider the *journey* in which this marathon happened and what followed this moment, this not-so-good marathon was actually exactly what I needed. This fall marathon was part of my training for an ultramarathon later in the winter. I had been training for a while, was familiar with the course, and felt ready for the race. Looking back, I believe my ego showed up at the start line and I started out too quickly for a long, 26-mile race. I finished the race but had to stop several times in a significant amount of discomfort and cramping. After the race, I was frustrated, mad, and disappointed with myself and my performance. After reflecting on this race and my frustration, I immediately signed up for another marathon a month later and applied many of my lessons to this race. The point here is that instead of ignoring the race, pretending it did not happen, I looked at it, stayed in the discomfort and used that leg of the journey to warm up and prepare for the next turn in my transitional journey.

Doing transitions training will not make this work easier, it does not make the uncertainty and self-doubt disappear. Performances like parenting, adopting, and building families—whether marked by a birth, adoption, or some other moment in the in-between—are often anxiety-inducing, worrisome, and uncertain. These parenting performances, these firsts, get better and stronger with practice and more performances. The paradox here is that the while we hold the performance up as "the" moment, the reason or motivation for the work, the best of these events happen when they feel more ordinary than extraordinary. The performance is important but I would argue that the performance is actually no more important than the warm-up and the practice and when we arrive at the moment where each of the stages of this framework is an equal priority, we will know that we are starting to recognize the importance and priority of the journey rather than focusing on the outcomes and the associated achievements. As I have said before, this transitions training, like a degree, promotion, role, or race, is more than training. It is an opportunity to awaken to these transitional moments. To attend to, stay with, and lean into whatever emerges and these actions, together will help us to notice, name, mark, and navigate these moments more effectively.

In the context of transitions training, courage involves risk-taking, a willingness to be vulnerable, and a learner. Courage and vulnerability represent another paradox where courageous individuals in these moments hold uncertainty, face risk, and experience emotional exposure. The idea of imperfection is critical to this work, our journeys and transitions and it reminds me of the Chinese parable of the two pots.

Daily, a woman carried two pots to the well, and in one of the pots she only brought back half as much water as the other. This pot was sad and ashamed that it was not contributing as much as the other pot due to several cracks in the pot. One day, the pot, with embarrassment and regret, apologized to the woman for not carrying as much water, for not being enough. The woman took both of the pots back down to the well, refilled the pots, and began the journey back to her home. As she crossed her doorway, she turned back to show the cracked pot the beautiful line of flowers growing on that side of the road. She shared with the pot that upon learning about the cracks in the pot, she planted seeds and the cracked pot may not provide the same amount of water as the other pot but it contributes beautiful cut flowers for her table.

This story shows us the power and gift of imperfection. During our transitions training and our performances, it is important to give ourselves grace for our unique differences and express gratitude for our own cracks. It is not possible to do this work without bringing our real and authentic selves into this work and into these moments.

CHAPTER 12: REFLECTIONS AND FINAL THOUGHTS

"What would it be like if I could accept life, accept this moment exactly as it is?" – Tara Brach

As I have said so many times before, I love the outdoors, working out, and pushing myself in all sorts of ways, mentally and physically. The Massachusetts winter and the 2020 pandemic introduced me, as you also already know, to the Peloton bike. I have grown to love this work and I am impressed with and appreciative of the trainers who lead the different training sessions. On one Saturday morning, I did a 75-minute ride to work on endurance as well as the discipline and focus to stay in my training zone over a long period of time. Towards the end of the session, the trainer suggested that the Peloton bike is more than a bike. I knew immediately what she meant.

The trainer reminded me that exercising involves more than physical activity. It includes an intentional practice of being present, paying attention to how we feel and what we think during our workouts. It involves learning to turn our voice of self-doubt into gratitude. While riding our bikes she reminds us that challenge leads to change and growth. Being uncomfortable is not a sign of weakness or being less than, it is part of our learning and getting stronger. The trainer reminded me that riding is not only about the performance or the data that shows up on my screen.

Riding my bike, running on road, earning an academic degree, or taking on a new role or job is as much about the journey as the outcome. While I am convinced that this transitions training framework is important to our ability to leverage these critical learning moments, I am also convinced that *what* you do in terms of selected warm-up and practice strategies is less important than *how* and *why* you do this work.

In school, whether as a student or teacher, I remember the opportunities to create what was often referred to as a "cheat" sheet or formulas sheet. It really was not a cheat sheet as the instructor gave us permission (or I gave permission) to use this tool on an exam. For those unfamiliar with this strategy, often in classes with lots of formulas, mathematical expressions, or calculations, instructors allow students to bring a sheet to class for reference. The idea is that students need to learn *how* to use the formulas rather than just memorize the formulas.

Here is the interesting feature of these cheat sheets—the preparation of the sheets *is* the studying. It *is* the work that prepares students to perform well on the exam. It was never about having the cheat sheet, it was about doing the work, focusing on which formulas were important, noticing how best to organize them, and attend to those that might be needed for the exam. Like this cheat sheet, this framework trains us to notice, name, and pay attention to and focus on our transitional moments. People do not need to worry about which strategies to employ or how long they should last. It is about committing to the work and, as Van Gogh reminded us, "by all means paint."

Tara Brach asks us to consider what it would be like if we accepted life just as it is. It would mean that we have been doing the work of the transitions training and coming ready to stay in the transitional moment and be present for whatever comes during those moments. In this book, we learned that everyone experiencing transitions and that these moments can be unexpected or expected but all of them include self-doubt, uncertainty, discomfort, and anxiety.

We have learned throughout this book that to do this work, we need to learn how to dance with the dissonance, adopt an attitude of grace, gratitude, and greatness, and learn how to be learners in this work which means we bring a beginner mindset to all of the steps and actions we take. Through all of this work and the stages of the framework, we also learned that reflection, feedback, and evaluation contribute to our ability to lean into and learn from these moments of dissonance and discomfort.

In thinking about and writing on the topics contained within this book, I am left with several takeaways. I would encourage you to think about your own takeaways and make a note of them somewhere.

CHECKPOINT:

For me, it is about:

- staying present.
- owning the moments and discomfort.
- quieting the voice of self-doubt.
- maintaining focus.
- adopting a "Gr" attitude and learning identity.
- remembering process over outcomes:
  - right-now victories for the sessions of training.
  - not perfection but progress.
- living with curiosity and ignoring the ego.
- paying attention to hinge moments.
- asking powerful questions of ourselves and others.

What is it about for you?

FINAL THOUGHTS

"Be where you are, otherwise you will miss your life."
– the Buddha

I spent so much of my early years moving from one milestone or one goal to the next. The irony of this is that I often believed that I would be enough or worthy, credible, smart, accomplished if I only could do _____ (fill in the blank). It took me a very long time to realize that if I am not enough before the goal is set and achieved, I am not going to be enough after the goal is reached. I also realized that in my anxiety, worry, and distraction of getting to that goal I missed the moment, the journey, and the amazing ups and downs, growth, and failure. I hope that this transitions training teaches each of us how to stay in the space in-between, to be where we are so that we do not miss those important journeys. It is not the milestones that matter, it is the in-between moments on the way to our goals where we learn, grow, and become.

My 96-year-old grandmother passed away in 2019 and I miss her every day. She was one of my most favorite human beings and I loved her with all my heart. As I think about my time with her and my grandfather, I remember that they were present for just about every significant milestone of my life. She was there when I graduated from high school and college. She was there when I was a part of winning field hockey or softball teams. She cheered me on and consoled me too many times to count. When I think about her now, however, I am not thinking about those milestone moments, I am thinking about our talks on her swing by the water, riding bikes at her house, playing golf on any given Wednesday morning, or just fishing, crabbing, and swimming off of her pier.

The thing I realize is that I miss the journey with her, I miss checking in with her just because I love to hear what she is up to. I miss talking with her on the phone to hear what she did today or to share what one of my kids said today, just to hear about her comings and goings. She taught me so much but one of the most important gifts she gave me was her time and presence. It did not matter whether she was working at her grocery store, at home making dinner, or just enjoying time on the porch, she was there, paying attention, asking questions, and leaning in to listen to my stories, my celebrations, and my sorrows.

In fact, I now host a podcast called *Tell Me This* and the name comes from something my grandmother used to say. Whenever anyone from her family (kids, grandkids, or great-grandkids) would come for a visit, she would lean over and say "Tell me this..." and this was her cue for, I am ready, present, and listening to your moment, I am staying, and being where you are because I do not want to miss anything.

I hope that this book can, in some ways, be the "tell me this" for each of us individually and collectively. Can we be intentional, disciplined, and prepared to engage in the work required to experience these important transitional moments, using this framework of warm-up, reflection, rest, practice, and performance to effectively engage in our transitional performances?

Thank you for reaching for the discomfort, staying with the curiosity, being present, and remaining in your journey otherwise you might miss something. Learning to notice, name, and navigate these transitional moments will contribute to our ongoing learning journeys.

REFERENCES

Allen T. D., Eby L. T., Chao G. T. and Bauer T. N. (2017) 'Taking stock of two relational aspects of organizational life: Tracing the history and shaping the future of socialization and mentoring research', *The Journal of Applied Psychology*, 102(3), 324–337.

Baikie, K. and Wilhelm, K. (2005) 'Emotional and physical health benefits of expressive writing', *Advances in Psychiatric Treatment*, 11(5), 338–346.

Baltes, P. B. and Smith, J. (2008) 'The fascination of wisdom: Its nature, ontogeny, and function', *Perspectives on Psychological Science,* 3(1), 56–64.

Bandura, A. (1997) *Self-efficacy: The exercise of control*. W. H. Freeman and Company.

Bar-Eli, M., Azar, O. H., Ritov, I., Keidar-Levin, Y. and Schein, G. (2007) 'Action bias among elite soccer goalkeepers: The case of penalty kicks', *Journal of Economic Psychology*, 28(5), 606–621.

Baumeister, R. F. (1986) Identity: Cultural change and the struggle for self. New York: Oxford University Press.

Beck, M. (2012) 'The Willingness Factor: Learn To Avoid Avoidance', Martha's Blog [Online]. Retrieved from: www.bit.ly/3B94VEX

Becker, G. (1964) *Human Capital*. New York: Columbia University Press.

Bierly, P. E., Kessler, E. H. and Christensen, E. W. (2000) 'Organizational learning, knowledge and wisdom', *Journal of Organizational Change Management*, 13(6), 595–618.

Bethea, A. (9 November, 2019) Brené with Aiko Bethea on Inclusivity at Work: The Heart of Hard Conversations [Podcast]. Retrieved from: www.bit.ly/3kcB5Ix

Bjork, E. L. and Bjork, R. A. (2011) 'Making things hard on yourself, but in a good way: Creating desirable difficulties to enhance learning', *Psychology and the real world: Essays illustrating fundamental contributions to society*, 2, 59–68.

Blatner, A. (2005) 'Perspectives on Moreno, Psychodrama, and Creativity', *Journal of Creativity in Mental Health*, 1(2), 111–121.

Bloch, D. P. and Richmond, L. J. (1998) *SoulWork: Finding the work you love, loving the work you have*. Palo Alto, CA: Davies-Black.

Borkoski, C. and Donaldson, S. (2020) 'Bridging media: Shared referents to connect the unfamiliar with the familiar'. Spring/Summer (34). NEFDC Exchange.

Brackett, M. A. (2019) *Permission to feel: Unlocking the power of emotions to help our kids, ourselves, and our society thrive*. New York: Celadon Books.

Bradley, G. (2008) 'The induction of newly appointed social workers: Some implications for social work educators', *Social Work Education*, 27(4), 349–365.

Breunig, M. C. (2017) John Dewey: Purposeful play as leisure. In Spracklen, K., Lashua, B., Sharpe, E. and Swain, S. (Eds.), *The Palgrave handbook of leisure theory* (pp. 355-370). London: Palgrave Macmillan.

Bridges, W. (2009) *Managing transitions: Making the most of change*. Da Capo Press.

Brown, A. C. (2020) *I'm Still Here: Black Dignity in a World Made for Whiteness*. London: Little, Brown Book Group.

Brown, B. (2010) *The Gifts of Imperfection*. Minnesota: Hazelden Information & Educational Service.

Brown, B. (2013) *Daring Greatly: How the Courage to Be Vulnerable Transforms the Way We Live, Love, Parent, and Lead*. London: Penguin.

Brown, B. (2016) 'Brené Brown Encourages Educators to Normalize the Discomfort of Learning and Reframe Failure as Learning', *About Campus*, 20(6), 3-7.

Bush, T., Abbott, I., Glover, D., Goodall, J. and Smith, R. (2012) *Establishing and developing high performing leadership teams*. Nottingham: National College for School Leadership.

Bussolari, C. J. and Goodell, J. A. (2009) 'Chaos Theory as a Model for Life Transitions Counseling: Nonlinear Dynamics and Life's Changes', *Journal of Counseling and Development*, 87(1), 98–107.

Carpenter, S. K. (2014) Spacing and interleaving of study and practice. In Benassi, V. A., Overson, C. E. and Hakala, C. M. (Eds.), *Applying the science of learning in education: Infusing psychological science into the curriculum* (pp. 131–141). Society for the Teaching of Psychology.

Cepeda, N. J., Vul, E., Rohrer, D., Wixted, J. T. and Pashler, H. (2008) 'Spacing effects in learning a temporal ridgeline of optimal retention', *Psychological Science*, 19(11), 1095–1102.

Cooperrider, D. L. and Whitney, D. (2000) A positive revolution in change: Appreciative inquiry. In D. L. Cooperrider, P. F. Sorensen, Jr., D. Whitney, and T. F. Yaeger (Eds.), *Appreciative inquiry: Rethinking human organization toward a positive theory of change* (pp. 3–27). London: Stripes Publishing.

Daly III, E. J., Martens, B. K., Barnett, D., Witt, J. C. and Olson, S. C. (2007) 'Varying Intervention Delivery in Response to Intervention: Confronting and Resolving Challenges With Measurement, Instruction, and Intensity', *School Psychology Review*, 36(4), 562–581.

David, S. A. (2016) *Emotional agility: Get unstuck, embrace change, and thrive in work and life*. New York: Random House.

Davis, J. and Atkinson, T. (2010) 'Need Speed? Slow Down', *Harvard Business Review*. Retrieved from: www.bit.ly/3mZwsEO

Davis, D. M. and Hayes, J. A. (2011) 'What are the benefits of mindfulness? A practice review of psychotherapy-related research', Psychotherapy, 48(2), 198.

Dehaene, S. (2020) *How We Learn: The New Science of Education and the Brain.* London: Penguin.

Dewey, J. (1916) *Democracy and education: An introduction to the philosophy of education.* New York: MacMillan.

Dong, S., Campbell, A. and Vance, S. (2017) 'Examining the Facilitating Role of Mindfulness on Professional Identity Development among Counselors-in-Training: A Qualitative Approach', *Professional Counselor*, 7(4), 305-317.

Dow, P. E. (2013) *Virtuous minds: Intellectual character development.* Downers Grove, IL: InterVarsity Press.

Duckworth, A. and Duckworth, A. (2016) *Grit: The power of passion and perseverance* (Vol. 234). New York: Scribner.

Duhigg, C. (2015) 'What Google Learned From Its Quest to Build the Perfect Team', The New York Times Magazine, 25 February. Retrieved from: www.bit.ly/2WPGfm4

Du Plessis, H. (2015) The Mindset and Posture Required to Engender Life-Affirming Transitions. Retrieved from: www.bit.ly/3DEErgs

Dweck, C. (2007) Mindset: The new psychology of success. New York: Ballantine Books.

Eccles, D. W. and Kazmier, A. W. (2019) 'The psychology of rest in athletes: An empirical study and initial model', *Psychology of Sport and Exercise*, 44, 90-98.

Eger, E. (2017) The choice: Embrace the possible. New York: Scribner.

Epstein, R. (2017) *Attending: Medicine, mindfulness, and humanity.* New York: Scribner.

Ericsson, A. K. (2006) 'The influence of experience and deliberate practice on the development of superior expert performance', *The Cambridge Handbook of Expertise and Expert Performance*, 38(685-705), 2.

Ericsson, A. K., Prietula, M. J. and Cokely, E. T. (2007) 'The Making of an Expert Harvard Business Review', *Expert Harvard Business Review*, July–August.

Erikson, E. (1959) Identity and the Life Cycle. New York: International Universities Press.

Evans, N. J., Forney, D. S. and Guido, F. (1998) Student Development in College Theory Research and Practice. San Francisco: Jossey-Bass.

Fenge, L. A. (2010) 'Sense and sensibility: Making sense of a professional doctorate', *Reflective Practice*, 11(5), 645-656.

Godin, S. (2008) *Tribes: We need you to lead us.* London: Penguin.

Graafland, J. H. (2018) New technologies and 21st century children: Recent trends and outcomes (Report No. 179). Paris: OECD Publishing.

Gray, J. A. (1987) The neuropsychology of emotion and personality. In S. H. M. van Goozen and N. E. Van de Poll (Eds.), *Cognitive neurochemistry* (pp. 171–190). Oxford: Oxford University Press.

Heckman, J. J. and Rubinstein, Y. (2001) 'The Importance of Noncognitive Skills: Lessons from the GED Testing Program', *American Economic Review*, 91(2), 145-149.

Hudson, F. M. (1999). The adult years: Mastering the art of self-renewal. Jossey-Bass Publishers, 350 Sansome Street, San Francisco, CA 94104.

Huff, J. (2013) Teaching New Leaders: A View From the Academy. In Cypres, A. (Eds), *Great Leaders Equal Great Schools: Alliances and Discourses for Educational Reform*. Charlotte, NC: Information Age Publishing.

Ibarra, H. and Obodaru, O. (2016) 'Betwixt and between identities: Liminal experience in contemporary careers', *Research in Organizational Behavior*, 36, 47-64.

Inhelder, B. and Piaget, J. (1958) *The growth of logical thinking: From childhood to adolescence*. (A. Parsons & S. Milgram, Trans.). New York: Basic Books.

Jensen, B., Sonnemann, J., Roberts-Hull, K. and Hunter, A. (2016) *Beyond PD: Teacher professional learning in high-performing systems*. Washington, DC: National Center on Education and the Economy. Retrieved from: www.bit.ly/3gYjDqv.

Kabat-Zinn, J. (1994) *Wherever you go, there you are: mindfulness meditation in everyday life*. New York: Hyperion.

Kaplan, S. (1995) 'The restorative benefits of nature: Toward an integrative framework', *Journal of Environmental Psychology*, 15(3), 169-182.

Kimiecik, J. C. and Stein, G. L. (1992) 'Examining flow experiences in sport contexts: Conceptual issues and methodological concerns', *Journal of Applied Sport Psychology,* 4(2), 144–160.

Kolb, D. (1984) *Experiential learning: Experience as the source of learning and development*. New Jersey: Prentice-Hill.

Kroger, J. (1993) 'On the nature of structural transition in the identity formation process', Discussions on ego identity, 205-234.

Kurzweil, R. (2006) *The singularity is near: When humans transcend biology*. New York: Penguin.

LeDoux, J. E. and Brown, R. (2017) 'A higher-order theory of emotional consciousness', *Proceedings of the National Academy of Sciences,* 114(10), E2016-E2025.

Liu, Y., Fu, Q. and Fu, X. (2009) 'The interaction between cognition and emotion', *Chinese Science Bulletin*, 54, 4102.

Malpass, A., Binnie, K. and Robson, L. (2019) 'Medical students' experience of mindfulness training in the UK: well-being, coping reserve, and professional development', Education research international.

Marcia, J. E. (1966) 'Development and validation of ego-identity status', *Journal of Personality and Social Psychology*, 3(5), 551.

Martin, A. J. and Marsh, H. W. (2003) 'Fear of failure: Friend or foe?', *Australian Psychologist*, 38, 31-38.

Masicampo, E. J. and Baumeister, R. F. (2007) 'Relating mindfulness and self-regulatory processes', *Psychological Inquiry*, 18(4), 255–258.

Maslach, C., Schaufeli, W. B. and Leiter, M. P. (2001) 'Job burnout', *Annual review of psychology*, 52(1), 397–422.

Maxwell, J. C. (2003) *Thinking for a change: 11 ways highly successful people approach life and work*. Brentwood, TN: FaithWords.

McGowan, C. J., Pyne, D. B., Thompson, K. G. and Rattray, B. (2015) 'Warm-up strategies for sport and exercise: mechanisms and applications', *Sports Medicine*, 45(11), 1523–1546.

Merriam, S. B. (2005) 'How Adult Life Transitions Foster Learning and Development', *New Directions for Adult & Continuing Education*, 108, 3–13.

Mezirow, J. (1997) 'Transformative learning: Theory to practice', *New Directions for Adult and Continuing Education*, 74, 5-12.

Mezirow, J. (2000) Learning to think like an adult: Cores concepts of transformation theory. In J. Mezirow & Associates (Eds.), *Learning as transformation: Critical perspectives on a theory in progress* (pp. 3-33). San Francisco: Jossey-Bass.

Moorhead, B. (2019). Transition and adjustment to professional identity as a newly qualified social worker. Australian Social Work, 72(2), 206-218.

Muenks, K., Wigfield, A. and Eccles, J. S. (2018) 'I can do this! The development and calibration of children's expectations for success and competence beliefs', *Developmental Review*, 48, 24-39.

Nagoski, E. And Nagoski, A. (2019) *Burnout: The Secret to Unlocking the Stress Cycle*. New York: Random House.

Nieto, S. (2005) 'Schools for a new majority: The role of teacher education in hard times', *The New Educator*, 1(1), 27–43.

Palmer, P. J. (1998) *The courage to teach: exploring the inner landscape of a teacher's life*. San Francisco, CA: Jossey-Bass.

Palmer, P. J. (2004) *A hidden wholeness: the journey toward an undivided life: welcoming the soul and weaving community in a wounded world*. San Francisco, CA: Jossey-Bass.

Patt, A. and Zeckhauser, R. (2000) 'Action bias and environmental decisions', *Journal of Risk and Uncertainty*, 21(1), 45–72.

Pennebaker, J. W. and Beall, S. K. (1986) 'Confronting a traumatic event: Toward an understanding of inhibition and disease', *Journal of Abnormal Psychology*, 95(3), 274–281.

Peterson-DeLuca, A. (2016) Top Five Qualities of Effective Teachers, According to Teachers, *Fresh Ideas for Teaching* [Blog] 5 October. Retrieved from: www.bit.ly/3mUXP2Q

Pieper, J. (1952) Leisure, The Basis of Culture. In Hochschild, J. P. (1999) *First Things: A Monthly Journal of Religion and Public Life* (p. 74).

Plass, J. L. and Kaplan, U. (2016) Emotional design in digital media for learning. In S. Y. Tettegah and M. Gartmeier (Eds.), *Emotions, technology, design, and learning* (pp. 131–161). New York: Elsevier Academic Press.

Radnofsky, M. L. (1988) The Mental Warm-Up: An Activity To Promote Quality Learning. Retrieved from: www.bit.ly/3kKeX8R

Resnick, B. (2019) 'Intellectual humility: the importance of knowing you might be wrong', *Vox* [Blog] 4 January. Retrieved from: www.bit.ly/3DI65Jq

Roediger III, H. L. and Pyc, M. A. (2012) 'Inexpensive techniques to improve education: Applying cognitive psychology to enhance educational practice', *Journal of Applied Research in Memory and Cognition*, 1(4), 242-248.

Röthlin, P., Horvath, S., Birrer, D. and Grosse Holtforth, M. (2016) 'Mindfulness promotes the ability to deliver performance in highly demanding situations', *Mindfulness*, 7(3), 727-733.

Ryan, S. (2013) Wisdom. Stanford Encyclopedia of Philosophy Archive. Retrieved from: www.bit.ly/3t7mimy

Saad L. (2020) Me and White Supremacy: How to Recognise Your Privilege, Combat Racism and Change the World. London: Quercus.

Sagar, S. S., Lavallee, D. and Spray, C. M. (2009) 'Coping with the effects of fear of failure: A preliminary investigation of young elite athletes', *Journal of Clinical Sport Psychology*, 3(1), 73–98.

Sawa, B. and Swift, S. (2013) 'Developing high-performing organizations: Keys to recruiting, retaining, and developing people who make the difference', *Leadership and Management in Engineering*, 13(2), 96–100.

Schlossberg, N. K. (1981) 'A model for analyzing human adaptation to transition', *The Counseling Psychologist*, 9(2), 2–18.

Schlossberg, N. K. (1984) 'Counselling Adults in Transition: Linking Practice with Theory'. New York: Springer Publishing Company.

Schön, D. (1991) *The Reflective Practitioner* (2nd ed.). San Francisco, CA: Jossey-Bass.

Skar, P. (2004) 'Chaos and self-organization: emergent patterns at critical life transitions', *Journal of Analytical Psychology*, 49(2), 243–262.

Smith (2021) CNN article: The benefits of approaching this year like a total newbie.

Sonnentag, S. and Zijlstra, F. R. (2006) 'Job characteristics and off-job activities as predictors of need for recovery, well-being, and fatigue', *Journal of Applied Psychology*, 91(2), 330.

Stephen, J., Fraser, E. and Marcia, J. E. (1992) 'Moratorium-achievement (Mama) cycles in lifespan identity development: Value orientations and reasoning system correlates', *Journal of adolescence*, 15(3), 283–300.

Sweller, J. (2011) Cognitive load theory. In Mestre, J. P. and Ross, B. H. (Eds), *Psychology of Learning and Motivation* (Vol. 55, pp. 37-76). Cambridge, MA: Academic Press.

Tang, R. and Braver, T. S. (2020) 'Predicting individual preferences in mindfulness techniques using personality traits', *Frontiers in Psychology*, 11, 1163.

The New York Times (2019) 181 Writing and Discussion Prompts From the 2018-19 School Year. Retrieved from: www.bit.ly/3yONUhP

Tsaousides, T. (2018) How to Conquer a Fear of Failure, *Psychology Today* [Online] 23 January. Retrieved from: www.bit.ly/2WKI9Ei

Tuckman, B. W. (1965) 'Developmental sequence in small groups', *Psychological Bulletin*, 63(6), 384.

Tugend, A. (2011) *Better By Mistake: The unexpected benefits of being wrong*. New York: Penguin.

Turner, V. (1969) 'Liminality and communitas' in *The Ritual Process: Structure and Anti-structure*, 94(113), 125–130. Chicago: Aldine Publishing.

Tyng, C. M., Amin, H. U., Saad, M. N. and Malik, A. S. (2017) 'The influences of emotion on learning and memory', *Frontiers in Psychology*, 8, 1454.

Vanderbilt, T. (2021) *Beginners: The Joy and Transformative Power of Lifelong Learning*. New York: Knopf.

Van Gennep, A. (2019) *The Rites of Passage*. Chicago: University of Chicago Press.

Wels, H., Van der Waal, K., Spiegel, A. and Kamsteeg, F. (2011) Victor Turner and liminality: An introduction, *Anthropology Southern Africa*, 34(1-2), 1-4.

Wenger, E. (1998) *Communities of Practice: Learning, Meaning, and Identity*. Cambridge: Cambridge University Press.

Wenger-Trayner, E. and Wenger-Trayner, B. (2015) Communities of Practice: A Brief Introduction. Retrieved from: www.bit.ly/2WNWRe7

Wingate, U. (2007) 'A framework for transition: supporting 'learning to learn' in higher education', *Higher Education Quarterly*, 61(3), 391–405.